Musical Theater and American Culture

Musical Theater and American Culture

DAVID WALSH AND LEN PLATT

 PRAEGER

Westport, Connecticut
London

Library of Congress Cataloging-in-Publication Data

Walsh, David F.
  Musical theater and American culture / David Walsh and Len Platt.
    p. cm.
  Includes bibliographical references (p.) and index.
  ISBN 0–275–98057–X (alk. paper)
  1. Musicals—Social aspects—United States. I. Platt, Len. II. Title.
  ML3918.M87W35   2003
  306.4′84—dc12   2003048238

British Library Cataloguing in Publication Data is available.

Library of Congress Catalog Card Number: 2003048238
ISBN: 0–275–98057–X

First published in 2003

Praeger Publishers, 88 Post Road West, Westport, CT 06881
An imprint of Greenwood Publishing Group, Inc.
www.praeger.com

Printed in the United States of America

♾™

The paper used in this book complies with the
Permanent Paper Standard issued by the National
Information Standards Organization (Z39.48–1984).

10 9 8 7 6 5 4 3 2 1

Copyright Acknowledgments

The authors and publisher gratefully acknowledge permission for use of the
following material:

Excerpts from S. Banfield, *Sondheim's Broadway Musicals*. 1993. Ann Arbor: The
University of Michigan Press.

Excerpts from H. Brogan, *The Longman History of the United States of America*. ©
Longman Group Limited 1985, reprinted by permission of Pearson Education
Limited.

Excerpts from D. Walsh, *American Popular Music and the Genesis of the Musical*.
London: Goldsmith Sociology Papers No. 1.

This book is dedicated to Joe and Elsie Walsh.

Contents

Preface

Musical Theater and American Culture began life in 1996 as a project with an even wider scope, covering dance and film musicals, involving Dave Walsh and a different collaboration. For various reasons, this arrangement broke down, and by 2001 Walsh had a first-draft manuscript that was essentially a sociology of the American stage musical. It was at this point that he heard I was working on a cultural history of the early West End musical (1894–1920) and approached me with a view toward producing a joint book on the West End and Broadway musical. There were several reasons why this project seemed problematic to me. Our books were different in style and methodology and understood historiographies of the musical in different ways; moreover, Dave's manuscript, although it needed work, already constituted a clearly formulated thesis, as did my own. Putting the two together at this late stage was not really practical, in my view. It did seem to me, however, that Dave's highly original approach to the stage musical really deserved to be published, and it was in this spirit that I agreed to work on his manuscript. Chapter 1, which had been published previously in a different form, required relatively little rewriting, although I did add some material on the early musical comedy. I produced some hard edits of the introduction and chapters 3 and 5. Chapters 2 and 4 were reorganized and edited, and chapters 6 and 7 formed out of combining a long essay on *Evita* with material on the megamusical. It was only in these later chapters, and in the material on musical comedy in chapters 1 and 2, that I contributed in any significant sense to the ideas of *Musical Theater and American Culture.* My role, then, was primarily a writing/editorial one. I also worked on the more mundane side of things—the appendix, bibliography, index, and so on. The point being that this work, somewhere between editing and co-authoring, was not easily named, until Dave, with great generosity, insisted that we describe the book as being co-authored.

I think I would accept Dave's contention that *Musical Theater and American Culture* might not have appeared without an intervention such as mine. And I would want to take joint responsibility for *Musical Theater and American Culture* in the sense of owning up to any faults and errors. However, it should be emphasized that this book is Dave's project in very substantial ways. He conceived it and developed it, and it is his enthusiasm for musicals that really underscores the ideas expressed here. I would only say how much I appreciate the opportunity to work on his material. This was made a real pleasure by Dave's patient and entirely positive responses to my rewrites and, again, his unstinting generosity.

LP

Many others have contributed to this book. In particular, the authors would like to thank Salley Vickers, without whose active encouragement and constant support the book might not have seen the light of day; Mike Pickering, who offered the most thoughtful and thought-provoking comments on various drafts of the book; and Martin and Susie Gates, who gave the authors an inside knowledge into the creation and production of musicals. A number of academic colleagues, through their comments, helped in the shaping of the book. In this respect the authors would like to thank Les Back, Stephen Banfield, Paul Filmer, Paul Gilroy, Robert Gordon, Val Rimmer, and Helen Thomas. Other non-academic friends but informed enthusiasts of the musical produced stimulating debate. Here the authors thank Mary Ashwin, Jim Birkett, Sue Bunnett, Dale Idiens, Roger Harris, Bill Harrison, Alan Rebbeck, and Julia Whitburn. Undergraduate and postgraduate students taking the course in Contemporary Culture and Artistic Practice in the Sociology Department at Goldsmiths College, London, contributed very much to the authors' knowledge of the musical through their dissertations. Finally, and here a deep debt of gratitude, our thanks to Jen Tarr and Greer Rafferty for their help in transforming manuscript into typescript.

DW and LP

A Note on the Text

Originally *Musical Theater and American Culture* was illustrated by many quotations from the lyrics of songs, especially, of course, songs from musicals. The authors tried for several months to get copyright permissions to use these materials but in the end were defeated, sometimes by difficulties in finding copyright holders, sometimes by demands for large fees to quote just a few lines, but most often by companies simply refusing to respond to our requests. We make the point in *Musical Theater and American Culture* that the musical has been neglected by academics as a area of study, and we suggest a number of reasons as to why this might be so. To these must be added the further problem of a copyright culture that, to put it mildly, is not very conducive to serious academic work. In face of these obstacles, then, we have had to make do with the titles of songs and glosses. We give below a list of the song titles thus used, and, where appropriate, the shows they appear in, indicating where they are alluded to in the text. This will enable cross-referencing with, for the most part, easily available sheet music, should the reader be so interested. Authoring details of shows listed in the text appear in the appendix.

"Old Black Joe"	by Stephen Foster	page 27
"I'm a Yankee-Doodle Dandy"	from *Little Johnny Jones*	page 46
"Maxim's"	from *The Merry Widow*	page 56
"Girls at Maxim's"	from *The Merry Widow*	page 56
"Off to Maxim's"	from *The Merry Widow*	page 56

Introduction: Analyzing the Musical Sociologically

THE VIABILITY OF THE MUSICAL

Musicals, like all popular texts and forms of art, have an explicitly reflexive relationship with the societies from which they stem. As well as reflecting the historical and cultural character of society, they voice society's own sense of its life and values. The combination of song, dance, and drama, which distinguishes musical theater from other theatrical genres, is linked both to historical circumstances and ideological beliefs. The lyrics and formal qualities of movement, rhythm, and structure create a fantasy that is at one level escapist but which is also not just entertainment. The musical show offers a characteristically open, direct, and ideologically unapologetic expression of the ideals, dreams, anxieties, feelings, fulfillments, and frustrations of its audience. Conventionally, musicals work to produce a utopian view of life, and their pleasures can be found in the ways in which they can lead into realms where qualities that audiences' real lives lack can find visual and verbal expression. Musicals articulate values and ideologies through the crafted order, disjunctions, and restraint of their narratives. They can become powerful vehicles of popular collective expression by articulating symbolically, in the patterns of their narrative, lyrical harmonies, and dance, the tensions and reconciliation of everyday relations between individuals and society.

Yet in the upsurge of critical and analytical interest in popular culture that has occurred during the second half of the twentieth century there has been a strange neglect of the musical, especially the stage musical. While there are a number of sociocultural studies of the film musical,[1] there have been no comparable studies of the stage musical other than specific historical accounts of its development,[2] some musicological studies[3] and preliminary studies for a more systematic approach.[4] One reason for this may be the uncomfortable way in which the musical straddles the high/low cultural divide. It is too "lowbrow" musically and dramatically to interest high-art critics, yet it is too conventional and mundane for cultural critics of popular music forms such as jazz and rock.

But this neglect is a mistake for a variety of reasons, all of which establish the significance of the musical both as a popular form of entertainment and as art. In the context of American society, which is its source, it has been a primary and accessible voice through which the American way of life has expressed itself to the people of the United States and to much of the rest of the world. In this respect the musical became a theatrical expression of American national and political identity with a long history and tradition. It had deep roots and was formed through a whole variety of nineteenth-century forms of live American popular theater—ballad opera, vaudeville, burlesque, blackface entertainment and the minstrel show, melodrama, farce comedy, the operetta, and musical comedy. In this the musical was dependent for its resources mainly on folk and popular traditions of song-and-dance and their essentially vernacular nature. The history of the musical was largely, until the last decades of the twentieth century, the history of the relationship between American popular culture and society as it changed from the nineteenth century on to make the musical not simply an index and reflection of American society but a popular genre that helped to form, articulate, and instantiate its shape.

Now the musical has spread worldwide, originally as part of the process of the global spread of American culture wrought by its rise to power as a (now the) dominant world power, but also through the position that America achieved as the absolute symbol and epitome of modernity. Central to this has been the commodification of popular culture in terms of its capitalist-industrial production. In America itself, live theater had become well established in commercial terms by the turn of the nineteenth century and flourished progressively, except for the hiatus of the Great Depression, throughout the twentieth century with the development of Broadway in association with the music industry of Tin-Pan Alley. As radio and film took away the audience from live theatrical entertainment, and most specifically vaudeville and variety in the 1920s and 1930s, the musical became the primary form of live commercial theater. Commerce had always been the basis on which the musical was created and produced. However, as the costs of the musical rose (and it is a highly costly form of live theater) so commercial considerations became even more preponderant. On Broadway this meant that the viability of the musical steadily came to rely on longer and longer runs to ensure that costs could be amortized. In the 1920s and 1930s a Broadway musical would be highly profitable on a run of 500 performances; by the 1960s, the required run for financial viability was closer to 2,000 performances. In this context, the creation of a musical for Broadway had to be envisaged with a very close eye on its commercial success as a "hit" (this, too, would be true of the West End stage).

This essential link between commerce and musical theater has developed even further since the 1970s as the capitalist commodification of popular culture has transformed the musical into a global phenomenon. Here the musical has ceased to be an American genre. Through its exportation, theatrical provenance, and success, the musical has become a popular and contemporary artistic form that has opened up to composition and production that is non-American—to the point, indeed, where American creations within it have been, at least commercially, challenged and overtaken by the latter. What has emerged has been the "megamusical" and with this the musical as very big business indeed. The megamusical is not just a big musical of the traditional Broadway kind but part of a global business in which "capital investments are larger, markets are bigger, more international and more numerous, and stakes are higher than ever before in the history of popular music-theatre production" (Burston 1997, 205). So, as Steyn notes (1997, 165), by 1990 *Cats* (1982) had earned $860 million worldwide (by the end of its run in London in March 2002 it had earned $2 billion); *Les Miserables* (1986) had earned $450 million; *Phantom of the Opera* (1988) had earned $430 million; and *Miss Saigon* (1989), after only one year, had earned $25 million. The return of profits on *Cats* alone, for its investors, was 200 percent per annum over the first 15 years of its life. In terms of audience numbers, to take two examples, *Les Miserables* had been seen by 40,000,000 people by 1997 and *Cats* by 50,000,000 people by 2002 in 300 cities. Broadway and the West End musicals more specifically have annual audiences of 4,000,000. The commercial viability of any particular musical may be in doubt, but the commercial viability of the musical per se is not. It flourishes as popular live theater in this respect, now most particularly in three predominant world centers for music theater—New York, London, and Toronto—which are interlinked in terms of the exchange of productions and are the primary originating sources of productions that travel out to other parts of the world.

The huge audience for the musical speaks volumes for its vitality as a musical theater genre even if many musicals, individually or as types, do not. To paraphrase Irving Berlin, there's no business like show business, but for every hit there are plenty of turkeys that are destined to fold. For all the difficulties of individual success, however, there is virtually no major city worldwide that does not stage musicals. In the three world centers of musical theater, musicals dominate live theater in the sense that they represent at least half of major commercial live theater production and account for as much as two-thirds of the audience for it. Moreover, this audience combines both social variegation and social differentiation.

Increasingly, and in response to the differentiation of popular culture that has accompanied the social diversity of modern society, the musical has taken on a variety of forms that appeal to, and are specifically directed toward, particular audiences—for example, "art" musicals, "chamber" musicals, "rock" musicals, "conceptual" musicals, and megamusicals. But megamusicals together with revivals of classic musicals are the only live theater (except for pantomime) to draw in the lower classes in significant numbers—some 25 percent of the audience—as well as the young, again representing some 25 percent of audience totals. As with all live theater audiences, in London over 50 percent of the audience is female and predominantly middle class (in its widest form).

That the demand of the audience for commercial productions of the musical is primarily a demand for new musicals and not revivals of classic musicals is highly suggestive of the continued viability of the musical. This is true of all three centers of music theater, where the proportion of musicals produced is two-thirds new to one-third revivals. Although it must be noted, too, that there are very large numbers of semiprofessional and amateur companies for which the musical is a staple diet. This means that a huge number of revivals occur outside the commercial theater axis. For example, there are over 4,000 productions of Rodgers and Hammerstein musicals annually staged worldwide.

The musical, then, is not just a genuinely popular theater but, more importantly, it is very much a living form. No other live theater has this degree of creative contemporaneity. Even "straight" theater now has a much more limited scope for the major commercial production of new plays. In terms of live music theater, the composition of new operettas virtually died out with Friml and Romberg in the United States and Coward, Ellis, and Novello in Britain. As for opera, Puccini and Richard Strauss (with a few exceptions) were the last composers to create operas with a genuinely popular appeal to audiences. In this respect the musical comes closer to the cinema or even sporting events, rather than live theater or concerts, as a genuinely popular cultural phenomenon, especially as live theater and the concert have increasingly become revival-led and therefore focused around production and performance in these terms.

The musical continues to be creatively vital in another sense, one which is very much tied to its developmental history and tradition. A steady musical and dramatic advance can be detected in musical comedy from the early Princess Theatre musical comedies of Kern and Wodehouse in the 1920s through to the shows of the Gershwins, Porter, and Rodgers and Hart in the 1940s. The advance continued throughout the 1950s and 1960s in the works of Lerner and Loewe, Bernstein, Loesse, and Styne, and into the 1970s and beyond with shows by Kander and Ebb and Sondheim. But even more of a dramatic advance came with the development of the "book" musical, first in Kern's *Show Boat* (1927) and then through the

Depression works of the Gershwins (*Porgy and Bess*, for instance) on to the classic Rodgers and Hammerstein shows and to conceptual musicals such as Kander and Ebb's *Cabaret* (1966) and Sondheim's "modernist" musicals. Even rock musicals have developed an increasing degree of dramatic and musical sophistication, evident in such shows as *Tommy* (1993) and *Rent* (1996), as have megamusicals, like *Evita* (1978) and *Les Miserables*. Indeed, it might be said that the megamusical, with its through-musical composition, has produced a certain revivification of the operatic form (albeit perhaps to the detriment of the more traditional and distinct musical). Certainly the transformation of the musical from mere entertainment to art, both as music comedy and as music drama, has given stature and legitimacy to the musical as a form of music theater. This is evinced in Europe by the fact that certain musicals have been represented as art and produced by virtue of this status in state-subsidized theaters. In Austria, Germany, and Eastern Europe, for example, musicals are very often produced in the opera houses of major cities; in the United Kingdom, *Kiss Me Kate* (1948) and *Pacific Overtures* (1976) have been produced by the English National Opera, *Les Miserables* and *The Wizard of Oz* (1902) have been produced by the Royal Shakespeare Company, and the Royal National Theatre has a long string of musical productions to its credit—*Carousel* (1945), *Guys and Dolls* (1950), *Lady in the Dark* (1941), *My Fair Lady* (1956), *Oklahoma* (1942), *Singin' in the Rain* (1952), and *South Pacific* (1949). The Donmar Theater, too, in London, has been instrumental in producing the musicals of Sondheim.

Normally, however, the musical has been a genre of commercial theater and largely continues to be so. The musical is a popular cultural phenomenon not only because it has historically been a powerful vehicle of popular collective expression, but because it remains so in terms of its continuing creative vitality and its commercial viability. It requires no subsidy to keep it alive because its very popularity gives it lifeblood.

WHAT IS THE MUSICAL?

Put simply, the musical is musical theater composed out of an integrated and vernacular genre of song, dance, and speech. Central to its nature is the organization of the relationship between text and music, but this organization has taken a number of forms that establish various subgenres of the musical and a variety of hybrid relationships between them. It could be argued that this hybridization, in the end, shaped a larger distinction that was central to the history of the Broadway musical in terms of its form and structure: the distinction between the song-and-dance show and the book musical. The later form, it could be and has been argued (see Block 1997, 8–9; Lamb 2000, 172–73), involved a transformation of the musical from popular entertainment to popular art and thus the

transformation of the musical into a music drama of comparable stature to
opera and operetta, although sustained by its own aesthetic conventions.

Indeed, the tendency of many historical, theatrical, and musicological
studies has been to see the musical as a continuation of the operetta within
an American context. Bordman (1980) argues the case for this on the basis
of two claims. The first is that of form. Operetta means only a little opera
and, in this, the operetta is essentially a semidramatic work, partly in dialogue and partly in song, often comic but with modern characters and
music patterned on folk song with a relatively subordinated accompaniment. Against this yardstick, Bordman measures the musical and its subgenres. The revue, for instance, becomes an operetta that has no plot.
Musical comedy is understood in terms of the cynicism and sarcasm that
contrasts to the romanticism of operetta. The book musical is essentially
the same as operetta in having an integrated plot and music. Moreover,
and perhaps even more crucially, Bordman insists that the musical springs
from the entry of operetta into America through Offenbach, Gilbert and
Sullivan, and the early "Golden Age" in Viennese operettas of Johann
Strauss, followed more prominently by the later "Silver Age" Viennese
operettas of Lehár in particular.

This study, however, argues differently. It insists that it is a mistake to
see the musical as a form of operetta. To do so makes it impossible to
understand the character of the musical as an artistic phenomenon of popular culture that is reflexively tied, in terms of its genesis and development, to American society and its culture. European operetta played a
significant part in the emergence of the musical, but it was drawn upon in
a particular way and assimilated rather than simply "copied." The musical took on board both the format of operetta and, perhaps more fundamentally, the substance of musical comedy as it evolved in Britain, but it
nativized them within a genre that became its own. It did this both
unevenly and in a variety of different ways in respect of its own different
subforms. It is here that we can come to recognize the emergent specificity
of the musical as a genre of music theater creating a tradition that found a
primary basis in American popular culture and the forms of live theatrical
(and home) entertainment that were engendered within it. Studies by
Kislan (1980), Mates (1987), Block (1997), Steyn (1997), Erenberg (1984),
and Lott (1993) clarify how nineteenth- and early-twentieth-century burlesque, vaudeville, minstrel show, farce comedy, and melodrama were
crucial theatrical resources on which the musical drew for its genesis and
development, and Hamm (1979) shows how its musical composition had
a major basis in a continuous and flourishing tradition of American
indigenous popular song. The musical historically took up the primary
structure of such songs (i.e., verse and refrain), which gave it an easy
accessible musicality. With this the musical also became marketable

because of its simplicity, memorability, and repeatability. The significance of this will be made clear in a later part of this introductory chapter.

The musical, then, is quite distinct from opera and operetta on a number of grounds, some developmental and cultural and others aesthetic. Banfield (1993), for instance, insists that the musical is characterized by its own general *melapoesis,* which distinguishes the character of its songs. By this he means that vernacular song is an interplay between the verbal and musical elements, which entails a unitary perception dependent on both of them. Melapoetic integration, then, is one where the first without the other is impossible—lyrics cannot be separated from music, or music from lyrics. Lyrics without the music make no sense because metric beat is not just lyrical but musical—that is, part of this beat is the silent beat provided by the music. So the interplay between lines of verse and lines of music is the essence of this vernacular song, and interplay is simultaneous, successive, and directional. Operetta, by contrast, subjects lyrics to the music, which is why it can be described as a little opera.

Block reinforces this view of the distinctness of the musical by considering Kerman (1998) and Kivy's (1988) analyses of opera as music theater and pointing out where this has relevance, or not, to the musical in its structure and forms. Kerman in *Opera as Drama* argues that the aesthetic value and integrity of opera as art depends upon its validity as music drama—and, with this, assembles a series of canonic masterpieces on the principle that, in opera, the composer is the dramatist. Here Kerman insists "on music's primary role in defining character, generating action and establishing atmosphere" (see Block 1997, xvi). This emphasis on the determining character of music is problematic, of course, when applied to the musical. It imposes a specific model that cannot be generalized to include all music theater. It might apply to operetta, which is based on the same aesthetic as a "little opera," but not to musical comedy. Yet, Block argues, some value can be given to the operatic analysis of the musical in its integration of text and music as music theater if we use Kivy's extension of this analysis in terms of the distinction he draws between "textual realism" (music that sets "meanings and not words") and "opulent adornment" (music that sets "words, not meanings"). This distinction, Block argues, can be thoughtfully used to characterize the distinction between the typical early Broadway musical (mainly of the 1920s and 1930s) and what it would later become (from the 1940s)—that is, between the "song-and-dance" musical and the "book" musical. The latter is one in which the text (the "book") becomes the foundation of the musico-dramatic integration of the musical as opposed to song-and-dance per se. By its very nature, the musical is a song-and-dance theater essentially characterized by its popular and vernacular nature, but it can be claimed that it did move into a more comprehensive (and potentially more sophisticated) genre of music drama in its book form. The movement toward integration through the book can certainly be traced within the history of the Broadway musical and can be treated, in this respect, as a development by both its leading composers, as a form they were actively striving for, and its critics, as its most satisfactory completion (see Block 1997, 8–9). An argument can be made, then, that the musical transformed itself from popular entertainment to popular art in this way—the musical as music drama—to constitute a tradition (as exemplified in the history and development of the Broadway musical) that is an aesthetic project. This would develop further as cinematographic forms of music-text integration entered into the stage music to offer new structural possibilities of narrative and dramatic fluidity derived from film rather than melodrama.

But, still, it is important to emphasize that the musical is a *popular* music theater whatever form it takes. It is, crucially, a theater fostered within a commercial context, and this also plays a major part in its character. The tradition through which it developed and took aesthetic shape was subject not only to the structural and institutional conditions of commerce but also purposed an aestheticization of the musical tailored to the requirements of commerce. It is a moot point whether the development of the early song-and-dance musical into the later book musical, although a product of historical development and compositional intent, constitutes a simple divide between the musical as entertainment and the musical as art. One is on much safer grounds with this distinction when discussing how these two types of musical integration operate in the three previous subgenres in the musical: the revue, musical comedy, and musical plays. Whichever, to treat the musical in terms of an exclusively operatic model grants it artistic stature on aesthetic grounds but entails the reduction of the popular element in its character (particularly as entertainment). Instead of finding the validity and status of the musical as the exploration and extension of its tradition within the parameters of this popularity, it is the very diminution of the demotic that somehow guarantees an increase in "artistry."

In this study it is argued that any degree of operatic practice in the development of the musical has to be set in relation to its popular and commercial context even as book integration becomes central to its late Broadway form. Consequently, the divide between the song-and-dance musical and the book musical is treated here as a difference in the musico-theatrical structure of integration and not as an entire transformation of its aesthetic integrity and quality. The musical becomes more reflexively fashioned as a "realist" kind of music theater in this change, although it should be pointed out that this constitutes a potential loss as well as a gain. As Block suggests, where the "principle of textual realism" (book integration) replaces the "principle of opulent adornment" (song-and-dance), it leads to the "abandonment of cleverness, wit, autonomous memorable tunes—in favor of integrated and more operatically constructed musicals filled with techniques such as leitmotivs, foreshadowing, thematic transformation, and classical borrowings, however convincingly employed for various operatic purposes" (1997, 8). These remain variations within the parameters of a popular format where the use of operatic techniques may subvert the specifically populist character of the musical by elimination of the autonomous "hit" tune. At the same time the popular may also subvert the truly operatic (tunes may lose their autonomy but not their memorable tunefulness if the musical is to find favor with an audience). Narrative may replace cleverness and wit but it must still remain within a recognizable framework of vernacular meaning and comprehension in order to be accessible (as with the music) to the tastes of popular culture.

In American popular culture it can be argued that commerce and the form of the musical find an agreement that is central to the musical as music theater and which the Broadway musical enshrined and institutionalized to give the musical its tradition and characteristics as a popular genre. It is therefore quite mistaken of Swain (following Kerman) to insist on treating the Broadway musical in essentially operatic terms, to fail to distinguish the musical from opera, and so to constantly judge the musico-dramatic qualities of the former in terms of the latter. This ultimately leads him to disparage the musical in favor of opera as true musico-drama on the grounds of an alleged inability of the former to articulate and express tragedy. For Swain, "though a number of its best plots have offered opportunities for tragic composition, Broadway music has generally failed those moments" (1990, 205). Its history has been a music history of missed chances and unanswered challenges. In opposition, Banfield argues that the musical is its own kind of music theater and drama and is not seeking to be opera. Comparing the two, Banfield points out that, even with regard to sung-through musicals, the musical "can often not just move in and out of the drama but in and out of itself, and is more dramatically agile...than...most opera" (1993, 7). The good musical is one that does not fall into the trappings and conventions of the opera but keeps faith with its own self as a genre and, where it tragedizes, it does so in terms of its particular agility.

Centrally this agility comes from the "vernacular" and the "popular" that characterizes the musical as music theater. These origins have two interrelated sources, which are explored extensively in chapter 1. The first is the historical genesis of the musical in American popular culture. It emerged as a theatrical expression of the national and political identity and life of the United States of America and the myths, beliefs, and dreams that largely formed themselves in terms of a popular culture, as befits a society that is ideologically egalitarian and formally democratic in its conception of itself as the first post-Enlightenment "new nation." The musical thrived and developed as a popular voice for and expression of the growth of the

United States into the very epitome of modernity and, eventually, a global superpower. In this the musical was an American product and artistic form, which evinced and celebrated the American way of life. But it did this within the framework of very specific American forms of popular live theater and entertainment in which song-and-dance predominated and which came to be organized through the emergence of a commercially effective, highly institutionalized, and hugely profitable theatrical system catering for and partly creating a popular audience. By the end of the nineteenth and the beginning of the twentieth century, this merged with Tin-Pan Alley to create a powerful music business. The relationship between musical theater and popular culture was thus solidified to provide the economic, technical, and artistic conditions to make, promote, maintain, and develop the musical. What was created, then, was a mass and popular culture that could accommodate changes wrought by the social transformation of the United States, at least at the level of entertainment.

The musical owes its own and special integrity as popular music theater and art to what would seem to be the paradox of its historical constitution—what Steyn (quoting George Abbot, a major figure over decades in the production of Broadway musicals) argues has always been the guiding principle and Broadway's first rule: "forget art: does it work?" (see Steyn 1997, 4). This paradox is central to the musical. It is as an art founded in commerce and entertainment that the musical remains faithful to the popular, its resource and lifeblood. One might go even further to argue that the musical is conjoined with America at a deeper level—that its musico-dramatic structure metaphorically captures the New World in terms of the way the United States formally (through its Constitution), ideologically, and popularly set out to cast and establish itself. It saw itself as the model of post-Enlightenment civil society in an attempted realization of the ideals of political thinkers from Locke to Rousseau. So "the new world needed new forms, forms which could combine music with words and drama in ways the Viennese [the primary font of operetta] had never foreseen. Opera and operetta were absolute monarchies ruled by composers: the American Republic would make a musical of checks and balances, of collective congressional will, of composers and lyricists and librettists and stagers" (Steyn 1997, 38). Put less hyperbolically, this establishes the musical as a truly American genre and, in this, a music theater made by and for its popular culture.

HOW TO STUDY THE MUSICAL

Musicals have an explicitly reflexive relationship with the societies from which they stem, like all popular texts and works of art, so, as has been suggested above, they are properly analyzed in terms of what Geertz has termed the "thick description" of culture (1975, 10). The organization, construction, and meaning of musicals must be treated in terms of how they are lodged within, and lodge within themselves, the cultural and social structures of the society of which they are a social expression and with which they are reflexively engaged. In this, the interest that sociology has in social and cultural phenomena is met through an investigation of the musical in terms of an examination of the general social and cultural form/forms of life that are the musical's foundation. But the study of the musical must also proceed by taking this up ideographically through an investigation of the actual and intrinsic practices that constitute the musical as a genre artistically embodying these forms in its character and composition.

In this context, the current study seeks to offer a sociocultural analysis of the musical as a phenomenon of popular culture specifically originating in American society. It interprets the musical in terms of a reflexive relationship to America, tracing its development in relation to the development of national identities. It sees the musical as a vehicle for American myths, ideologies, and dreams, one that gives voice to their collective expression as a popular articulation of society and its values. *Musical Theater and American Culture* is a musicological or dramaturgical study only inasmuch as music, dance, and drama are the means through which this expression and articulation are structured and organized as music theater. Similarly, this study is not a theatrical history per se, although it does recover and address that history. The aims here are both to examine how a tradition of music theater was established out of live American popular culture and entertainment and to understand the systematic spread of the musical throughout America, by way of its commercialization, commodification, and transportation. With this, *Musical Theater and American Culture* examines how a large and varied mass audience was created, stimulated, and engineered by the commercially effective, highly-institutionalized, and massively profitable character of this theatrical system because it could accommodate changes produced by the transformations of American society. In a sense, then, this study provides a social history of the musical, which, as Block says, is missing (1997, 11). It explores the social, political, and cultural issues that the musical has engaged, expressed, and formed. The central issue of the book is to show how the musical arose from the popular culture of American society and evolved as America translated and reshaped its Enlightenment origins in ways consistent with the creation and consolidation of the capitalist-industrial/bourgeois society *par excellence*.

Ideographically, this is taken up through an examination of specific musicals that can be seen as canonical only in the sense that they offer key examples, through their popularity, of works that evince and chart this process. These are addressed precisely in terms of their historical, social, and cultural setting and in the ways their narratives, lyrics, and formal structures of movement, rhythm, and structure engage, articulate, and shape a sense of culture and society. Here the book argues that musicals can be examined in terms of the musico-theatrical particularities through which their social and cultural setting is represented and varied in terms of a show that is characteristically an open, direct, mythological, and unapologetically ideological expression of the ideals, anxieties, and frustrations of its audience. Generally the mythopoetics of the musical cultivates a highly utopian vision of life. For America this has meant that the musical, reaching a peak, perhaps, in the "classic" book musical, has always been a powerful threnodist of the American Dream, in its many forms and transformations. It has articulated the American Way as a millenarianist end of ideology. But is has also seen the "good life" of the American Way as being undermined by changes in American society itself and even exposed as its own ideology. The musical has increasingly become an interlocutor in relation to a fragmentation, both positive and negative. It has engaged a variety of new and different forms that often set out to show the rotten teeth in the utopian smile of the American Dream as well as harvesting the social differentiation and disintegration of the American community. If a new utopia is projected by the contemporary musical, it is not American musicals that are so much the vehicle of this but the megamusical, which is an altogether different creature created out of and by global capitalism and a globalized culture industry. Here musicals and their composers, producers, directors, performers, and technologies have become international.

Musical Theater and American Culture, as a work of "thick description," is, of course, an interpretation and not a legislative sociocultural analysis or historical narrative of the musical. What it attempts to do is open up a way of systematically addressing the musical in terms of how it is located in and reflexively creates itself within cultural life. But it does this by exemplification—that is, through examining musicals as works that constitute the musical's tradition and genre. So, to follow Geertz, the book's theoretical and methodological stance is to treat society and culture as primarily a context, and not as a unilateral causal determinant, in terms of which the musical can be socioculturally described, understood, and analyzed as "popular" music theater. A historical narration is required because this context has a temporal reality that is constitutive of its intelligibility.

NOTES

1. See, for instance, Altman (1987); Feuer (1993); Babington and Evans (1985); Barrios (1995).

2. The best known are Bordman (1981, 1982, 1985, 1986); Ewen (1959); Gänzl (1995); Kislan (1980); Mates (1987); Morrden (1983); Gänzl and Lamb (1989); Lamb (2000).

3. See Banfield (1993); Block (1997); Swain (1990).

4. For example, Lawson-Peebles (1996); Walsh (1996); Burston (1997); Steyn (1997).

CHAPTER 1

The Genesis of the Musical in American Popular Culture

The musical is a particular and American genre of popular music theater and this chapter sets out to trace its nature in these terms. The underlying sociological argument is that the musical not only reflects the historical, social, and cultural character of American society, but also voices that society's own sense of its life and values. It originated and developed as a primary and widely accessible voice through which the American way of life came to express itself to Americans. The form comes from the various genres that live popular entertainment and theater took in nineteenth-century America.

BALLAD OPERA

What the early British settlers in the eighteenth century brought to America with them was the ballad opera, of which John Gay's *The Beggars' Opera* (1728) is the classic example. This itself appeared in Britain in opposition to the domination of Italian *opera seria. Opera seria* had its source and basis in Europe as a cultural expression of the centralized monarchies that constituted the political-state organization of European society at this time and for which it provided a major part of the politics of spectacle in terms of which such monarchical regimes culturally sustained their form of regime and government. As such *opera seria* had a particular symbiotic relationship with its social setting that made it court opera *par excellence*. Although, in Britain, it was commercially organized, and not a court enterprise, it still remained tied to this social setting, as this commercial organization was sponsored by the court aristocracy

through the Royal Society of Music. It provided for its audience an idealized and legitimizing portrait of the nobility and its world as one of high
moral ideals and action. It was, then, a primary artistic embodiment
of "civilization," to use this term in Elias's sense (1994). But from the
middle of the eighteenth century on, *opera seria* came under increasing
attack politically, ideologically, and aesthetically in Britain. Following the
restoration, parliament, and with it a new bourgeoisie (as Britain transformed into a mercantile economy), asserted itself through an attack on
monarchical power and aristocratic privilege. This was increasingly sustained by a growing intellectual establishment fed on Enlightenment philosophy and the development of what Habermas refers to as a "bourgeois
public sphere" (1974) that created a civil society functioning as a republic
of private individuals (operating in salons, coffeehouses, debating societies, and so on). They thought of themselves as constituting an educated
public divorced from, and entitled to engage in, critical debate and confrontation with the state and the traditional aristocratic-estate organization of society. America was to be born as the first fruit of this—
essentially as a post-Enlightenment society. This new "bourgeois public
sphere" established itself as an arena of debate with the development of
the print media through journals, broadsheets, pamphlets, and periodi-
cals, a sphere that, in turn, was institutionalized in two further ways.
First, there was a reconstitution of the family from an institutional order
of affinal relations to a sphere of intimacy that led to an affirmative eval-
uation of ordinary life, the economic activity it entailed, and the participation of the patriarchal head of the household in the public arena. The
family, then, was no longer seen as just a reproductive unit or a property-
owning entity but as a locus of subjectivity, one where humanity was
reconceptualized by making personal closeness the basis of the family
bond and the family idealized as the purely human realm of intimate
relations between human beings. Second, the "bourgeois public sphere"
was associated with the emergence of a world of letters, particularly in
terms of the sentimental literature of the period, which reinforced this
sense of humanness through its content of subjectivity and intimacy, the
creation of an author-reader relationship that implied an empathy
between individuals psychologically that was interested in what was
"human" in self-knowledge, and the production of a literary public
sphere developing the modern idea of culture as an autonomous reality
and a commodity culture now claiming to exist for its own sake and as a
means of communicating subjectivity. This literary public sphere established institutional bases for its extension into the political sphere rang-
ing from meeting places (such as coffeehouses) to journals to various
other webs of social relations (through salon culture, for example). It
became a realm of rational-critical discourse that was open in principle
(however elitist in practice) to anyone with access to cultural products

who as readers, listeners, and spectators could participate by availing themselves via the market of objects that were subject to discussion.

In consequence *opera seria* came under a series of attacks. Ideologically, its aristocratic and feudal ideals and values of duty, loyalty, courage, and compliance could no longer be seen as holding any relevance. The portrayal of such values, in high-flown tragedies set in mythical and historical contexts where gods and noble heroes and heroines were the protagonists, no longer appealed to an audience that had reconstituted its sense of the nature of humanity and human life. The implied politics of *opera seria* did not correspond with the newly emerging democratic ideals of the Enlightenment and the rising bourgeoisie. Aesthetically, the extremes to which musical embellishment, spectacular production, and dramatic formalism had raised itself in *opera seria* led to its ridicule and to the demand for reform of opera in the direction of simplicity, directness of expression, and a more human characterization of the dramatic personae. In this emerging bourgeois world in Britain, *opera seria* came to be the subject of abuse as exotic and irrational entertainment (as figures such as Pope, Swift, Lord Chesterfield, Walpole, Johnson, Goldsmith, and so on attacked it). As part of this broadside, and in the ideological and political spirit of the critique of it, "ballad opera" emerged as a primary popular theatrical form.

This kind of opera fused a comic libretto of a satirical and sentimental nature with popular song as the accompaniment to, commentary upon, and focus for the drama itself (see Price 1989). So ballad opera provided the foundation for what became the central characteristic of the musical: popular drama, largely about the contemporary world, organized and expressed through contemporary and vernacular music and dance. Ballad opera was imported from Britain into America in the eighteenth century by British settlers who provided an enthusiastic and popular audience for its satirical critique of British government and society. They interpreted it from an American point of view, central to which were the anti-British sentiments that had brought them to America in the first place and later led to their commitment to the American Revolution. Quickly, however, Americans began to write their own ballad operas attuned to American society, defined as autonomous, democratic, and opposed to European government and culture. America was thus understood, at a popular level, as a revolt against authority in favor of the common man (notwithstanding the real political nature of the American Constitution, which was of an altogether less egalitarian character). In popular music theater the result was the construction of parodies of European operas and plays that challenged the rules and conventions of the older form, satirized historical and contemporary events, and attacked the despotic political regimes of the old European order. But ballad opera of this kind also, and more largely, entered into the generation of popular American music theater through its specific help in the creation of burlesque.

BURLESQUE

This American form of ballad opera, leading to burlesque, was distinctive: a form of travesty that used sprightly folk tunes to convey the social and political content of its theater. Burlesque, through this popular musical representation of characters and action in comic and satirical scenes, was already creating an embryo-form of musical comedy. Using the *olio* and *pasticcio* (which could be fitted into any form of theatrical or musical entertainment as well as being freestanding theater in its own right), little music dramas of a popular nature were created that utilized familiar American material, simple songs and music, and ordinary human characters.

Burlesque also built into itself a second thread, which was primarily a result of its adult male audience: stage nudity. This was not so much integrated into the travesty but interspersed to produce a complete comic and satirical song-and-dance show composed of scenes, sketches, interludes, and dances. From the early 1830s on, the burlesque included a *tableau vivant*—a living picture of nude women (although "nude" at this time meant women in tights) who stood on stage, without moving, to the accompaniment of an orchestral piece. The result was to create the female entertainer (the *soubrette*), playing a breeches role, who would eventually, in the burlesque, become transformed into the nude star-turn. And slowly, too, the *tableau vivant* turned into the *chorus dansant*, which remained in an unadorned state. Thus, in the burlesque, the female star and the singing-and-dancing chorus line of girls originated. These were central to the form of the musical as musical comedy as well as to the revue. Moreover, the form of the burlesque made it easy to commercialize and spread to a popular audience. It was cheap and easily transported, and this—along with its strong element of nudity—made it easy to join up with the "honky-tonk" shows with their singing-and-dancing girls that had appeared in the dance halls and saloons of the American West, as well as with the "showboats" of the Midwest. The latter combined the dual function of entertainment and prostitution in a primitive and virtually all-male society so that the purveyance of sex was a large part of their business.

But burlesque grew in another way too: the "minstrel show," highly popular in mid-nineteenth-century America, added itself to burlesque. The net result was that by the 1870s burlesque had developed into a girlie-show based upon music, dancing, comedy, and speciality acts. There it remained throughout the heyday of its popularity up to the 1930s. Slowly and surely, sex and smut replaced satire as its central element, particularly as variety and vaudeville took comedy to itself. However, this, too, had future consequences for the musical, because the increased orientation toward sex and titillation led to an emphasis on dance to generate erotic movement in the nude women performers. In this way dance now became effectively established as part of American popular theater culture.

Once established, the burlesque show was very effectively sustained and institutionalized through a theatrical system that systematically financed and commodified it. This system, known as the *wheel system*, consisted of a number of centralized theatrical management companies, each of which subcontracted the theaters of all the major towns within a geographical area and then put together a burlesque show rotating through them. At the completion of the rotation another show was sent out, and so on. In this way, theater, show, and audience were structured into a tight relationship with one another. The profitability of the show was guaranteed while the appetite of the audience was stimulated and satisfied by an established and regular venue for a constant stream of new shows. At the same time the management, by controlling shows and the theatrical circuit, could and did foster new artistes and acts but simultaneously kept their demands under control. Both were necessary for burlesque to survive and thrive, but demonstrated the way in which popular entertainment was to become a business that was not only "show business" but "big business." The musical would become an essential commercial venture as a result and this, as much as its artistic provenance, would emerge as a vital part of its character. The overall result was to give a high degree of homogeneity to American live popular culture, because it came to be tied to its effective commercialization and commodification.

But, if sex and smut came to play a large part in the success of burlesque, this was its eventual undoing too. It thrived on its risqué and unrespectable character because its audience was largely male and lower class. But by the last decade of the nineteenth century and the beginning of the twentieth, the industrialization and urbanization of America had developed a large middle class. This typically was not only family-organized and centered on a domestic existence; its identity was also specifically established in terms of respectable bourgeois values. Burlesque was rejected by it as totally unseemly. But it was this class that began to take over as a primary audience for theater particularly as, from the First World War on, the cinema drew away the lower- and working-class theatrical audience. So burlesque was squeezed as the new middle class took to the respectable music theater of vaudeville, the revue, and the musical comedy, while the working class went to the movies. The initial response of burlesque was to try to import vaudeville and musical comedy into itself. But this, in the end, was an unworkable solution. The popularity of the real thing drew away audiences and artistes. Burlesque was reduced to a constant recycling of the same stuff, and audiences declined even further. Eventually it could only fight with all it had left to offer—nudity and sex—but this meant it degenerated into the striptease show. In reaching this apotheosis of what had always constituted a major element of its audience appeal, it lost its other sources of vitality (particularly satire). More than this, however, it was the emergence of other and more glamorous sources of sexual titillation (the revue) operating in less seedy venues that finally killed off burlesque. It was left playing in dilapidated theaters, standing in prime positions in city centers that had a huge real estate value: with a declining audience there was more economic value and profit to be made in knocking the theaters down than in keeping them going. By the 1930s burlesque was dead as popular entertainment in America. It had created the embryo of musical comedy in its spoofs, parodies, and travesties, but this would need transformation from horseplay to wit and from sketch to full-blown narrative before musical comedy could use it.

VAUDEVILLE

In many ways the death of burlesque was precipitated by its sister form of popular entertainment in America: vaudeville. This too entailed a large element of comic song-and-dance and was just as easy to put on and transport, but it operated on an altogether more respectable level, which allowed it to attract and keep a huge and, even more importantly, socially varied audience. Between 1860 and 1920, vaudeville became the primary form of popular cultural entertainment in America: by 1913, there were 2,973 vaudeville theaters in the country. It ended only when cinema, then radio, and finally television replaced it, and its effect on the musical, particularly musical comedy, was key.

Originally vaudeville was called "variety" and it grew up with the burlesque as a bill of songs, dances, and speciality acts, which traveled easily because of its small economic and artistic requirements and the fact that it could be fitted into any kind of show from concerts to circuses, minstrel shows, plays, and burlesque. In the end, it would even become part of the silent film show. But variety took two forms, the respectable and the unrespectable. The former was initially performed in the theaters, museums, and concert-halls of the cities, particularly in eastern America, and had a relatively socially varied audience. The latter placed it, together with burlesque and to a certain extent the early minstrel show, into a popular entertainment milieu that was lower class and, to a large but not exclusive extent, male. This meant that it was performed in the box-houses, saloons, and honky-tonks of the western frontier to ally itself with their wider world of drinking, gambling, and prostitution. In the cities, this kind of variety was saloon-connected. It was part of that popular amusement that existed on the boundaries of dance hall environments and red-light districts. The saloon was essentially a lower-class and male preserve and the variety show that developed in association with it was one in which its audience came to see singing, dancing, and comedy skits, but in a form that entailed both rowdiness and audience/performer intimacy. Thus the male audience, frequently lubricated with drink, booed the villain, encouraged the hero, and either approved or saw the failing low comedian off the stage entirely. For this reason, variety remained largely male until it was cleaned up and thoroughly established in the concert-salons and theaters of the city through its renaming as vaudeville in the mid-1880s. This was a calculated move on the part of theater managers, led by Tony Pastor's Theater on Fourteenth Street in New York, to create a larger audience and to capture the respectable dollar of the emergent and growing American bourgeoisie. This growing middle class had, at least ostensibly, abandoned the traditional forms of stage entertainment during the 1850s as they became imbued with, and distinguished themselves in terms of, middle-class values of decorum, gentility, and restraint. Moreover, this respectability was tied to the creation of a family life that separated the public from the private sphere to create a domestic sphere that was the specific province of women and required of them that they become not only the epitome of virtue but also its guardians. As such, respectable women had to be protected from the more disorderly and overtly sexual environments. Initially this led to the creation of specifically middle-class forms of entertainment—the concert hall, legitimate theater, and private social functions—although the circus remained an acceptable traditional entertainment. With variety now turned into vaudeville, this form of popular entertainment could attract the bourgeoisie, and this helped to move American popular culture into a middle-class world, if not entirely to bourgeoisify it.

Vaudeville established itself as a national popular entertainment in several ways. First, it spread nationally through the ease with which it could be transported. The completion of the railroad system by the 1880s permitted vaudeville troupes to extend their operations and create a large and socially diversified mass audience. On this basis, vaudeville circuits were established throughout America. Second, vaudeville had a unified content that established a tight format of song, dance, comedy, speciality acts, and drama. This institutionalized its whole structure by creating and fulfilling uniform audience expectations, supplying and training acts, and establishing economic conditions for its viability and success. Third, it focused on American themes, particularly on ethnic and racial groups as sources of comedy, and on using sentimental ballads, popular songs, and dances of the day (including ragtime, jazz, and syncopation) to do so. Song-and-dance, then, was at the very heart of vaudeville, not only in its many forms (ballads, minstrel songs, dialect songs, juvenile songs, character songs, and a whole variety of dances) but also because its other acts were dependent on music too.

Vaudeville also played a valuable role in the social integration of American society by virtue of its character, content, and national dissemination. Because it primarily depended on talent, and on a wide, novel, and diversified variety, it became a vehicle for entry into and social mobility in American society for ethnic groups. Not only did it portray these ethnic groups in its acts so the audience could identify themselves, but, as it included them, they could laugh at themselves with a sense of being part of the American world, if not as yet entirely part of its family. Full incorporation into the latter by particular ethnic groups always depended on the pull of older immigrant groups moving up the ladder of social mobility and institutional power and the push of new immigrant groups entering America to take their place as the lower orders of society. At the same time, members of ethnic groups could achieve mobility as performers in this context. Vaudeville was certainly, and almost entirely, the major vehicle of social mobility for black Americans.

Black Americans, as they entered the cities of America following the end of the slavery, mainly inhabited what was the milieu of disreputable entertainment and the red-light districts with which this conjoined—the world of burlesque, free-and-easy clubs, saloons, dance halls, and brothels. In such venues they found some measure of neighborhood authority outside of white hegemony where they could express aspects of cultural identity with relative freedom. Many of the early hot spots in this milieu were run and frequented by blacks, and it was in the cities that blacks developed ragtime and jazz. The city offered social and political protection that promoted "cabarets, rookeries and saloons devoted to the worlds of entertainment...[where] sportingmen, and crime developed and prospered" (Erenberg 1984, 23). Within this context black Americans could establish a place for themselves. The musical vitality of jazz and ragtime developed here would eventually make its way out and become absolutely central to white popular musical culture and entertainment in the early-twentieth century, albeit in sanitized versions.

So, through its uniform nature and complete dissemination through America, vaudeville was creating a homogenized form of live popular culture and entertainment that was specifically based on song-and-dance and appealed to all walks of life in American society through its variety, topicality, respectability, and entertainment value. Moreover, it carried an essentially urban entertainment to the whole of America. This was a crucial part of the creation of an entertainment industry, because it could center itself through and flourish within this urban foundation to become the "culture industry" that Adorno and Benjamin[1] identify as the basis of the commodified and mass popular culture that is produced by capitalism and first, and particularly, emerged in America as the most developed and developing of capitalist societies. Until the 1920s, when cinema effectively began to replace it, vaudeville played a major part in creating the star, promoting popular song, and creating dance crazes. It did this through nationwide tours and the repetition of the same kind of show from coast to coast. Its popular and commercial theatrical culture was a crucial source of the musical, particularly the comic form. The cinema helped eventually to kill it off as its audience deserted to the superior glamour and technical resources that film could offer, and radio and TV completed this process, because initially what they offered was vaudeville in one's home.

THE MINSTREL SHOW

The minstrel show is not, as the majority of its American historians have it, entirely indigenous to America.[2] But it did take on a very particular shape and importance as popular theater in America in relation to the serious social and political problem of slavery. The argument that the minstrel show is indigenous to America is based on the claim that it originated with T. "Daddy" Rice's early 1840s song-and-dance act in ragged clothes as "Jim Crow" with which he toured the whole of Northeast America "imitating" black life and particularly the life of the plantation slave. Some critics have argued (see Mates 1987) that this set up a key type in American folklore, which came to be known as "Jim Crow" because of the name of Rice's act. But more recent evidence shows that minstrelsy was an English as well as American phenomenon[3] and that the two interacted throughout the nineteenth century. It is true that the minstrel show format was primarily shaped by American troupes in the 1840s (and this was taken up and adapted in Britain) but it is not clear that Rice was the originator of the form or that it was solely American. Charles Matthews took "Negro" impersonations from England to America in the 1820s,[4] and Rice certainly used English sources for his own farces. Following his visit to London, he essentially reproduced Maurice Dowlin's burlesque *Othello* (1834) in his own burlesque of the same name, even if he substituted American for English songs. Moreover, after his return to America, Rice started to integrate the English dandy and the blackface "Negro" in his farces primarily in the character of Zip Coon (the stereotype of the urban dandified black). Rice was not even alone in giving Yankee impersonations (which were possibly blackface) in London: Danforth Marble, James H. Hackett, George "Yankee" Hill, and Joshua Silbee were doing this before Rice's first visit (see Ramshaw 1989). The sources and materials of all these acts were American, as were Matthews's in part, but the origins of minstrelsy were not solely in America and the extent to which Rice was its progenitor is open to doubt.

However, slavery and its institutionalization in the American South gave the minstrel show a particular context and serious topicality in America. Slavery in this period was not only the basis of the agrarian plantation economy of the South (and through it a primary basis of the whole American economy until the end of slavery) but also an emblem of the divide that opened up between the South and North from the mid-nineteenth century on. It provided the moral and ideological cause around which the Civil War conflict came to rally. What was at stake was the whole nature of the political and social order that would constitute the United States and fulfill its revolutionary foundation as a post-Enlightenment civil society. The Founding Fathers of America had envisaged a modern and democratically organized society, but one that was primarily rural and agrarian in its social and economic foundations, albeit with capitalist and commercial overtones. What emerged instead was a full-fledged capitalist-industrial, urban, and bourgeois society. This would become the material foundation for the instantiation of the new and modern society of America, becoming, ultimately, the primary vehicle for the realization of the American Dream and the transformation of America into a world power.

From the inception of the United States and into the 1850s, then, the southern states politically dominated the Union through their control over its Constitutional organization as a result of the economic might of the plantation economy. "King Cotton" was indeed the king of the American economy, and slavery was its foundation. The society of the South was a reflection of this: a rural, racialized society organized in terms of a hierarchical class structure of "poor white trash," yeoman farmers, and plantation aristocracy. This structure was, of course, based upon and produced by the slave system. It was an oligarchical rather than a democratic world, despite the Constitutional framework of the political system through which it was ruled. The North, by contrast, although still primarily agrarian at the time of the Civil War, was in a process of transition to a commercial and industrial economy, and neither its agricultural system nor its commercial and industrial enterprises had a use for slavery. Rather, the slave system could only be a barrier to the progress and development of its own economy. Northern agriculture was based on the family farm and this was an easily self-sufficient and productive unit for developing the agricultural economy. Moreover, it had a symbiotic relationship with the growth of commerce and industry because it needed the support of a good and extensive system of roads and towns to create and organize a market for its produce and to get it to consumers. The whole economy of the North had its basis in free labor, and its interest was the continuing extension and development of this.

Both economically and politically, the South stood in the way of the North. From the 1840s the North began to politically articulate and organize itself in the pursuit of its interests and future in terms of a growing opposition to and from the South. The battle was fought out in terms of state rights within the Union and the westward extension of the frontier to carve out new territories and create new states of America. The American Constitution had been designed as a political system that created checks and balances between the forces and interests at work in the social composition of its original immigrant society and chiefly through the creation of itself as a federation of states (a union) and not a centralized state. What the South saw in the North was an attempt to transform the Union into the latter through the incorporation of new territories and states as free. This could only be to the detriment of its own position and power, now dependent on maintaining the Union as a federation by asserting the rights and autonomy of states as against central government. Throughout this period, the South insisted and fought for the right to extend slavery and the plantation system into these new frontier territories and the new states carved out of them. The North, on the other hand, saw the preservation of the Union as crucial for both the existence of America itself and its progress and development, which would need to have its foundation in an agricultural, commercial, and industrial economy based on free labor. This, it believed, could be secured Constitutionally and peacefully through the extension of the Union along its frontiers and the incorporation of these expanded territories into it as free territories from which free states would be carved out. In this its understanding was that slavery would simply die out as a redundant economic system. That it would not do so is what inevitably forced the conflict between the North and South into a civil war. The whole foundation of southern society was utterly determined and shaped by slavery: the end of a slave-based economy could only be the end of this society, just as the North and its society could not prosper if slavery continued. Ultimately the North would win because, as Brogan puts it, the Southern planters had inherited "a labor system which, though extremely profitable, was also degrading, dangerous and unstable" (1990, 296). Southern society depended on rule by tyranny and violence at every level by this white aristocracy: over slaves, over other white sections of society, and over wives and women generally.

The South seemed at first, and this is what its rulers believed, to be impregnable, but "the foundations were rotten. Its defenders proved incompetent and their incompetence was as much a result of slavery as any other aspect of Southern life" (Brogan 1990, 298). But the South was economically and politically strong enough to bring the Union into disarray throughout the 1850s through its manipulation of the constitutional system and its threat to secede if its demands were not met. It was also sufficiently united ideologically and militarily powerful to make the Civil War a drawn out and bloody one.

Abolitionism provided the ideological framework around which the economic and political conflict between the North and South could rally and find moral purpose in its causes and pursuit. Entirely northern, it grew from its initial foundations in 1831 into a highly vociferous, active, and eloquent movement in the next 30 years, and it made its case in terms of the Enlightenment values that it took the American Revolution to enshrine and from which America would emerge as the civic and civilized embodiment. In these terms slavery was an evil degradation and sin that had to be purged from the American soul. William Lloyd Garrison sums up and expresses precisely what the issue and task was in the journal that he founded in 1831, *The Liberator:*

There are, at the present time, the highest obligations resting upon the people of the free States to remove slavery by moral and political action, as prescribed in the Constitution of the United States. They are now living under a pledge of their tremendous physical force, to fasten the galling fetters of tyranny upon the limbs of millions in the Southern states; they are liable to be called at any moment to suppress a general insurrection of the slaves; they authorize the slave owner to vote for three-fifths of his slaves as property, and thus enable him to perpetuate his oppression; they support a standing army at the South for its protection; and they seize the slave who has escaped their territories and send him back to be tortured... This relation to slavery is criminal and full of danger: IT MUST BE BROKEN UP. (Garrison 1835)

The task was pursued by the abolitionist movement with a total and single-minded vigor. But despite this, the movement did not prevail, and nor could it, because it did not understand the South as it was and how slavery was the key to its power and prosperity. Abolitionists "could not, they found, preach or pamphleteer the South into repenting its sin; and in the North, when they were not attacked as 'nigger-lovers', they were avoided as bores, and denounced as agitators whose activities threatened the existence of the American Union" (Brogan 1990, 302). But, despite this, abolitionism would change the course of American history. "They had found the weakness in the citadel [of the American South]. The slave-holders rejoiced in the profits of slavery and exhibited the utmost arrogance in personal behavior; but underneath they were profoundly insecure." Abolitionism forced this insecurity into a total suspicion of the North. The defensive position that the South had taken up in relation to the growing economic and political power of the North was now completed:

The abolitionist contention, that so long as the sin of slavery continued, America could not hope for peace and liberty, began to seem fearfully plausible to some; so, to others, did the belief of the Southern "fire-eaters" that so long as the South continued in the Union, slavery could not be safe. Both sides, without ever abating an instant their own self-righteousness, began to believe the threats and fear the anger of the other: double paranoia was hastening the patient's death. (315)

The Democrat coalition tipped south as northern politicians left it to realign themselves through the creation of the Republican Party in 1854 as an exclusively northern party. This became committed to the preservation and extension of a United States based on free soil and willing to promote commercial and industrial growth. By 1861, the state of the Union was in disarray. Its traditional federal order could no longer be sustained nor could a new order be introduced by peaceful and constitutional means.

The North/South conflict had steadily grown into the clouds of war, and this alone would be decisive in the making and breaking of the old Union.

The minstrel show gathered these political and social forces, conflicts, and transformations into itself as it formed into a popular cultural entertainment that both recognized and, in part, diffused them for its audience. The diffusion lay in a portrayal of black life that assuaged the anxieties provoked by the institution of slavery, both in itself and as a potential cause of war. Two immediate, and essentially racist, forms of diffusion could be offered by the minstrel show in terms of an attempt to reduce the threat of blacks and slavery. The first was ameliorative. The show created an idealized, romanticized, and exoticized portrait of black life on the plantation in which the slaves were pictured as happily content with their lot. Indeed, was this not the favorable light on which southern propagandists of slavery constantly sought to present the South and its plantations? Was it not, as they said, a world of so many "Sambos—bewildered darkies with childish joys and fears, lazy, affectionate and stupid" (Brogan 1990, 292), who, because of the essential inferiority of their nature, needed to be taken in hand and given the food, care, and protection that only slavery could offer? They required and even deserved the authority and government of the superior white man, and it was only fair that they should work for him in exchange for the benefits that plantation life conferred upon them. The happiness of their lives upon the plantation, as pictured by the minstrel show, made blacks and slavery seem quite unthreatening and deflected any inquiry into its truth. What this picture did not reveal (although this is not entirely true of all early minstrel shows) is the appalling degradation that slaves endured on the plantation.

This savage and violent reality the southern audience for the minstrel show did know, but the show could brush it aside in a second diffusion that simply pandered again to racism and justified it, albeit in an ambiguous way. On the one hand, it captured how the feelings and fears of this audience truly pictured the "sambo": "a marauding ape, lusting for fire, death and white women" (Brogan 1990, 292) who had to be kept in submission at all costs. Erenberg points out how the minstrel show actually recognized the danger of black sexuality, in particular, through its way of handling it. There were no females in the cast and the black characters had no more than comic characteristics. Until the 1870s, women were prohibited from attending minstrel shows, by which time these shows were changing through absorbing so much from other forms of popular entertainment. Moreover, the white actors who blacked-up would always let on that they were, in reality, white. Black sexuality was an omnipresence feeding the show but ambiguously represented as both animalistic and comic. To place it in this way sustained the racist stereotyping. To have brought sexuality on stage otherwise would have created a quite different problem for its audience, particularly in the South. "[Stage] black men had to be comic types, for a serious black man could be too appealing and hurt the stereotype...given the racial and sexual codes, blacks could not have been pictured as desiring a stable emotional sexual life" (Erenberg 1984, 19). Moreover, "sex is an emotion tied too closely to will, and for whites, a display of black will was unacceptable." But even as the audience had its racism confirmed, not just in terms of sexuality but in the general stereotyping of the black character as one of an inferior nature, it could also put the fears in this to rest too. By viewing blacks and slave life as a source of entertainment, the audience could console itself with the thought that there was, perhaps, no real danger of these fears turning into reality.

With the Civil War, the abolition of slavery, and the reconstruction of the South, however, the minstrel show moved steadily toward a more frank and vicious racism in which the ape in the "sambo" moved more to the forefront. Again the historical context suggests why. The debacle that was reconstruction abolished slavery and enfranchised the black population without replacing the former by a new economic system. The effect, in the South, was to create a new racialized battle over land in which the South was simply left to get on with it. The South turned into a backwater in which the superiority of the past and a nostalgic longing for its return would now become a dominating ideology well into the twentieth century and find a degree of authentication in popular culture.

At the same time, these events stimulated the racism of the northern audience. Freed slaves moving off the land and into the northern towns and cities in search of work and a new life found themselves feared and vilified by the white population and suppressed by new forms of social, economic, political, and legal discrimination. This is not to suggest that a northern audience for the minstrel show had approached it without racist prejudice before this point. All the evidence and experience of the abolitionist campaign in the North show that the population of the North was racist. Abolitionists were most frequently denounced as "nigger-lovers" in the North as in the South. But the North did not have a large black population of its own until this point. It had accepted and fought for the northern cause primarily for the economic and political advantage that would be brought to itself by the end of southern domination of the Union. It supported the Republican Party as the political agent of this, but it did not consistently understand the abolition of slavery as a necessity for the moral salvation of America. Its morality lay elsewhere and, indeed, fitted in with the racism of the minstrel show. The population of the North, both family farmer and urban worker, had a lively interest in freedom and their rights and recognized the American Constitution and its democratic political system as the condition for their preservation. But it reserved the exercise of this as a prerogative of whites when faced with the thought, and possible reality, of extending such rights and the advantages to blacks. In the minstrel show's stereotype of the northern urban black character—

"Zip Coon" or "Jim Dandy"—they found the moral justification for their racism.

[He] was a creature of impulse, who got drunk, danced about wildly, got into scrapes, and put on airs. He was the overdressed urban black who stepped beyond his position and always bungled the job. Because he indulged himself, he could not share the values of the popular myth of success. He was racially incapable of self-control. Thus in the minds of northern whites the urban black was doomed to failure in the egalitarian cities and the western frontier. (Erenberg 1984, 19)

Better then for blacks was that once-idyllic alternative life on the plantation, and this view united the northern audience with that of the South and found its reflection in the way in which the minstrel show started to emphasize the "Jim Crow" character more—the plantation black—after the Civil War.

But there is also evidence that the minstrel show—at least in its earlier format—was not entirely a racist parody of black lives and cultures, designed to entertain by mockery. Part of its initial impetus and thrust was to try and capture black life in a genuine (however naive) representational sense through the recreation of black dress, manners, humor, and speech using plaintive black melody (particularly that associated with spirituals) and black dance. These were treated as a spontaneous product of black culture and assigned value in their reproduction as a basis for entertainment. There was, in this sense, an educational element in the minstrel show, insofar as it sought to treat itself as a portrayal of the black man that was drawn from real life within a black setting. Although the focus was humorous, some of the darker actuality of this life entered into the portrait of the burden that slavery imposed upon blacks. Stephen Foster's melancholic, sentimental songs—and he was a major figure in the composition of songs specifically created for the minstrel show—often brings this to the fore. The famous "Old Black Joe," with its evocation of an afterlife free of trials and tribulations, and brutality, is entirely representative of this tradition.

This sense of valuation is supported by the way in which the minstrel show, in its work songs and spirituals, tried to bring to life not only the black cultures of American society, but also of other indigenous subcultures of the time and the lives led within them. Logger songs, riverboatmen songs, wagoner songs, and cattlemen songs entered to create a rich panoply of the every and workaday world of America. They were brought under the minstrel show as a unifying umbrella of popular entertainment that took itself around the whole country. This extended to dance within the show as it similarly gathered up ethnic jigs and clog dances to marry them up with rhythmic black dance. A strong part of the unifying synthesis of the minstrel show was how it found parallels between such elements. These parallels stem from the social expansion and transformation that America was undergoing from the mid-nineteenth century. Mates captures this as he seeks to explain the particular popularity of the minstrel show and its wide audience on the American frontier (see Mates 1987). For a white audience, the minstrel show could enable a degree of identification in the midst of its racism through the way it took, in its less vicious forms, the savagery out of the black world and its problems. In this way, it could then transform itself and the mood of its characters (particularly in the sentimentality of its songs) from bitterness to that of homesickness, frustration, and nostalgia. So the black could become a kind of Everyman caught up in the travails of the frontier and the newly emerging and raw industrial world in which displacement was also the adjunct of development.

But the minstrel show had another and crucial unifying role in the shaping of American popular culture, which was indigenous in a different kind of way. This kind of show started on a small scale, at first copied by the circus. It rapidly established its format through two archetypal black characters: Jim Crow, the lackadaisical rural plantation figure, and Zip Coon, the northern urban dandy. It presented them, and their life and black culture, primarily as a culture of humor, song, and dance. Specifically, the format of the show was set up in three parts using a small cast who undertook the whole of it. In part one, sentimental songs and comic routines were performed between an interlocutor and two comedians (Mr. Tambo and Mr. Bones). Part two consisted of speciality acts. Part three offered a specific representation of black life ending in a crude choral walkaround at the end. Throughout there was a mixture of solo and chorus songs, dance, comedy, burlesque, variety, and spectacle. But now these constituted an integrated song-and-dance show; a true music show in which the organized finale provided a prototype for the whole tradition of theatrical dancing in the musical. Moreover, it was entirely flexible in its ability to absorb any new theatrical element, and in this sense helped to create a form of music theater that created homogeneity out of synthesis. As it did this, it began to divorce itself from the circus to become a show in its own right, but more, it began to create song and dance of its own. Songs were especially created for it and so was dance. Both embraced and were increasingly influenced by and orientated to ragtime and jazz. Now the minstrel show not only offered American music and dance but opened the door and gave a venue to new composition by American composers and new forms of dance.

The minstrel show was of the greatest importance in terms of live popular theatrical entertainment between 1840 and 1880, but particularly from 1846 to 1854. Not only did it travel all over America, it was also often the first entertainment to come to new communities, introducing the integrated format of a song-and-dance show that offered both new American song and dance as well as those already established. In this way it made a substantial contribution to the development of American popular culture, moving it on creatively with this framework as its indigenousness. But, post–Civil War, the minstrel show grew altogether larger and more gimmicky with its absorption of other forms of popular entertainment. It could now no longer travel as a result. The day of its topicality had disappeared and the South dropped out of view as the preoccupations of the victorious North moved to its own industrial development and the expansion of America to the West. By 1880, other forms of popular musical theater had begun to overtake and replace it. Eventually, its various elements were taken up by these other forms: variety acts went into vaudeville, the speciality acts went into revue, and the satirical elements moved back into burlesque.

But the minstrel show left a crucial legacy for the musical to draw upon as it thematized America culturally and theatrically brought its worlds to vernacular life for a mass audience, presenting them as worlds to be found in, given expression by, and experienced in terms of song-and-dance. In this it continued the move that this chapter argues is evident in the various forms of live American popular theater. It was a move to a considerable degree of homogenization that proceeded through synthesis. In all its varieties, live American popular theater tended toward song-and-dance inspired by the essential and constructed unifying Americanness of its nature. This found its basis in a reflexive address on the "experience" of the world with America as its referent.[5] It was a world of America's making, with a popular culture that was always the culture of a "new" world. Within this popular culture, the black voice found a first hearing in the minstrel show, but a highly problematic one. It largely disappeared from view in terms of the white population after the end of the popularity of this kind of show in the early 1880s and would not resurface until the end of the nineteenth and the beginning of the twentieth century as ragtime and jazz. Then it would be massively influential in molding popular music, music theater, and entertainment generally. But there black mobility has largely stayed. In the main, America has permitted blacks to be a source of entertainment and this, in a major sense, is how black cultures have entered into the popular culture of American society with its primarily white power structure. This cultural importance has produced very little structural change. However, black music was central to the synthetic homogenization of American popular culture, particularly as America came to be seen and declare itself as the pinnacle of modernity. America did not formally declare and enact itself as a world power with an international mission and responsibility to lead all other societies until it finally abandoned isolationism in the Second World War. But its leadership in the processes of modernity was well established before that, in the early twentieth century, when it began to penetrate the popular cultures of the rest of the world, particularly Europe, on this basis. The specificity with which American popular culture was received and incorporated in the non-American world gave a sure sense of the degree of its homogeneity.

MELODRAMA

This entrenchment of a song-and-dance culture also found a further contributor in the straight legitimate theater. The minstrel show was largely performed outside the legitimate theater, often in association with the circus, which was why it was able to travel widely throughout America. But the legitimate theater also fostered song-and-dance through the main form it took: melodrama. Though we may laugh at melodrama today, as the audience for it eventually did, it was originally viewed as serious drama and constituted the main fare of the legitimate theater in Europe and America. Melodrama was a highly standardized form of drama. This explains part of its appeal to audiences, who knew what to expect from it and how to understand, appreciate, and enjoy it. Moreover, as drama, it worked within and expressed the moral conventions of its own time, which gave it force for its audience and supplied it with serious intent and, consequently, artistic legitimacy.

As drama, melodrama is characterized by a predictable plot that emphasizes the theme of vice versus virtue. The villain of the piece engages in evil machinations directed toward the heroine, who is eventually rescued by the hero, and poetic justice is effected through the punishment of the villain for his evil. The characters are essentially flat and one-dimensional: the villain is entirely villainous, the heroine is pure-hearted, and the hero is completely noble. None of them change during the course of the action. So the tone of melodrama is one of both sentimentality and romance in a conventional moral context, but, importantly for the growth of a song-and-dance culture, the acting is both physical (which betrays its pantomime origins) and declamatory. In addition, the setting is normally realistic even if historical. In this form melodrama could easily be understood and identified with, particularly when its audience was drawn from a mass and unsophisticated social background and culture.

Melodrama's form also explains how it became the legitimate theater of America, in the form of small, permanent stock companies performing on small resources. Melodrama meshed perfectly with this system because the predictable plot and stock characters required only a limited number of actors. But the style of acting that characterized melodrama required that actors be able to sing and dance as well as act; melodrama readily made itself available to pantomime, dance, and music, which became a strong and established part of it. So melodrama contributed to the development of music theater in America as another song-and-dance strand in its culture. At first, pantomime in melodrama took the form of a dumb-show performed by dancers using placards before the play began; this set up what was to follow but also entered into the way in which it was acted. Music was brought into the play to stress emotion by vividly and explic-itly articulating, in musical terms, the action, the characters, and their moods. The end result was the development of melodrama as a dialogue-with-music kind of drama.

The element of dance in melodrama was just as important for the emer-gence of the musical. This had two aspects. First, the very pantomimic style of acting in melodrama required a balletic and physical approach. Second, dance proper was performed both as part of scenes and in *entre-actes*. This was by no means disconcerting for the audience, since dance was a constant feature of all other forms of entertainment that they attended, from the circus through minstrel shows to variety and bur-lesque. Melodrama as the legitimate theater of America entailed the train-ing of actors to dance, sing, and act and to relate all three to one another. Indeed, for much of its life, melodrama did not really distinguish between acting, pantomime, and ballet in any strict way. Moreover as melodrama increased its popularity, its music and dance element also increased; in turn, the number of specialist theatrical performers in these areas increased and whetted the appetite of the audience for more.

The effect, in relation to American theater, was twofold. First, from the 1860s balletic and dance troupes began to perform in their own right, at first through foreign importation but then on an indigenous basis. Sec-ond, and more generally, dance was incorporated into theater as part of its dramatic tradition. The seeds were sown for the precipitation of that other major contribution of America to music theater—modern dance—which finally exploded in the twentieth century. The dance element that is central to the musical is different from the ballet content of eighteenth- and nineteenth-century European opera, where it acted largely as a kind of divertissement and not as a vehicle through which the drama was articulated and enacted. Moreover, the dance that American music the-ater incorporated into itself was to be modern dance in all of its forms.

By the 1860s, then, a song-and-dance popular culture and entertain-ment had been well and truly entrenched in American society. The theater emerged as a central agent in the development, dissemination, homoge-nization, and popularity of forms that were musical and centrally allied to American life. Theater was largely popular theater in America. But the combination and integration of its parts into the musical required a fur-ther catalyst, which historically turned on how the revue and the musical comedy utilized and reconstituted the available theatrical ingredients; and, crucially, on the appearance of the operetta in America as a model of music drama.

THE BLACK CROOK (1866)

A number of commentators have treated *The Black Crook* as the first musical (see Kislan 1980; Green 1986; Steyn 1997), albeit as more happenstance than deliberate creation.

Steyn, for instance, writes of the fortuitous circumstances bringing together William Wheatley's problems, notably his huge barn of a theater and an expensive commitment to *The Black Crook*, which apparently had a ridiculous script, with some entirely unlikely solutions. This involved a Parisian ballet troupe stranded in New York after a theater fire. Engineering an unlikely marriage between a poor play and some one hundred "underdressed coryphées," Wheatley created a smash and, according to Steyn, incidentally ended up "inventing the American musical" (1997, 3).

Steyn hits upon the truth that *The Black Crook* had all the ingredients of a musical, but the music was by a conglomeration of various composers and not specifically composed for the show. Moreover, its plot was little more than the standard fare of melodrama set in a typically exotic location (the Harz Mountains of Germany). *The Black Crook* could not be described as an integrated song-and-dance show. It was, to a large extent, a variation on the extravaganzas of popular theater. Yet Steyn also captures the vital ingredient that makes *The Black Crook* a crucial harbinger of the musical. It was the first musical show to "bring on the girls" in a really big way—this had been done before but never with this degree of lavishness. Moreover, and despite the loud and thunderous denunciation of it by church leaders, it managed to do so with a considerable degree of social legitimacy, as is evinced by the "respectable" audience who flocked to it. As Thomas puts it, drawing on Freedly (1978), "the real attraction of...[*The Black Crook*] was the all-female troupe of dancers...The advance publicity...spoke of the enormous cost of the production, the elaborate settings and the ballet troupe whose premiere danseuse is bewitchingly beautiful and exceedingly graceful" (1995, 38). This gave it respectability, but it was intent on conserving the risqué by extending the boundaries of permissibility into the arena of the respectable. "The publicity and attendant rumors led to the expectation that dancers would be scantily clad, and women attending the show wore long veils so they would not be recognized." So *The Black Crook* bridged the gap between risqué and respectable by being, as the reviewer of the *New York Herald* so succinctly captured it, "nice but naughty." The "girls," as "the chorus line," were to become an indispensable part of the musical and, more often than not, the chief reason for the show was precisely to show them off. Its popularity for its audience stemmed from this central ingredient. *The Black Crook* managed to clean up its "girlies" sufficiently to gain access to the growing urban middle class and its family audience spawned by the commercial and industrial development of America while preserving the glamour and sexual allure that was a necessity for the musical to emerge and flourish as a genre.

But Mates (1987) puts his finger on what *The Black Crook* had much more crucially inaugurated for the musical. Even more important than issues of format, it took a major step in the commercialization of popular theater in America since it established a new form and organization of theatrical management as big business—as "Broadway." The musical would need this economic institutionalization and, as *The Black Crook* did, it would involve the investment of huge sums to produce a spectacular event with star performers who were advertised precisely as such to create and capture an audience. *The Black Crook* heralded the engineering, organizing, and marketing of the musical show in terms of a particular image and reputation that would capture the customers. Here then the musical began life and developed its tradition as commercial theater and, with this, *The Black Crook* gave to Broadway its attitude and first rule as pointed to in the introduction to this study, "forget art: does it work?" (see Steyn 1997, 4). Art would certainly come to the musical as it extended and deepened its form, but almost always in association with commercial viability. Even now, in an era when the musical has become much more self-conscious about its artistic stature, artistic success that is not a commercial success at the same time poses a serious problem.

By the 1860s a popular culture of song-and-dance had become entrenched in American society. The theater emerged as a central agent in its development and dissemination to create a homogeneity that, though synthetic in construction and multiple in its forms, was primarily musical in character and tied thematically to the American world. But further assimilations and synthesis were needed to produce the musical. These emerged from the revue and musical comedy as they utilized the now available and familiar ingredients, and also from the appearance of operetta, which acted as a model for the music drama into which the musical would eventually develop.

American culture was beginning to take shape creatively and artistically and starting to assert its dominance, but it retained its particular integrity as popular culture. Its dominance as the culture of a contemporary world stemmed from and matched the steadily emerging political and economic status of America as the epitome of modern liberal democratic and capitalist society. The primary basis of American popular culture was commercial and was increasingly constituted as a culture industry. To that extent, much of it would be little more than passing and profitable fodder of its entertainment industry just as the frank attachment of this culture to American society would be little more than an ideological reflex. Most musicals would have this character. But the best would be more. They would penetrate their American world in particular ways and not simply feed off it. Some became subtly discriminating in their Americanness, deciding the how and why of their committed expression of the American and where and in what it lay. But it was necessary that the musical should never forget it was "showbiz." It was impossible for the musical to offer its unique music theater without this. The reflexive and critical capacity of the musical as popular American art was thus inextricable from "entertainment value," and it was this latter that gave most of the huge number of musicals that were created and produced the character of nothing more than simply commodified assembly-line products of an entertainment industry.

REVUE

The revue per se was a mid-nineteenth-century French invention originating in Paris as an annual show using sketches, songs, and dance to review the past events of the year and satirize them. It therefore had a distinctive unity as a show. In Europe, the revue eventually turned into the cabaret. However, the revue in America started earlier (in the 1820s), arising out of the ballad opera, and only becoming influenced by the French form when it had already made its own way through American theater and even then only in the British version of the French revue. The revue as it became formalized in the 1890s, then, as a subgenre of the musical, derived from a relatively long-standing tradition and was very much American in character.

As we have seen, ballad opera was itself satirical drama that used popular music. Its popularity in America lay in providing tools for a dramatic critique of the old European world as a defense and celebration of the new and democratic world of America. Its satirical nature, then, was an expression of the American experience and attitude, in combination with the rejection of the past that the immigrant nature of American society entailed. This explains why the satiric is a constant feature of American humor, as is its other face—the optimism, sincerity, and idealism that allies itself to what is new. So ballad opera was the first beginnings of the revue, which emerged separately in the form of one-man comic shows that toured the country in the 1820s and 1830s. These shows used popular songs in skits that mimicked famous figures of the day, mocked recent events, and satirized contemporary society, spoofing the artistic successes of the time. In time they became more elaborate, drawing in many more performers and moving into *olio*, extravaganza, variety, vaudeville, burlesque, and the minstrel show, stimulating them to develop comedy sketches and using musical performers and abbreviated musical scenes performed by monologists and comedy teams. But, at the same time, the revue element in these shows preserved a certain distance because of its central emphasis on the importance of words and not just the use of music. This made revue a form of drama and therefore a genuine form of the musical. To achieve this, however, the revue had to take from its associations with other forms of popular music and dance theater: from the minstrel show (where it was frequently housed) it took the fantasia of speciality routines by individual performers, from variety and vaudeville it took the comedy and variety acts, from burlesque it took extended satirical sketches, and from the "extravaganza" it took the sumptuously-clad girls. It organized and melded these ingredients into a single show with a unified theme or concept that was provided by an examination of contemporary foibles and follies through sketches, music, and dance, which were essentially theatrical in nature. The show was clothed in a lavish spectacle of magnificent scenery with huge composed tableaux and a big chorus line of beautifully dressed girls. The revue form finally established itself definitively in the first decade of the twentieth century, with British musical revue playing a consolidating but not causal role in the second decade.

The situation of the theater in America at this point made the revue a readily exploitable commercial possibility. First, there was a lull in other kinds of popular American theater at this point—burlesque was increasingly too indecent for a family audience; melodrama had had its day; European and British operetta had dried up and American operetta had yet to properly establish itself; and although there had been fledgling attempts at farce comedy, musical comedy had yet to emerge. Second, the revue provided an opportunity to take over and legitimize the popular element of the burlesque—the chorus girls with their routines—and place it in a more respectable theatrical context for a more respectable audience. Third, the revue was normally put on during the summer, when its light and frothy comedy and satire could be suitably staged either in theaters that lacked air conditioning or in open-air roof theaters. Finally, by 1900 America had become an industrial and political superpower seeking to celebrate its newfound status and foster its prestige by seizing upon what was new and distinctive in its own homegrown culture. Revue also now had the institutional and commercial organization, and large and affluent audiences, to support it.

However, until 1907, with Ziegfeld and the first of "Follies Show" a fine line separated the revue from vaudeville on the one hand and musical comedy on the other, since comedy, popular song, and popular dance were the major ingredients of all three. Ziegfeld changed this situation by creating a sophisticated revue show that satirized the events, personalities, and shows of the day, and contained popular songs specifically penned for it; an extravagant chorus line; and the greatest star-singers, star-dancers, and star-comedians of the day. Moreover, he converted the girlie-show element of the revue into a respectable, legitimate, and important part of the musical by eschewing vulgarity in favor of beauty, taste, and artistry. Although the allure of female flesh continued to be the major element, all aspects of the revue were now being specifically written and composed for it, acted by a single cast, played by good orchestra, and organized and directed by a single producer to create an integrated and distinctive musical show. In this form the revue became a major vehicle for the popular music and dance culture of America. It actively sought out new popular music and dance crazes, providing a major commercial venue through which to test, advertise, and spread them and an artistic venue for composers, lyricists, and writers to flourish. Every American popular composer of note during much of the twentieth century took this route at some point. Moreover, the revue was an ideal testing ground for its contributors because, although it was unified in content, it used many contributors on a collaborative basis so no one had to take the risk of creating a whole show. At the same time, the revue became the place of the star as comedian, singer, and dancer, bringing forward new talent and showing off the established. Finally, the revue gathered weight as well as entertainment value because it promoted music, writing, and choreography of a very high standard but in a style that was now essentially and distinctly American. This gave it—and the musical generally—artistic legitimacy while still keeping it within a popularist context.

OPERETTA

The operettas of Offenbach (the creator of the form in the early 1860s) arrived in America from 1867 and enjoyed an immediate popularity. This stemmed from their bourgeois character; the wit, satire, and absurdity of their plots; and admiration for their musical and dramatic sophistication. But their popularity was short-lived because of the very nature of the host society and its theater. First, the tendency was to put Offenbach's operettas on in the original French, which broke the contact with, and limited, the audience for them. Second, they required considerable technical and artistic abilities and resources. And finally, but critically, Offenbach was too risqué for the American bourgeoisie.

So it was only with the British operettas of Gilbert and Sullivan, starting with *HMS Pinafore* (1878), that operetta took off in America. *Pinafore* took America by storm, and in 1879 there were 90 companies touring with it. This, followed by other Gilbert and Sullivan operettas, became a staple diet of American musical theater. Indeed, *The Pirates of Penzance* (1879) actually opened in New York before London in an attempt by Gilbert and Sullivan to capitalize on their American success but more specifically to protect their royalties against piracy by American companies.

The success of Gilbert and Sullivan is not difficult to understand. The audience could understand the dialogue, appreciate the jokes, and enjoy the tongue-twisting lyrics because burlesque, variety, and melodrama (and, indeed, nineteenth-century American comic literature) had prepared them for it. Through a novel form of musical play, the audience could actually follow and enjoy Gilbert and Sullivan as drama. Equally important, Gilbert and Sullivan operetta was wholesome and clean. This distinguished it from French operetta.

Viennese operetta now rapidly followed into America. This again was specifically bourgeois, but it introduced sentimentality, glamour, romance, and exoticism into operetta, thus heavily reducing its comic content. Most importantly, it figured the waltz as its central musical form. This was originally a courtly dance but had now become a popular middle-class social dance with lasting consequences. It became the waltz that was to characterize operetta's treatment of romance. Steyn captures this admirably: "decorous, restrained formal movement blossoms into giddily confident, sweeping lyricism [becoming] ... the most potent stage metaphor for intense, intimate romance" (1997, 35). The musical would capitalize on this romantic potential, using the waltz in its traditionally stereotyped gender relations, and in terms of the romance plots leading ultimately to marriage and a happy-ever-after ending. Thus operetta affected the dance in the musical in a very specific, dramatic way. Steyn, again, captures this when writing of the Silver Age operettas of Lehár and Kalman that were to follow Strauss. "Where previously show dance had meant marches, drills, ballets, big chorus set-pieces, the Silver Age operetta introduced dancing not by dancers, but by the characters in the drama... [it endowed] it with a far more alluring image, establishing a line that led through Vernon and Irene Castle to Astaire and Rogers and beyond."

But, through the waltz, operetta moved away from realism and comedy toward romance and escapism. American operettas remained entirely operettas, with their high romanticism and exoticism, and it is interesting to see how, in the period when they particularly flourished (1914–30), they corresponded to the high romanticism and exoticism of much silent film and most likely for the same escapist reasons. American operetta was no more than and no different from European operetta. It was not the musical, although it did make an eventual contribution to the musical, specifically the book musical, through its legacy as a musical play. But the music (vernacular song and particularly the ballad) and drama (contemporary realism) that essentially form the basis of the book musical came from elsewhere: the popular tradition of American musical, dance, and theatrical culture. One look at *Show Boat*, the first book musical, shows how different the musical is from operetta, however much both are musical plays.

Operetta managed to gain a foothold in America because of its celebration of a plush and secure bourgeois world, a *belle epoque* to which there now corresponded an American version. It coincided with the emergence of a new bourgeoisie and ruling elite within American society and politics and the establishment of America as a society materially based in a mod-

ern capitalist economy. As this class developed, it had largely and systematically disengaged itself from American popular culture and its forms of
institutionalized entertainment. This new and established urban bourgeois class sought to distinguish itself from the lower orders not only by
what it perceived as its more refined moral standards and capacity for
work, but also in leisure terms. It was for this reason that it created entertainments consistent with its position in a culture conceived hierarchically.
Respectable men and women, then, established what was appropriate for
them to attend together.

As part of the process of this discrimination, the American higher bourgeoisie began to show appreciation for the values of an older, more aristocratic European civilization. Once seen as a decadent culture, Europe was
rapidly becoming important to the identities of fashionable American
urbanites. Here, in an ironic turnaround from the earlier American identity
which constructed itself in opposition to old Europe, operetta, itself the
product of a similarly emergent European bourgeoisie celebrating its social
and political arrival, became appealing to this new American bourgeois
class. Operetta was moral in a bourgeois sense, well-bred and with just that
touch of snobbish sophistication (which Europe could now be seen as offering) to appeal to a legitimate and arriviste audience wanting more than just
the democratic and socially undifferentiated delights of traditional American theatrical entertainment. It also had sufficient audience appeal to
attract socially aspirant immigrants seeking entrance to the middle classes,
an appeal much enhanced through operetta's rose-tinted and escapist
spectacles. But operetta still had to find some native dimension to place
itself within an American legitimacy. In its raw European state, however
appealing—and Lehár's *The Merry Widow* (1907) infinitely appealed—
operetta clashed with other sides of American society that were part of its
essential modern nature and Americanness. It was converted initially into
American bourgeois life and love by Victor Herbert under the sign of
Europe, but ultimately such a sign could not be maintained as an adequate
representation of America. Operetta could be fashionable and emblematic
of middle-class taste, but it could not truly be reproduced as a New World
taste.

Operetta, in the end, always remained well-bred because of its associations with opera, which, in dramatic terms, largely constricted its plot and
character as the accessories of music. The content of operettas, to a large
extent, was greatly stylized, artificial, and cultured, incorporating romantic characters with high-flown feelings and inhabiting exotic locales in a
variety of imaginary never-never lands. This came to have a dramatic
edge in Offenbach and Gilbert and Sullivan, where it was deliberately
used as a device for satirical comment on the contemporary world. Otherwise operetta rapidly degenerated into nice tunes, fantasy, and escapism.
Certainly Strauss's operettas pushed in this direction even if Lehár's tried

for a more sophisticated, knowing, and dramatic ambience in relation to the contemporary middle class and its deeply ideological morality of romance and marriage.

The musical, however, moved in a different direction, even in respect of the romantic, to realism in character, plot, and locale and the use of vernacular music to create the drama. The waltz was also given a vernacular character, but the overwhelming history of the vernacular history of American music lies in the dominance of 4/4 time and not 3/4 time, which it strengthened with syncopation. As Steyn points out, songs would have narrower ranges (see 1997, 40), but they would meet the demands and fit the contours of conversational speech. Operetta tends to sacrifice words to music to sustain its appeal to romance and so develops the drama through the rhapsodic emotionalism of the latter rather than through the lyrical qualities of the former. This tends to leave the drama on only one note (the highest) and in one world (the clouds). The operetta could only voice the contemporary through its own confines to develop a moment with a very limited history. It created a light musical play and set its characters dancing, but its stylized dimensions closed it off from the vernacular. Indeed, it prolonged its life after the musical had become entrenched through making the foreign and exotic its own special territory on Broadway. Friml and Romberg, its chief exponents after Herbert, mainly inhabit a world that is American only inasmuch as it represents an escapist attempt to present a fantasy other world.

MUSICAL COMEDY

It was musical comedy that more effectively helped free the play and its music and dance for the vernacular, to make it move toward and become a musical. Musical comedy was definitively established at the close of the nineteenth century and beginning of the twentieth century, primarily in Britain and America. But again there had been a proto-form of early American musical comedy.

The period 1870–80 saw a vast wave of immigration into America—some seven million over this period, the majority of whom were British, Irish, German, and eastern European, although Scandinavians and southern Europeans were also substantially represented. They stayed largely in the cities of the northeast, particularly New York and Boston, to become an urban population. This was made possible because America established itself as a primarily capitalist-industrial economy between 1865 and 1890 and New York became the real capital of it. It was the country's greatest industrial city as well as its greatest port and financial center. This industry was not initially organized mainly on the basis of factories, but in terms of huge numbers of workshops supplying consumer goods. Much of the work could also be done in the home. Huge tenement areas were rapidly built on both the East and West Sides of New York to house this new immigrant workforce on which its industrial economy thrived. What developed within New York (as it did in Boston and other major north-eastern cities) for this immigrant population, was what Lubell calls the "Tenement Trail" as an equivalent to the track westwards:

It was not so long as the Oregon Trail or the Long Drive, but it took years or decades to get from its beginning to its end. A family which started...on the Lower East Side would gradually promote itself to better accommodation as its savings and income mounted, until eventually it could cross the rivers into the boroughs of the Bronx, Queens and Brooklyn. The places it left behind were never empty: other families, intent on making good, followed closely behind. (Brogan 1990, 412)

The flow of immigrants continued to peak in a third wave between 1900 and 1910 when ten million more arrived, but this time from much more diverse origins. The British, Irish, and Germans were no longer a major part of this migration pattern, largely because the birth rates of these societies were falling as a result of industrializing economies. Slower-rising populations were thus more easily absorbed.

Edward Harrigan, the New York impresario, was first to fix upon and realize the potential of this new immigrant population as an audience for popular theater. He invented farce comedy as a comic play that lovingly, and with some degree of accuracy, tried to depict the everyday life of immigrant society in terms of its aspirations and the conflicts between the different ethnic groups within it as they attempted to make economic and political headway in the New World. His was essentially a situational comedy founded upon the immigrant situation itself and, in that respect, distinct from the boy-meets-girl scenario and the subsequent romance and marriage that hitherto had been the staple diet of musical comedy. In this respect Harrigan offered closely observed comic slices of everyday immigrant life in the American city, with particular reference to how the ghetto lives and customs of particular ethnic groups were organized. His shows focused on the rivalries between these groups and their involvement in local structures of patronage operating through the political machine of the city and its Boss politics. The primary dramatic vehicle of this farce comedy was hummable tunes, and it sought to engage its audience through a combination of laughter and tears. The music was used in overtures (entre-actes), incidental music-and-song to enclose a very rough-and-tumble style of comic acting and interplay between characters given particular and stereotypical ethnic identities.[6] Audience participation was specifically invited in sing-along songs and free-for-all scenes in which farce comedy abounded. They were still not genuine musical comedies, because the music was not fully integrated with the play and they were unsophisticated in their style and themes. But they lasted for twenty years up and into the 1890s. Their demise at this point explains the final trans-formation through which the definitive form of the musical comedy as a subgenre of the musical emerged.

By the 1890s, a large part of the immigrant population for whom these shows had been specifically designed had now left the tenements to find a more secure and solid position in American society and so had put behind them the life and tribulations that farce comedy portrayed. Their aspira-tions and interests changed as their entry into the "melting pot" of Amer-ica came to fruition in a newfound improvement of their conditions and affluence. "The big city still holds out its promise of improvement, though unfortunately, in the late twentieth century, the promise seems to be more than a little delusive. But in the nineteenth century, the promise was kept, and not only in New York. Most of the immigrants had left home in hopes of bettering themselves, and their letters home were full of proud claims that they had done so" (Brogan 1990, 412–13). They had done so because America had undergone an industrial revolution between 1865 and 1890. No longer the provincial America of the Revolution, eagerly gazing west-ward (rural in residence, outlook, and occupation), it was now a

continental nation, hugely rich and productive, populous, harshly urbanized, heavily industrialized, infinitely various in its ethnic origins, it religions, lan-guages and cultures, transformed into the first fully modern society by its rapidly evolving technology; and yet still, for good and bad, recognizably the country of George Washington who founded it and Abraham Lincoln who rescued it. (387)

It is interesting how the musical ultimately itself formulated these changes in the seminal work that created its classic form, Kern's *Show Boat*. Here the transformation is topicalized and dramatized to encompass a self-conscious constitution of the nature and tradition of the musical and its form of music theater.

But the absolute establishment of musical comedy, however compelling its American form became, was far from being entirely homegrown in terms of its origins and early development. It depended to a significant degree on the importation and incorporation of British musical comedy. By the 1890s Britain too had become a modern society that saw both the social triumph of the middle class, with its particular values and domestic life, and a respectable working class whose attitudes and aspirations con-verged with those of the middle class in terms of propriety and ambition. The impresario George Edwardes, who ran the Gaiety Theatre in London, formerly a center of burlesque, had begun to recognize and set out to cre-ate a musical entertainment for this new modern society that put moder-nity at its very center.

There are some doubts about which of the early Edwardes produc-tions can lay claim to being the first "authentic" West End musical comedy. McQueen-Pope was probably alone in thinking that a very early burlesque, *The Great Metropolis* (1874), witnessed "if not the actual birth of musical comedy, at least the birth of English revue" (1949, 154). *In Town* (1892), produced by Edwardes, but at the Prince of Wales, has also been seen as the first musical comedy, or at least as a decisive break with burlesque and an important intermediary on the road to the full-fledged product. Its book, however, was wildly underdeveloped, providing not much more than a modern setting for Arthur Robert's comic routines. It was, in many ways, a series of "turns" dressed up as a plot, a variety entertainment in disguise. The claims of the next two productions from Edwardes, *A Gaiety Girl* (1893) and *The Shop Girl* (1894),were, however, very much more substantial, and it is these shows that sometimes have had to compete for the title of first "real" West End musical comedy. Some commentators have argued for the latter. Most, however, would place *A Gaiety Girl* as the serious innovator, and it is not difficult to see why.

The crucial element here was not Sidney Jones's score, which was lively enough but derivative, as most early musical comedies were in this respect, but rather the levels of integration between Harry Greenbank's song lyrics and the play narrative, and, above all, the coherency of the comedy script written by "Owen Hall" (the pseudonym of Jimmy Davis). It was this play, with its relatively natural dialogue and topical, risqué jokes that really woke up the critics, and the censors, to the idea that something new might be happening on the West End stage. The *Times* reported on "a comic opera of a somewhat advanced type" where "licence is pushed further than has ever before been attempted in our day" (15 October 1893). The *Era* had more difficulty in distinguishing precisely what this "sometimes sentimental drama, sometimes comedy and sometimes downright variety show" really was, but recognized the dialogue as being "brilliant enough and satirical enough for a comedy of modern life" (October 1893)—as, indeed, it often was:

Gladys Stourton: I would love to go far away and fight the Zulus and Matabeles. I
  would love to fight for my country.
Harry Fitzwarren: You mean you would love to fight for *their* country.[7]

A Gaiety Girl was an outspoken show, and it was crucial to the definition of "gaiety" as an idea. If at one time the word had simply designated a "jolly" crowd roaring their approval of showgirls' legs, "gaiety," with Edwardes's new production values and Davis's intervention, now took on altered and fuller dimensions. The old voyeurism was still there, but in a new designer style, and it was accompanied by a politicized spirit, a *joie de vivre* expressed as a fin-de-siécle antidote to conservative values and in terms of a thorough embracing of modernity.

In Davis's play the disposition for modernity came to life not just in periodic jokes made at the expense of the religious, legal, and military establishments, but through the main plot dynamic of the piece, which became a staple of early musical comedy. This turned on a sustained confrontation between vibrant modernity and outmoded tradition, represented in *A Gaiety Girl* by a group of young actresses on the one hand and a group of snobbish female aristocrats on the other. They meet initially at a military barracks where the aristocrats, chaperoned by Lady Virginia Forest, are looking for husbands. The Gaiety chorus girls are "bright young things" from town invited down to lunch by Major Barclay. For Lady Virginia, however, these women are highly problematic—not just socially inferior, but a positive impediment to her matchmaking ambitions. "Actresses," she says, "stand terribly in the way of the best families." On first being introduced by her nephew (Charley) to the Gaiety girl he will fall for (Alma), Lady Virginia sinks despondently into a chair. Alma's spirited response shows no sign of embarrassment or deferment: "your aunt seems delighted with the introduction Charley. Are the upper classes always as cordial as that?" As the play develops, the two groups of women move even further apart, with Alma being accused of stealing a diamond comb by the end of the first act. However, the play becomes increasingly insistent on interrogating this difference. It points out parallels between the women, which, without exception, elevate the status of the Gaiety girls. When they are accused of being "fast," for example, because they appear in bathing suits, they respond with a song that turns the criticism back against their aristocratic counterparts, who are accused of being far more "loose" in their pursuit of a "fellow with money" than the actresses themselves. The rest of the play articulates a curious reversal, where the Gaiety girls take on the dimensions of aristocratic grace, as they appear "like young Duchesses going into a drawing room." At the same time, the traditional aristocrats learn that gaiety is irresistible. "High spirits might be vulgar," as one of them points out, "but for all that we mean to indulge in them." By the end of the show an astonishing *volte-face* has been accomplished. Old tradition and conventional wisdom have been displaced. The tired elites not only know this; they also learn to embrace new ways. Among the last lines of the play are those that give Lady Virginia's blessing to her nephew's forthcoming marriage. "I'm glad you are going to marry a gaiety girl after all, Charley," she tells her nephew. "In a year or two, she will be all the rage of society."

In this way *A Gaiety Girl* positioned "gaiety" at the very center of an imagined bourgeois bohemia. Its entirely appropriate gaiety girl/aristocrat metonym announced musical comedy as *the* contemporary musical theater of the late Victorian stage. With considerable boldness, Davis had taken the word that designated the essential musical comedy theatrical space, and the troupe of singer-dancers who were to take London by storm, and from its associations concocted the first "real" West End musical comedy. Gaiety, with Davis, became an idea, an attitude taken toward the modern, as Max Beerbohm knew when he recognized the new Gaiety theater as "a temple" serving the idea of gaiety, "that special and peculiar sort of gaiety with which we have always associated [musical comedy]."[8] Just as "decadence" was a key signifying concept for some intellectual communities of the 1890s, so "gaiety" was to become something of a rallying point, but for a very much more mainstream cultural identity. If decadence was the defiance of languid individualism against the "leveling" of contemporary life, the kind of gaiety involved in Davis's formulation produced something like the opposite: a carnivalesque indulgence in joie de modernity.

All these elements, then, were combined in Davis's play. It was superficially iconoclastic, enough so to delay its license until the very last moment, but its central impulse was more inclusive. It staged modernity as an all-accommodating fun and sent out invitations to join in. Those that declined were, by definition, old-fashioned, or bluestocking, and certainly redundant. The next Edwardes hit, *The Shop Girl*, with its department store setting, was perhaps more immediately recognizable as "modern," but in its dialogue, costume, and staging followed in the footsteps of *A Gaiety Girl*. For the *Times*, the "picturesque treatment" of modernity in the one was replicated in the other. "The whole scene" of *The Shop Girl* was "entirely modern, like that of *A Gaiety Girl*, which appears for the time to have set the fashion." In this review *The Shop Girl* became an "imitation" of *A Gaiety Girl*, albeit a triumphant one, "for all concerned" (26 November 1894).

Both shows became hugely popular. *A Gaiety Girl* transferred from the Prince of Wales to Daly's and played a total of 413 performances. By 1894 the show was on tour playing to audiences in New York, Boston, Washington, Brooklyn, Pittsburgh, St. Louis, Chicago, Milwaukee, and San Francisco. After touring for a number of years, it returned to London for a short run at Daly's in 1899. *The Shop Girl* played 546 performances at the Gaiety, before a disappointing run in New York, which took exception to the play, some have said because of political tensions between Britain and the United States over Venezuela. These were the first, then, of a string of West End musical comedies to be taken to Broadway and beyond, including *An Artist's Model* (1895), *The Geisha* (1896), *Monte Carlo* (1896), *A Runaway Girl* (1898), *Little Miss Nobody* (1898), *A Greek Slave* (1899), *Floradora* (1900), *Kitty Grey* (1900), *The Messenger Boy* (1901), *The Toreador* (1901), *A Chinese Honeymoon* (1902), *San Toy* (1902), *The Silver Slipper* (1902), *The Cingalee* (1904), *The Medal and the Maid* (1904), *The School Girl* (1904), *The Duchess of Dantzic* (1905), *The Orchid* (1907), *The Earl and the Girl* (1905), *Sergeant Brue* (1905), *The Catch of the Season* (1905), *The Blue Moon* (1906), *The Spring Chicken* (1906), *The Little Cherub* (1906), *The Dairy Maids* (1907),

Miss Hook of Holland (1907), *Havana* (1909), *The Belle of Brittany* (1910), *Our Miss Gibbs* (1910), and *The Arcadians* (1910).

The essential point about almost all these shows was their self-conscious modernity, from their *mise-en-scène* through their narratives and characters to the magnificent bedeckment of the characters in the very latest fashions. They captured a newly emergent audience and became instant style-setters. West End musical comedy gave modernity cachet, appealing to both men and women by virtue of an artistry that was fashionable and modish. In essence they featured the contemporary world through their working of modern social setting and usage of colloquial speech in the dialogue and lyrics of the songs. Their songs had more of a recitative than an aria-like volume and so dovetailed with the action. The comedy fostered a mood of lightheartedness rather than heavy sentimentality and featured a new kind of heroine who was an idealization of the new middle-class sense of femininity and the proper aspirations of womanhood. Though she was comparatively lowborn, she worked hard and finally attracted a wealthy suitor, on the basis of her merits and feminine qualities, to marry and live with him in affluent, domestic bliss. This staple rags-to-riches story now became, in an infinite variety of settings, the diet for a rash of British musical comedies up until World War I, performed in a style that was skipping, tripping, quipping, swinging, and dancing.

But, crucially, they celebrated the modernity of the British modern world and so carried an ethnocentric and celebratory sense of Britain as a nonpareil civilization. This British musical comedy rapidly crossed to an American music theater that could easily assimilate its committed and stylish modernity because in its key respects it corresponded with America's own new modern world. It had to be nativized to a certain extent to accommodate the more overtly egalitarian and democratic ethos of American society, but this was easily accomplished because of America's own exuberant and self-conscious trust in modernity at this point.

The figure who brought this about was George Cohan, with his immediately imitated music comedies. His shows were self-consciously American and expressed the bullish mood and politics of America at the turn of the twentieth century. By the end of the nineteenth century, the wealth and production of America had outstripped that of the Old World. It had become a self-sustaining continental economy that had no reliance on overseas trade. This was celebrated in Chicago at the World Columbian Exhibition of 1893, which was visited by 28 million people. It was accompanied by a faith, in Americans, "in their country and its destiny [that] now assumed an almost triumphal aspect" (Brogan 1990, 456). This announced itself in terms of a claim to the furtherance of world progress with America as the vanguard. It was precisely in these terms that Robert La Follette and Theodore Roosevelt would launch a new political party in

1912, the Progressive Party, and muster the power necessary to dominate the whole period from 1897 to the First World War. The basis of this power was the huge middle class that had developed with industrialism and urbanization; a "new class, conscious of its power and numbers and . . . confident in its ability . . . [as it] was anxious to get hold of American society and remake it according to plan" (Brogan 1990, 460).

Cohan sought to formulate and match this on a popular artistic level with his shows by concentrating them around the growing and common social attitude that was now emergent in order to create a wide and socially varied audience. This was enunciated as a jingoistic patriotism intertwined with a persuasive and deeply felt optimism that replaced satire and social criticism. He needed to tap an affluent audience as well as the gallery to pay for his shows, particularly as the latter audience was beginning to desert theater for the cinema and the silent film. That desertion was as yet limited since silent films could only compete with melodrama and straight comedy (which they could mimic and technologically improve upon), but not musical shows. His solution was to create shows that insisted upon materials drawn from America in terms of characters, experiences, settings, and music. He set their tone in terms of them proceeding at an energetic bustling pace to match the exuberance of the times, with memorable songs as their center point. This made them strongly contrastive with operetta. But, above all, they were pitched to tap a citified and affluent audience whose material desires, and the promise of their delivery, were set at the heart of the show's business. Cohan was reorganizing the British musical comedy and farce comedy by directing the appeal to an American, particularly middle-class, audience. The romance of British musical comedy was transposed from a pure tale of love and marriage to an optimistic celebration of American life and the possibilities of success for everybody. So Cohan created a musical play constructed about ordinary types of "guys" and "girls" and used contemporary popular music and vernacular language (particularly slang) as the means of its organization and expression. The Americanness of the show lay, then, in the refined and urban blend of those historical ingredients that made up the elements of the popular music and dance culture and theater of America. It melded them into a unified structure through the vernacular incorporation of melodrama to create a musical play but also to celebrate the very essence of America and the American way of life and its superiority over all others. This is caught quintessentially in, perhaps, what is the most famous of all songs from a Cohan show, "I'm a Yankee-Doodle Dandee."

Success and progress were America: in its model lay the true and real possibilities and destiny of modernity. Now American musical comedy had gained a foundation.[9] But there was more to musical comedy than this specific effect. In Cohan's shows the New World that the American Revolution set out to found in the creation of the United States had now moved from a raw and declared promise to a triumphant proclamation of realization. The American Dream and its expectations were now equated with capitalism and the frontier of expansion along which America and its dream was made complete. This frontier was now not just geographical but also implicated the economic expansion of capitalism to incorporate all members of American Society within its fold. In these terms, America was presented as creating and gathering the fruits of its essential modernity. Now it was ready to take on the world and spread the virtues of its modernity abroad (see Jacobson [1997]). This American Dream started to be advanced as a reality that need not be exclusive to America; rather, the American example was turned into a messianic message directed toward the whole world.

By World War I, then, the musical had become established in terms of the two subgenres, the revue and music comedy. The latter, together with operetta, had created the "musical play," which would become the source of the future major development and ultimately classic form of the musical as the book musical. It had come to fruition by virtue of a series of interrelated and conjoined conditions that were particular to American society and culture.

The musical owed its genesis to the particular nature and historical development of American society. The federation of the United States created itself as the first modern civil society in a deliberate attempt to realize the ideals of political thinkers from Locke to Rousseau. In this respect America was established in opposition to the Old World of Europe, as a society that was formally democratic and ideologically egalitarian, destined to become, as it popularly described itself, "the home of the free." This was the promise extended not only to its members but also to future immigrants who flocked to its shores between its foundation and the First World War. At the same time, through industrial revolution and frontier expansion, America's institutions, values, and life came to stand as the very epitome of modernity and emblematic of the future "progress" of all society. With this came a renewed ideologization, mythologization, and articulation of such values and these were celebrated in specifically American forms of artistic practice.

The culture of this celebration was primarily a popular culture orientated to the modern post-Enlightenment political and civic ideals on which America was founded. This popular culture largely found expression in forms of entertainment and theater as a culture where song-and-dance predominated. These retained an eclectic capacity for absorption and synthesis in relation to the many and varied strands of American life as America grew to full status as a modern society and world power. Whatever the variety of the elements that were collected up by the musical, this culture also developed a high degree of homogenization. At one level this was incipient in the very foundation of the United States, in terms of its modern political and civic system and the ideals and values that were entrenched by it and translated by the popular mind into America as the "land of the free" and, later, the "melting pot." Such "assimilation" was given a constant real and structural foundation in terms of the processes of immigration and frontier expansion that played a major part in the historical development of America in the nineteenth and early twentieth century. The myth of the frontier proved to be a powerful symbol that wove present and past into one unity of life that was "America" for its population, despite its various social and ethnic diversities, just as the accomplishment of frontier expansion fully realized the project of the American revolution: the creation of a federation of the United States of America. Now the American Dream of social mobility and prosperity for all was transformed from prospect into practice, not only through the geographical expansion of its frontiers but also with the social transformation that expanded the frontiers of an increasingly urban environment. What slowly emerged, for all of the diversities within American life and society, was an increasingly national culture, consolidated by the bourgeoisification entailed in the process. This culture was expressly nationalized in terms of popular entertainment and theater by the centralization, commercialization, commodification, and institutionalization of its forms, transported to every part of America to constitute a largely urbanized popular culture rather than a pure folk culture (whatever myths of "folk" it invoked). Feuer (1993) has tried to argue that the Hollywood film musical constantly created itself around an ersatz sense of folk to disguise its mass-produced nature for its audience. By comparison, she argues, the live popular entertainment and theater of the nineteenth and early twentieth century was genuinely folk and so organically connected to its audience. But she mistakes the nature of this live popular entertainment theater, which was commercially organized and commodified by the theatrical system that produced it and increasingly grew into big business by the turn of the twentieth century. It was indeed indigenously American in its nature and its popular voice, but it cannot be separated from its commercial organization and was, actually, part of the transformation of American society wrought by the capitalist industrial revolution and the penetration of popular culture by the culture industry. This culture industry became a national one with the industrial revolution and the creation of a national railway network, effectively completed by the 1880s, which made it possible to transport the same forms of popular entertainment and theater to all parts of America on a uniform basis. The theatrical system was thus permitted to both centralize its operations and organize itself in mass terms using the city, and eventually and primarily New York, as its base. With the transport and commerce revolutions, a commercially effective, highly institutionalized, and immensely profitable theatrical system was created. It was one that merged itself with the music business in general to make an associated branch of Tin-Pan Alley. The result was to solidify the relationship between musical theater and popular culture to construct not only the leading edge of American popular entertainment, but also to provide the economic, technical, and artistic conditions that successfully made, promoted, maintained, and developed it.

NOTES

1. Benjamin (1973) shows how the development of the culture industry is an inevitable consequence of the technological transformation of art and its media by mechanical reproduction. He argues that the effect of this is to produce a mass popular culture that is manipulated by the capitalist system to produce a passive affirmation of the system, so destroying the possibilities of a culture that is creative and critical. See also Adorno (1967) and Adorno and Horkheimer (1993).

2. For a full critique of this view, see Bratton et al. (1991).

3. See, for example, Bratton et al. (1991). More general problems of examining the history of American theater in isolation are addressed in Postlethwaite and McCouchie (1989).

4. For an account of Charles Matthews, see Nathan (1946, 191–97).

5. Pickering (1997) critically examines the need to address "experience" in terms of the historical analysis of culture in order to provide a sociological reading of culture.

6. See Hanes Harvey (1996). She examines stereotypes specifically in terms of Scandinavians. Gilbert (1940) describes a wider range of ethnic "types" and also ethnic performers who played a major part in their portrayal.

7. References to this show are taken from the unpublished manuscript in the Lord Chamberlain's Plays collection at the British Library, London.

8. See Max Beerbohm, *Around Theatres*, quoted in Hyman (1975, 131).

9. The history and development of American musical comedy is specifically addressed by Bordman (1985); Green (1986); Smith and Litton (1981). For a treatment of operetta in this context see Trauber (1983).

CHAPTER 2

Broadway: The Roaring Twenties, Black Culture, and the Song-and-Dance Musical

FINDING ITS FEET: THE ESTABLISHMENT OF THE MUSICAL AS A MUSIC THEATER—OPERETTA, MUSICAL COMEDY, AND THE BROADWAY MUSICAL

The period between the beginning of the twentieth century and the end of the First World War saw the musical develop as music theater in its various subgenres of revue, musical comedy, and musical play, or book musical. But until the 1920s there was a considerable overlap between these subgenres. This gave the musical a hybrid nature rather than the distinctive form that it would eventually take as the "classic" Broadway musical. What role to assign to operetta in the establishment of the Broadway musical, and thus to the nature of the musical as music theater, is, as we have seen in chapter 1, a problematic and contentious issue, which in the past has produced a mistaken genealogy of the musical and a confused notion of its American nature.

This is not, however, to deny the general importance of operetta in the development of the musical. Operetta was central to music theater on Broadway in its early period, and especially from 1900 to the First World War. But so, at this point was musical comedy and many of the works that appeared and became popular hits at this period were a combination of both—*Floradora* (1899), for instance, as well as *The Sultan of Sulu* (1904), *The Wizard of Oz* (1902), *Miss Dolly Dollars* (1905), and so on. The operettas that did appear, whether homegrown, like *Naughty Marietta* (1910) and *Sweethearts* (1913), or European imports like Lehár's *The Merry Widow* (1907) were subjected to a particularly American nativization, in two ways. First, they were largely reconstituted in terms of an American context vis-à-vis theme, plot, narrative, and character. This had the effect of vernacularizing the shows as American popular culture. Second, they were incorporated into the institutional organization of American theater. In this, the now well-established American music industry, occupying a central place in popular culture publishing, played a major part. The focus of the industry was the commercial production and creation of "hit" tunes in which it systematically sought out, popularized, and established the newest trends. A symbiosis was fashioned between the industry and the tastes of its audience through the industry drawing upon and relating to a familiar, everyday world and life. It was an industry that centered upon vaudeville as the primary venue in which new hits were plugged, but it also fostered the practice of interpolation—that is, the insertion into the musical of the hit tune that was calculated to appeal to the public but which had no particular, if any, relation to the musical's plot or its characters. No matter what the specific form of musical theater, then, be it revue, musical comedy, or operetta, such insertions were entirely characteristic of Broadway and flavored its nature. The self-contained hit tune would be a major element of the song-and-dance musical. Moreover, the institutionalized popular theater of America entered centrally into the composition of its music theater to make it very much a performer's and not a composer's art, especially in its earlier stages. Mordden (1984) classifies what kinds of performers these were. There were the earthy singers who commissioned and put over interpolations, the star comics seeking "business" and out-of-context quips, the vivacious prima donnas and soubrettes of quasi-operatic vocal commitment and the accompanying matinee idol of the same ilk, the girls, and the glamorous chorus line. In terms of this and the music industry, then, the audience could expect a wide variety of American popular music to enter into the musical of this period irrespective of musical subform. This was music composed in relation to its own theatrical character—a stophic story ballad ("After the Ball"), a rhythm number ("Yip-I-Addy-I Ay"), a nostalgic strain ("Love's Old Sweet Song"), a spoon ditty ("Shine on Harvest Moon"), or a coon song ("Under the Bamboo Tree").

Under such influences operetta was to fade from view in American popular entertainment until the beginning of the twentieth century. In part, this had to do with theatrical conditions themselves. From 1885, the supply of European operettas dried up, so there was nothing to import. American variety had largely been replaced by vaudeville and been successful in attracting a respectable middle-class audience. Musical comedy, a new European import, created an equally stylish and modish alternative to operetta, and one more suitable to nativization in the context of American theatrical traditions and forms. Thus European musical comedy was regenerated as an expression of American society and culture, becoming an epitome of modernity and a powerful realization of the American Dream.

When European operetta reappeared in America, as "Silver Age" operetta, it did so as a form united with this American musical comedy as well as with America's indigenous popular theatrical heritage. This development was consistent with the developing bourgeoisification of American popular culture and entertainment and the institutionalized conditions of American theatrical entertainment. The American bourgeoisie was rejoining the world of American popular culture and popular entertainment, but it did so as a native audience seeking native entertainment in a native theater. American popular culture was being reconstituted and rehomogenized through its growing bourgeoisification but institutionalized, in this, by the extension of the already commercialized and commodified structure of popular theater. In short, the music industry was to seize upon this process of bourgeoisification to fashion and reinforce the popular stage.

Thus Erenberg (1984) charts the return of the American bourgeoisie to American popular culture and entertainment as part of the dynamic that was to transform American society from a culture of work to a culture of consumption attendant upon the economic success and development of its economy at the turn of the twentieth century. Now, the Victorian values of work, self-discipline, and gentility in which the bourgeois elite had sought to distinguish itself were replaced by a new-style public dream where vitality took over from gentility, with consumption, rather than the work ethic, becoming constituted as the new and primary focus. In gender relation terms mutuality took over from sexual separation, both in terms of audience and the representation and signification of modern life that they enjoyed. The cult of personality began to conflict with the imperative toward good character. As it came from below as well as above, the new dream could be aspired to by all social groups in America and so it reengaged the democratic foundations of the nation. Now American institutional popular theater and music entertainment was beginning to celebrate and promote this consensus by utilizing preexisting theatrical forms and traditions to invent new genres.

Another major problem with operetta, especially in its earliest of forms, was the difficulty of fitting it into the institutional structure of the American theater system. It required relatively huge staging and production and highly sophisticated artistic resources, and these only the theater companies of the large urban centers could provide. Even if its form and content would not have made it difficult to promote in terms of the tastes of the majority audience for popular theater, as opposed to an elitist urban bourgeoisie, it could not be presented to any audience outside of the major cities, and only in certain of these, for purely practical reasons. New York predominated here as it steadily became the industrial, commercial. and financial heart of the American economy throughout the later decades of the nineteenth century. In the regions outside of the theater dedicated to burlesque, the minstrel show, and variety, the other main institutional theater primarily consisted of local stock companies who engaged in musical entertainment and "legitimate" plays (notably melodrama). No stock company could have produced and performed operetta. It required elaborate sets, a large orchestra, and performers and musicians who possessed formal musical (i.e., music academy–produced) abilities and skills. The stock company had none of these. This kind of operetta could not be toured either; it was far too elaborate and expensive. The Gilbert and Sullivan operettas were different; they did not need such resources, and touring companies could be (and were) put together to take them through all of the regions of America. But they were also quite distinct from Viennese operetta in other ways. They were much more easily assimilated into American popular theater—as we have seen above, not only were they recognizably close, in terms of their satirical comedy, to the travesty element in burlesque, but their tongue-twisting lyrics and play upon words was part of the currency of much popular American literature and the comedians and comic acts of popular theater and entertainment of the time. Moreover, the music was constructed, however skillfully, in a format of popular accessibility that made it more obviously tuneful in terms of American popular music. If into the bargain Gilbert and Sullivan sent up the "Old World," that was fine. Finally, in terms of the incipient, and as yet moralistic, bourgeoisification of American popular culture, Gilbert and Sullivan were wholesome and clean in their satiric comedy. Gilbert and Sullivan, then, fitted into American popular culture and its (institutionalized) theater and forms of entertainment. This permitted it to have such influence on the development of the musical.

This fit between Gilbert and Sullivan and American popular culture and its theatrical entertainment is repeated in the influence that Silver Age Viennese operetta had on the development of the musical. But this arrived at a new stage of the capitalist and bourgeois transformation of America and its culture, where "America" was beginning to resonate strongly not just as the promised land of rural new opportunity, but also as the very center of modern sophistication. There was always a tension in this enunciation between the urban version of the American Dream and its representation as a mythological ideal with its roots elsewhere—in a rural idyll of community and frontier. The latter sought to produce an originary sense of the American Revolution and the society designed and founded by it in an enlightened and democratic opposition to the Old World. But the tension was most often reconciled in the musical (both stage and film) through the survival, recovery, and triumph of the values of this rural order even within an industrial and citified context. Thus the hero/heroine and the narrative normally remained ultimately and optimistically true to traditional American values of self-integrity, where honest worth and achievement found a reward in success. A civilized society was seen to be dependent on the creation of relations of love, marriage, the family, and society. As an achievement, "making it" was not seen as sin, but as an American virtue, and was appropriately rewarded. The urban materialization of this reward in terms of affluence and consumption could therefore find a place in relation to traditional American values. So, a new sense of the American Dream in terms of the frontier emerged with the industrialization and modernization of America. Instead of the frontier being a geographical one pushing west territorially, it became an urban one pushing back the barriers to social advance through social mobility. Cohan's musical comedies were very much awake to this development, as were Ziegfeld's revues. Lehár's *The Merry Widow* also arrived at the right time to capitalize upon it.

The Merry Widow (as indeed is the case with the other imports into America of Viennese Silver Age operetta) was, both theatrically and socially, distinct from Golden Age Viennese operetta. For one thing, it was altogether more modern in terms of its setting in time. The world it celebrates is the modern one of the 1890s, a world in which the bourgeoisie has now triumphed as a ruling class to create and impose mores of its own on its society (and its life). These entail values, habits, tastes, and consumptory patterns stemming from the socioeconomic conditions of its social position and political power. There was now a self-bred "haute" in the haute bourgeoisie that needed no aristocratic disguise to legitimate it. It celebrated its basis in industry and commerce. It had developed a proper delicacy of propriety and good breeding of its own to justify the display of wealth and affluence that it possessed. What *The Merry Widow* offered was a very modish world that was both plush and secure and now definitely knowing and worldly, not only in its attitudes, but also in the chic style, glamour, and gaiety of the life it portrayed. It avoided materialist cynicism but not the material life itself. Central to the romantic relationship between Prince Danilo, the hero, and Sonya Sadoyo, the widow and heroine, is the new bourgeoisie. In the mythical kingdom of Marsovia, Danilo now has a job—albeit as part of its bureaucracy—as attaché to the Ambassador of Marsovia in Paris (Baron Popoff), yet one in which the duties are not so onerous as to prevent him from leading the life of a playboy with his aristocratic and upper-class friends. However, Marsovia is a country of dwindling finances, and the plot revolves around Baron Popoff inducing Danilo to marry Sonya, an exceedingly wealthy bourgeois widow, to resolve the situation. She, although originally a peasant, had achieved this position through her marriage to a banker. They are brought together, but Danilo, not willing to be taken as a fortune hunter (as befits his aristocratic honor), and she, being wary of fortune hunters (as befits a haute bourgeois woman of wealth), fence together initially in their relationship. As they fall in love, the problem of wealth interfering with love is resolved when Danilo eventually proposes marriage but only after Sonya has teasingly professed to having no money. The ideology of the purity of the wellsprings of love and romance, then, is overtly preserved, but very much within a knowing subtext about the world in which it is now taking place. Here the bourgeois purse string has gained the upper hand to the extent of underwriting the national government. Even the aristocracy, caught up in capitalism, has to work or pretend to work by having a job. Romance and marriage must position and yield itself to these new conditions of modernity.

The appeal of such a show to an American audience was an appeal to its own haute bourgeoisie, similarly endowed as Sonya, for whom the subtext and its world was immediately recognizable as their own (and the new) world of America where they were masters. Yet *The Merry Widow,* as a European import, carried that additional and extra frisson for its American bourgeois audience in terms of European glamour. The glamour, styles, mores, and affluence of this world, in its transportation to America as a parallel world, could permit it to offer a focus too for the bourgeoisifying aspirations of the increasingly socially mobile immigrant population of American society.

The musical style of this kind of operetta was just as central to its transportation as its narrative. It was altogether less complex than that of its Golden Age predecessor. It did not require academically trained singers but only actors with good singing voices. So it could be accommodated to fit in with the now central figures of American theater in general and, most specifically, the matinee idol and the leading lady, who sustained the dramatic and acting style of this theater and were crucial to the creation of its audience. Also at the heart of *The Merry Widow* were the girls so entrenched in American popular theatrical entertainment and raised at precisely this same time into the newly legitimated and "artistic" essence of the American revue through Ziegfeld's Follies. The exciting and glamorous playboy life of Danilo and his upper-class friends in *The Merry Widow* revolves around the cabaret of Chez Maxim's and the girls who are its center. The operetta celebrates this central significance in two of its showstopping numbers—"Maxim's" and "Girls at Maxim's." As Danilo sings in "Off to Maxim's," the girls of shady reputation—Lolo, Dodo, Joujou, Loclo, Margo, and Froufrou—are his real passion, although he has to work between 2 P.M. and 4 P.M. before he can temporarily forget the responsibilities to "fatherland" and indulge his more hedonistic tastes.

These girls became a major element of the American entertainment industry in this period, through the construction of new forms of theatrical and cabaret entertainment in the large metropolitan centers of America. Designed to appeal to an American urban haute bourgeoisie, they represented what had become the new reward for hard work and success—pleasure and the high life.

The urban vision of success was different from the old Horatio Alger myth, [which] had glorified the man of willpower, self-discipline, and perseverance—the classic Protestant virtues...[Now]...having lived with the wealthy's style of conspicuous consumption, men and women from New York and around the nation became accustomed to the enjoyment of money. (Erenberg 1984, 42)

Bourgeois life had now begun to revolve around money and the gratification it could buy, and this increasingly found expression in pleasure and play. But it was pleasure and play that took on a democratic form in the sense that access to this new high life was open to all—the passport into it was money itself, which, in an increasingly affluent society created by industrial development, was possessed by growing numbers of the American population. A new urban bourgeois culture of consumption was being created in America, and its popular culture and theater and entertainment formed around consumptory tastes and ideology as more Americans joined this bourgeoisie.

Yet, in the very democratization of this culture, the new operetta was immediately locked into a relationship with musical comedy. This latter, too, was a tribute to a bourgeois America as it also idealized and ideologized its world, but at a much more egalitarian and domestic level, which gave it even more direct appeal. The primary theme of musical comedy is the story of the poor little rich girl who makes good and often becomes a star through her own activity. What it produces, then, is the haute bourgeois story and legitimation of social position, with its rewards now made common. Here individual ambition, effort, and work find success. Musical comedy enunciates the American Dream and the American way of its realization in very direct ways: it takes place in a world that is treated as one of equality where mobility rewards success. Modernity is, now, conceived as democratization through bourgeoisification. In this way meritocracy and democracy are reconciled in the American Dream to create a degree of unity in American popular culture that outfaces the social divisions of American society. In this, also, the process of bourgeoisification is effected by consumption as its symbolic marker and not just its material maker.

Ultimately, *The Merry Widow*, as an operetta, contributed to the development of the musical not because of its theme, but because it showed a form in which a musical entertainment could be transformed into a musical play where music was integrated into the plot and became a means for the delineation of character. It grounded this in popular music and dance and, most particularly, the waltz. Lehár's Silver Age operetta offered a model of a "musical play" for the musical. It was copied and nativized, particularly by Victor Herbert, to become a central part of twentieth-century Broadway music theater in the years leading up to the First World War. But the American form was always subject to the inclusion of popular song and comic routines coming from the other forms of American music theater, popular entertainment, and the music industry. This produced a more hybrid character, and in this came its eventual decline and replacement by the musical.[1]

The First World War produced a hiatus in operetta, not only as Austro-German imports were unwelcome, but also because anything that smacked of this heritage was subject to suspicion. American music theater and its composers turned, instead, toward specifically American musical idioms, which led the revue and musical comedy to thrive and consolidate at operetta's expense. In particular, the musical comedy now established a style and tone of its own, which would be constitutive of the musical as it also incorporated the opulence, spectacle, chorus girls, and comedians of revue. Catering to a large bourgeois audience and its aspirants, it combined popular song and dance, which became increasingly polished, stylized, and constructed in association with witty and sophisticated lyrics to match the growing audience sophistication. This larger bourgeois audience was increasingly attracted to revue as other forms of popular entertainment, particularly cinema, drew the lower classes more and more away from live theater.

Operetta did return temporarily postwar, but now in opposition to musical comedy, capitalizing in this opposition on its primary ingredient (romance) and its major musical vehicle for this (the waltz). The effect of the competition with musical comedy was to force the romanticism of operetta toward exoticism, passion, and nostalgia in a purely escapist world inhabited by impossible characters with high-flying romantic feelings. It was a flight from the everyday, but not alone in this: so were many of the melodramatic silent movies as they capitalized upon the exotic possibilities of cinema. In any event, the romanticism of operetta placed it in firm opposition to the realism of musical comedy.

Moreover, operetta's claim to represent "real" musical quality began to be challenged as the criteria of "good" music shifted—an entirely befitting development in terms of the songs and music being created in popular music by the leading American composers. What was "good" about operetta simply became reduced to what was academic about it. The American musical tradition was indeed a popular one, but it was far from being just "mass" culture in any negative sense (see Wilder [1972]).

Finally musical comedy was developing narratologically as well as in musical terms and in this sense too outstripping operetta. In England it had already begun to attract accomplished writers, including the playwright Mark Ambient (co-writer of *The Arcadians* [1909] and *The Light Blues* [1916]), J. M. Barrie (*Rosy Rapture* [1915]), P. G. Wodehouse (co-writer of, among many other musical comedies, the wartime hit *Kissing Time* [1919]) and Edgar Wallace (*Are You There* [1916]). The Princess Theatre productions of musical comedies by Kern, Bolton, and Wodehouse staged

American versions of likewise sophisticated musical plays within musical comedy.

Operetta survived for a while longer, even flourishing on Broadway, but as something quite different from the musical. Indeed, it finds its very apotheosis, as romantic musical melodrama, in the works of Rudolph Friml (*Rose-Marie* [1924]) and Sigmund Romberg (*The Desert Song* [1925] and *The Student Prince* [1924]).[2] It was the Depression that finally killed it, by making its particular form of escapism untenable. It is one thing to forget your troubles; it is another to disappear into a Ruritanian never-never land full of absurd characters with high-flown feelings mouthing poetic nonsense to one another. The musical, then, established itself quite otherwise in terms of contemporary American popular song and dance, vernacular language, and a "realism" of setting, drama, and character. Its music was 4/4 time, and now black music and dance was beginning to enter into and shape the character of popular music and entertainment, and with it, the musical. What remained as a legacy from operetta for the musical was the "book" that the musical slowly took up and then came to make its own, on its own terms.

BLACK CULTURE AND POPULAR SONG AND DANCE

It is a supreme paradox of American popular music and dance that it has been centrally shaped by the black culture of America when, in all other respects, black Americans have largely been oppressively positioned and structurally excluded by American society. But the character of this paradox becomes clearer when one examines the relationship between black and white America in terms of the particular ways black America came to gain a presence in American popular culture. Specifically, it is important to note the role of blackface entertainment and the minstrel show in this. Minstrelsy, as we saw in chapter 1, was the first public acknowledgment by whites of black culture and played a highly significant part in the determination of the imaginary social consciousness in terms of which race relationships in American society found expression at the level of popular culture. But it did this in a highly ambiguous fashion, around what Lott (1993) calls a "love and theft" axis. Here blackface acts and the minstrel show entailed an investiture in black bodies that seemed both to try on the accents of blackness and so demonstrate the permeability of the color line, and yet derisively reject the reality of actual black culture. In doing so, it constructed a particular structure of feeling, which is that of American racism and through which black and white American culture has largely interrelated. But crucially, the minstrel show was able, through its position as the primary popular entertainment from 1846 to 1854, to effectively become a national American culture. The consequences of this created a vehicle by which black culture could enter the dominant (and white) popular culture of America and fund its entertainment and art forms.

Toll (1974) has argued that, in certain respects, the minstrel show was a celebration of "blackness," becoming, in this way, a public forum for a slave culture with liberating consequences. It was not, at least originally, simply a manifestation of anti-black prejudice, although it would eventually degenerate into a racist lampoon of black culture. The appreciation of the minstrel show shown by many of the abolitionists bears this out in part. For example, one anonymous contributor quoted by Horace Greely in the antislavery *New York Tribune* wrote:

Why may not the banjoism of a Congo, an Ethiopian and a George Christie, aspire to an equality with the musical and poetical delineators of all nationalities?...Absurd as it may seem [negro minstrelsy] to the refined musician, it is nevertheless beyond doubt that it expresses the peculiar characteristics of the negro as truly as the great masters of Italy represent their more spiritual nationality...[And] has there been no change in the feelings of the true originators of this music—the negroes themselves?...Plaintive and slow, the sad soul of the slave throws into this music all that gushing anguish of spirit which he dare not otherwise express. (September 6, 1855)

Or again, Mark Twain writes of the "happy and accurate" representation of the minstrel show and how "if I could have the nigger show back again in its pristine purity and perfection I should have but little further use for opera" (Twain 1924, 50). Moreover, this appreciation accompanied the fact that, at one level, the minstrel show attempted a degree of authenticity in its portrayal of black culture. Southern notes that,

to obtain materials for their shows, the minstrels visited plantations, then attempted to recreate plantation scenes on the stage. They listened to the songs of the black man as he sang at work in the cotton and sugar cane field, on the steamboats, and in the tobacco factories. The melodies they heard served as the bases for minstrel songs, and they adapted the dances they saw to their needs...The musical instruments originally associated with plantation "frolics" became "Ethiopian" instruments—banjos, tambourines, fiddles and bone castanets. (1997, 91–92)

But Lott (1993) also shows how this was still married to the more general consciousness produced by the minstrel show as popular entertainment that centrally carried an ambiguous racism in its representation of black culture. The key to this general structure lies in what was being presented as the "peculiar characteristics of the negro." Even the apologists of the minstrel show applauded it as a version of blackness entailing an essentialist sense of black as a kind of pristine naturalness that was both good and intrinsically valuable. This was emphasized in the way such supporters celebrated it. In her "Entertainments of the Past Winter," published in the *Dial* in 1842, Fuller, for instance, remarked how "all symptoms of invention are confined to the African race who, like the German literati, are relieved by their position from the cares of government... 'Jump Jim Crow' is a dance native to this country, and one we plead guilty to seeing with pleasure, not on stage, where we have seen it, but as danced by children of an ebony hue in the street" (1842, 52). Black culture, then, was understood in folk terms but its blackness was seen as an expression of a nature relieved of culture (in the sense that the absence of rule is its preeminent condition).

The minstrel show also focused on "blackness" in terms of the black body and particularly the male black body. But here "naturalness" was identified as a threat. The preeminence of this kind of association points to the particular place and popularity of the minstrel show in the North of America and to the white working class that was its audience. Already, in the early nineteenth century in the North, there was a sizeable black population that

because of the greater proportion of white to blacks in the North, [where] blacks were acculturated more quickly and more completely... offered blacks autonomy to develop their own cultural institutions... [and]... in addition, the various circumstances of the North, including densely populated urban spaces and residences with separate access, helped generate autonomous black association. By the early nineteenth century free blacks and slaves alike gathered in taverns and dance houses, engaged in festivals and parades, generally constituted an acknowledged... public presence. (Lott 1993, 40)

This population was one with its own particular world of stylistic characteristics. The presence of black culture led to a continuous and increasing familiarity with it among whites as "working-class whites and blacks in many instances shared a common culture of jokes, games and dances" and "lower class subcultures in northeastern cities saw extensive elbow-rubbing among apprentices, servants, slaves, journeymen, sailors and laborers; bullbaiting and footracing, masques and street fighting were indulged by whites and blacks together" (Lott 1993, 47). It was in this working-class context, then, that the minstrel show operated in the North to become part of white popular entertainment and theater. There it began to both express and disguise the interests, concerns, humor, and fantasies of its working-class audience.

Primarily this meant that the minstrel show became a loud and rowdy form of theatrical entertainment incorporating many of the traditions of the burlesque with its skits and parodies. In this it gave raucous expression to a popular republicanism and egalitarianism that served for a working-class commitment to the newfound land of America. But this very egalitarianism involved a racist edge. As it parodied and stereotyped, the minstrel show simultaneously invoked blacks in terms that, as Lott argues, "provided displaced maps or representations of working-classness" (1993, 68). It provided a convenient mask through which to voice class resentments of all kinds, resentments directed as readily toward black people as toward upper-class enemies.

Structurally, the newly emerging capitalist industrial order of America based on free labor was changing the character of American society to create a world (in the North) where "the crafts were fairly quickly proletarianised, splitting former self-sufficient artisans into masses of wage workers on the one hand and select groups of industrious mechanics and industrial entrepreneurs on the other" (Lott 1993, 70). Moreover, Irish and German immigration soon segmented that community even further, transforming the American working class by the mid-1850s into a largely foreign-born population. The result was to create a resentful working class who saw themselves as being "dispossessed by the new industrial America and its emergent bourgeoisie... Fearfully identifying this situation, as one of becoming 'like the blacks', [they] countered it with the language and violence of white supremacy" (71). The minstrel show gave vent to all this in complex and ambiguous ways. Through minstrel shows blacks were delineated as inferior, incompetent, stupid, effeminate, and cunning. At the same time, these shows allowed an identification of the white working class and blacks through parodies of black males that emphasized a powerful sexuality, trickiness, and a potential for violence. Some of these characteristics implicitly endowed blacks with characteristics that a working-class white culture positively sought to assimilate for its own identity (a naturally given masculine identity) as a culture of virility, street wisdom, and fighting prowess. Embedded in white working-class race malice, then, was a disguised envy of the black male. The minstrel show's use of black culture for entertainment entailed a fascination and identification. This gave black culture the potential for acceptance as well as rejection. The black as "native" was beginning to enter the hitherto white hegemony of American culture, but at a level that could appropriate black culture into the American world as part of its folk tradition without disturbing the white structure of power within it.

The ability of the minstrel show to represent and incorporate the "folk" of American society placed its importance for the emergence of national American popular culture. Central to the arguments of those American literati who had valued the "authenticity" of the minstrel show was their view of black American culture as a true "native" American folk culture. Although the America of the 1840s could find a unifying and legitimating ideology in the Enlightenment, which had been the support for the American Revolution and the Constitution, its cultural heritage was still one with a European foundation. Black culture, on the other hand, could be presented as folk culture that was indigenous, and significantly, at one level, on a par with the cultures of Europe. At the same time, for the lower class who found only entertainment in it, the minstrel show supported their sense of indigenousness: "eclectic in origin, primitive in execution, and raucous in effect, [the minstrel show] virtually announced itself as one of our first popular institutions" (Lott 1993, 64). This was further nationalized through the way the minstrel show began also to embrace and draw from other indigenous American subcultures of the time, to create a panoply of the every and workaday world of America. Moreover, it also began to develop a native cultural indigenousness theatrically through the song-and-dance material specifically created for it by such figures as Foster. The character of much of this new song specifically related to the America of this time. Mates (1987) points to the essentially sentimental character of these songs and the way in which they were capable of transforming the savagery and bitterness of racism into homesickness, frustration, and nostalgia. So the black, as seen in the previous chapter, could become a kind of Everyman appealing to all those caught up in the travails of the newly emerging raw frontier and the industrial world of the America of the 1840s to 1860s. As Lott puts it, minstrel nostalgia caught

all the forces in American life that seemed to be pulling the country apart...black-face songs spoke at once to restless immigrants moving West, recently transplanted rural folk in cities, and rootless urban dwellers beginning to experience the anomie of modern metropolitan life: turning the South into a kind of timeless lost home, a safe, imaginary childhood, these songs proved supremely satisfying to a wide variety of white audiences. (1993, 190–91)

The minstrel show faded only when it lost this nationalizing role. The once newly emerging and now established capitalist, financial, and industrial bourgeoisie rejected it as a lower-class amusement situated in the dance hall, the saloon, the burlesque, the penny press, and the dime museums. Real culture for them implied the more genteel cultural activities of the concert hall and the legitimate theater. Temporarily, this caused a divide of American culture into high and low, although the parlor song remained an entertainment shared by the bourgeoisie and working class.

There were further reasons for the decline of the minstrel show. Not only did it deflate the pretensions of the emerging middle-class culture of science, reform, education, and professionalism, it also imaged, in the lively behaviors of its cast and audience, the threat of class riot. More importantly the white working and lower classes would desert the minstrel show too as they became integrated into post–Civil War modern capitalist America to find a social mobility and affluence that ultimately united labor with capital in a growing process of bourgeoisification. By the end of the 1860s, although it continued for another 20 years, the minstrel show had done its work as a unifying American cultural entertainment to be superseded by other forms, but, in doing so, it had crucially introduced black culture to white society. This would continue, at first in a more limited and essentially negative racist context, but it carried a crucial residue for the future, the identifications between "nativeness" and/or "naturalness" and black culture, song, and dance that would later be mined and appropriated as a rich resource. In this, the minstrel show and blackface acts had also left an amazing popular cultural entertainment and theatrical legacy that imposed its imprint even on film where blackface played, as Rogin (1998) has shown, a central part in the way in which American cinema was Americanized by its choice of popular entertainment over form.

After the Civil War and the abolition of slavery, large sections of the black population moved either into the cities of the South or to the North to find work and establish a new communal existence for themselves. This was further reinforced by immigration to the North during and following the First World War. To a certain extent, the last decade of the nineteenth century brought a period of new opportunity for blacks and women in education, the arts, and business. Bolstered by the degree of economic success that sustained it, together with their largely segregated existence, blacks "developed their own institutions and culture...[and, in particular]...black music makers developed a distinctive style of entertainment and music fitted to their own personal needs and expression of their own individuality" (Southern 1997, 316). This was not, then, a culture served up for white consumption, but a self-referential culture centrally involving the emergence of ragtime, the blues, and jazz. Blues excepted, because it was a rural black cultural phenomenon, these were created out of and in response primarily to this new urban black culture and its audience, which differed significantly from that of the old slave and rural Southern black culture. In the city, black culture underwent a process of secularization and the venues of its new music and dance expression—the juke joints, honky-tonk night spots, saloons, dance halls, and cabarets—became the sporting-life districts of the cities. But also, and significantly, from 1900 in New York, the West Side of Manhattan developed as a black bohemia where the new music and dance flourished. This would create Harlem after the First World War as the undeclared capital of black culture and, with this new urban black music and dance, a more potent relationship between black and white society was established, although it simultaneously traded off the original introduction between the two.

At first ragtime and jazz figured only in the hot spots of the city, but then they also began to enter into the other forms of popular theatrical entertainment, such as burlesque and variety, to feature eventually in the song-and-dance acts of vaudeville and, through this, to become appropriated, established, and distributed through the music industry. What was new, however, was the nature of the white American society in which this was taking place—the character of the audience that had begun to receive and appropriate ragtime and jazz. The American bourgeoisie rejoining the world of popular culture came out of the economic success and development of the American economy by the turn of the twentieth century but, as shown above, this entailed the transformation of American capitalism from a culture of work to a culture of consumption. Now bourgeois values were fostering a dream of the "good life" as opposed to the classic Victorian values. This dream was concerned, as we have seen, with energy and consumption, reward rather than self-discipline, mutuality rather than sexual separation, and personality rather than character. It was a dream that all social groups in America could treat as an aspiration and, in this way, a hegemonic voice that reshaped American popular culture. The capitalist commercialization and commodification of it, through the development of the American culture industry, effectively funded its institutionalization.

It was in these terms that new black music and dance entered white and now bourgeoisified popular culture, offering to provide the source of vitality, freedom, and pleasure that the bourgeois dream of the "good life" sought to embody. Critically, it was the literal embodiment that was taken to inhere in black music and dance that became the basis of its white appropriation by this new American popular culture. In this, of course, the traditional stereotype of black as "natural," which historically constituted the white image of black Americans, was reasserted. The dance craze, perfectly symbolized by Berlin's great hit tune of the time "Everybody's Doing It," sweeping American cities between 1912 and 1916, illustrates the nature of this white embrace of black music and dance. Berlin's even greater hit, "Alexander's Ragtime Band," signified the major part that Tin-Pan Alley would play in securing black music and dance through its commodification. Both middle class and lower class, young and old began to flock to dance halls, hotel ballrooms, cabarets, and cafés to make dancing a regular and public form of entertainment. A tremendous expansion of commercial dance replaced the old and unrespectable lower-class dance halls and amusement parks. The social dance in these venues was now dance that borrowed the steps from black American dance, music, and culture in replacement of the old formal European steps. In this, as Erenberg notes (see 1984, 151), middle-class whites began to respond to body movement rather than patterned dance steps, and to a culture that was previously considered not just disreputable but as being exemplary of a kind of anti-culture. New dances tumbled out one after another—the Texas tommy, the bunny hug, the monkey hug, the lame duck, the turkey trot, and the fox trot, and then on to the cake walk, the Charleston, and the black bottom (note the animalism implied in the names of these dances). Here the more "natural" shuffle walk–steps involved greater intimacy between partners and implied a spontaneity that was quite at odds with the formal conventions of previous social dance. In all this, what was being sought was a release of the wilder elements and "natural" elements that had been suppressed by traditional bourgeois gentility, and it was found by turning to black culture and the red-light districts as the source for cultural regeneration.

But it was also a cultural regeneration brought by white appropriation and regulation in the process. With the dance craze came a host of popular dancers, none of whom were black, and of which Irene and Vernon Castle were the premier couple. As stars of the ballroom, musical comedy, vaudeville, and cabaret, they transformed and toned dance down to fit it for the respectable "civilized" and white bourgeois world of the middle class. As the *New York Times* reported, these new dances "smacked strongly of the Dahomey-Bowery-Barbary Coast form of revelry" but in being "trimmed, expurgated and spruced up ... [they] became a different thing" (4 January 1914). Dance became expressive rather than passionate, sensual rather than sexual, urban rather than primitive, and all established through the sublimation of and control over excessive bodily expression achieved by refining these dances through formalization. This was certainly an appropriation, but one that intervened in specific ways to construct a white version of what was understood as the passion of black dance.

This kind of process also characterized the appropriation of black music—at first ragtime and then, particularly, jazz. So it was not the black creators and performers of jazz who were able to establish themselves in the new popular culture, but "the white arrangers like Ferde Grofe, as if the sounds made by Duke Ellington, Don Redman, and Jelly Roll Morton came from nature. Improvisational skill, instead of being recognized in African American musicians, was overlooked as being central to jazz." In this way, jazz was seen as an instinctive music that needed work through the creative intelligence of white culture to fashion it from crude discord to melodious form and so establish it. It was Paul Whiteman, then, who became the acknowledged king of jazz and who would enunciate the idea of jazz as "the spirit of a new country ... the essence of America and the music of the common people," (Rogin 1998, 113) but his band excluded black Americans.

It was through this process that jazz became popularized with Tin-Pan Alley, selling any up-tempo music as jazz to make it consumable. In the first three decades of the twentieth century, black culture, music, and dance thoroughly penetrated bourgeoisifying American popular culture, but as a result of appropriation rather than on its own terms. It would, eventually, make a venue within itself for black performers, but it would be a slow process before their performances became black and not just "whitened."

In this respect, the contribution of black music and dance to the musical carries an ambiguous legacy, but one in which the musical arguably became receptive to black music and dance through the recognizable dues paid to it. On this basis, the musical was able to act as an aesthetic "melting pot" through which black America could make a substantive claim upon the heritage of American life and culture. Certainly black music and dance was a major element in inspiriting the song-and-dance musical. Even more important was how it stretched the rhythmic, melodic, and lyrical boundaries of popular song and the formal, representational, and expressive boundaries of popular dance. Indeed, as Gilroy (1993) argues, it was no mistake of popular white culture to recognize the expressive nature of black culture and the way this manifested in its music and dance.

BLACK CULTURE, JEWISH CULTURE, AND THE MUSICAL

Entering into the new relationship between black and white culture within the realm of popular culture was a particular bridge—the American Jews. The period 1890–1920 saw a great influx of Jews into the entertainment business as theater owners; managers; movie exhibitors; vaudeville owners, agents, and bookers; and Tin-Pan Alley song company owners. But this penetration went further to embrace and almost dominate theater and Broadway altogether. This period saw the emergence of the first great impresarios who were Jews—Cohan, Oscar Hammerstein I, Ziegfeld, and the Schuberts. So were the leading stars Jewish—Brice, Cantor, Durante, Jolson, and Tucker—as were many of the most important composers and lyricists—Arlen, Berlin, Caesar, DeSylva, Dietz, the Gershwins, Hammerstein II, Harbach, Kern, Rodgers, Schwartz, and Youmans. In some ways this followed the traditional economic route immigrants, and particularly Jews, had pursued historically as middlemen and, in America, this opportunity was open because, although entertainment was big business, it was not a central American industrial enterprise at this point.

It can also be argued that the structural position that Jews came to occupy on Broadway was made possible by Jewish history and popular culture and that this allowed it to successfully broker a relationship between black and white culture. A number of things stand out about Jewish history and popular culture that suggest a kinship with black culture, making for a degree of ethnic sympathy and dialogue between the two. First, Jewish culture, like black culture, is essentially diasporic and bound to geographic movement and immigrant status within the societies in which it found a home. Second, both blacks and Jews suffered historically from deep-seated hostility, prejudice, stereotyping, and exclusion, to which the response was to attune themselves to the requirements of survival both internally and through an understanding of the habits and desires of their oppressors. Third, for Jews, self-expression and the idea of upward mobility through entertainment came naturally from their European experience (see Slobin 1982, 44). Internally, American Jewish culture, like that of American black culture, used music to establish its identity and keep its community intact, while externally Jews utilized the ethnicity and the stereotypical roles assigned to "Jewishness" to enter the vaudeville theater, music halls, and burlesque houses as popular entertainers. But, being white, Jews were able to achieve a legitimacy and transform themselves into regular "melting pot" Americans in a way that was denied, at least initially, to black performers.

There were more specific structural and cultural forms of identification between Jewish and black culture. Within the city, Jews and blacks found themselves rubbing together on the streets of the jostling ghettos while also enjoying a further degree of interconnectedness through their mutual participation in its red-light and sporting-life districts. At the same time, Jews possessed a culture of embodiment and expressivity that at one level paralleled black culture but, particularly, shared the resource of a native and folk vitality that the newly emerging bourgeoisified white popular culture sought to mine for its own expressive and consumptory purposes. Moreover, Jews, as many commentators have shown, were distanced in some ways from Victorian codes of behavior. Marriage, for instance, was constructed as being an inherent good in Jewish culture, rather than a method of social control and sexual containment. Perhaps more importantly, the human body in Jewish culture was regarded with much less suspicion than in Western Christianity. At the same time, while Jewish culture was originally framed within a patriarchal familial structure, the American version of romantic love began to detach it from this mooring as the Jewish community became more and more assimilated. *Fiddler on the Roof* (1964), although set in Russia, is really about the Jewish-American experience of the breaking of the traditional patriarchal and familial Jewish community (and in this, illustrates how the book musical is always about America, no matter its specific settings). And finally, there were certain parallels between Jewish and black popular music. Drawing on the work of Goldberg (1958) and Idelsohn (1932),[3] Steyn argues that Jewish song uses the minor scale or at least has a minor character like that of the blue note of black music—"the third, fifth or seventh degree of the scale, with its pitch tweaked slightly to give it a bluesy, jazzy tinge...[is]...also characteristic of Jewish folk-song" (1997, 77). So the new American popular music of the musicals may owe a certain amount to Jewish as well as black popular culture—indeed, in the Jewish composers of the musicals, it may be that a fusion is at work rather than solely assimilation to the dominant cultural identity.

Certainly a degree of simulated substitutability of black culture by Jewish culture seems to be part of how black culture entered into the new modern white popular mainstream, which came from shared cultural elements and a common world of the ghetto and the street that the Jews of Broadway took over in bringing the "folk" to Broadway. The career of Irving Berlin—of whom Kern said, when asked about the nature of the musical, that he "has no *place* in American music. He *is* American music" (quoted in Steyn 1997, 82)—classically demonstrates this. Berlin, the son of an orthodox cantor, was "at home on the streets, that marginal land between his own culture and the culture of his new society...[The streets] could provide feelings of constant experiences of the self uprooted from a stable past" (Erenberg 1984, 74). Berlin worked, then, in the city's clubs, taking his speech and rhythms from its streets to vitalize and vernacularize the song and dance of the new modern popular culture (see Whitcomb [1988]). Or again, Sophie Tucker, who broke out from the streets in a performance style that was focused around a hearty earthiness. In this, she adopted three basic styles of song: "the sexually aggressive woman seeking physical love, the singer of dixie melodies, and the forlorn woman, a wise loser in the game of love" (193). Signally, in "deemphasising the ballad...[she]...and other pre-war singers in vaudeville and cabarets turned to the American streets and the Negro for the source of a new-style music" (193–94). But, in this, Berlin and Tucker represent the general transformation that American popular culture was undergoing and which Jewish impresarios, composers, and performers played a strong hand in fashioning. In fashioning it, they were engaged in making black music and dance the fashion. The problem was the degree of piggybacking involved in all this, which often ran counter to notions of cultural kinship and dialogue. Jews could carry this modern popular culture forward as they became upwardly mobile and increasingly Americanized and Americanizing—unlike the blacks, they could make a claim on Ellis Island and establish their bona fide American credentials as a legitimate part of New World folk. But, still, the door was now ajar for black musicians, performers, and composers.

Porgy and Bess (1935) poses most expressively whether and how much the influence of black culture on the development of the musical entails and conceals an act of theft or implicates respect and an act of inspirational homage. From its very first performance, as Swain (1990), Horn (1996), and Block (1997) demonstrate, it was accused of racism in terms of both its stereotypical and negative portrayal of black Americans. This, it was argued, continued the reductive tendency of minstrelization, particularly in the way this show frequently used a stereotypically "realized" version of black music in alliance with Jim Crow and Zip Coon—like portraits of character. On the whole, it has been poorly received by black commentators, who have rejected it as a white attempt to appropriate black culture and subject it to the bourgeois conventions, thus obscuring the harsh reality of the social deprivation of black existence and exploiting the expressivity of its culture. However sympathetic Gershwin may have been to black life and to black culture (he lived for a month on Folly Island off the coast of South Carolina to observe the Gullah community and described his experience as more of a homecoming than an exploration), he has been castigated for the presumption of the right to speak on behalf of the black world. Reviewers of the first production pointed out that folklore subjects recounted by an outsider were only valid as long as the folk in question were unable to speak for themselves, which certainly was not true of the African American in 1935. More potent still were the reviewers who wrote about *Porgy and Bess* in terms of fake folklore, a critique that has grown with time (see Horn 1996). Cruse has argued that, culturally, *Porgy and Bess* is a "product of American developments that were intended to shunt Negroes off into a tight box of sub-cultural artistic dependence, stunted growth, caricature, aesthetic self-mimicry imposed by others, and creative insolvency...[It] represents the most perfect symbol of the Negro creative artists' cultural denial, exclusion, exploitation and acceptance of white paternalism" (1996, 100–101). Dennison describes the content of *Porgy and Bess* in similar terms: "Perhaps, the secret of [its] success is that it is earthy, sexy, corrupt, violent, comical, irreligious, blasphemous, hypocritical, desecrating to the spirituals, immoral and altogether derogatory to the American Negro" (1963, 472).

Defenders of *Porgy and Bess,* however, such as Mellers (1964), Starr (1984), Swain (1990), and Block (1997), turn to its aesthetic and theatrical qualities and defend its dramatic and musical borrowing from black culture as an advance in the musical as music drama. Here much of the debate revolves around whether it should be considered as a musical or an opera, which stems from the fact that it has both "long since demonstrated a stageworthiness matched only by the memorability of its tunes" (Block 1997, 84). It also possesses a "wealth of unifying devices." In it one finds considerable "use of leitmotivs throughout the score, involving much motivic development in the orchestral parts" (Starr 1984, 75).

In the end, however, to call *Porgy and Bess* an opera rather than a musical may simply disguise a prejudice that refuses to accept that the idioms of popular music and a vernacular engagement with America cannot be expanded and made consonant with "high" cultural achievement. What such a classification comes from is the reduction of the "popular" in the musical to mere "entertainment"; what it ignores is the ability of a sophisticated music drama to work within the musical and theatrical conventions that make the musical popular.

Moreover, this kind of argument misses the main point of the critics of *Porgy and Bess*. Irrespective of what one calls this show and what wider status it is deemed to have, the fact of appropriation remains. It may be, again as its defenders argue, that this musical can be elevated to the point that it becomes a commentary on the wider human condition. But this latter persists in being registered in culturally specific ways in *Porgy and Bess,* and its musical idiom is also culturally precise. *Porgy and Bess* is "an artistic work for the musical stage, which uses a group of Black Americans as its subject matter" (Horn 1996, 120). The question, then, is not whether *Porgy and Bess* is appropriative—it clearly is—but how to read its appropriation. Whether it is inevitably "racist" in this respect, for instance, is by no means clear. It would be denial, as Horn argues, not to recognize that it creates a specificity of "race" in the world that it portrays and through the terms in which it constructs the reality of this world musico-dramatically. But *Porgy and Bess* never degenerates into mockery. The dramatic figures who inhabit the world of Catfish Row are responsible for what occurs in it. Now, "instead of an artistic conceit by means of which one group of people causes another, imagined, group to conduct their lives to music in order in some way to get at their souls, the people of Catfish Row reveal the musicality of their daily lives" (Horn 1996, 121). Rather, then, than treating Gershwin as the author who exploits the black world for his creation, his creation itself becomes central through its own intricate musicality. Once revealed, this musicality shows itself to be complex and varied. The people of Catfish Row draw upon a range of styles and approaches: collective religious expression, and expression in which individual and group are integrated; songs about work, again involving individuals and the group; solo songs with accompaniment; romantic duets; jazz-influenced singing about the city; and so on. In this context the idea of exploitation seems irrelevant or at least much reduced—Catfish Row cannot exploit itself. What happens is that material from these sedimented layers is "used by the people of Catfish Row to negotiate the relationships between concepts fundamental to their lives and to changes in those lives" (Horn 1996, 122). Gershwin has tried to achieve an acculturation of the black image through marrying it to bourgeois and white cultural conventions (music drama) and giving it equivalence. Musically, it does go beyond just the realization of black music and dance and it intensifies the dramatic possibilities inherent in them. This does not entirely work, because stereotyping persists even here, but the ambition of *Porgy and Bess* is to find integrity in black life and culture and not to caricature it. That this is the case is given support by the fact that only black artists are permitted to perform *Porgy and Bess,* and they continue to do so now. Certainly, *Porgy and Bess* advanced black song-and-dance beyond the realms of entertainment value and positioned it as a structural and dramatic component of a complex musical. The book musical also needed to use the rhythmic, melodic, lyrical, and expressive characteristics of black culture to forge its music drama, as much as musical comedy needed these to couch and eventually sophisticate its comic invention.

THE JAZZ AGE AND THE SONG-AND-DANCE MUSICAL

The era of the 1920s is often constructed, with some foundation, as the legend of America entering a world of carnival now read as its nature. The decade following the First World War was a decade of triumphal capitalism that produced a general vote of confidence. Major cities, particularly New York, saw the building of truly gigantic skyscrapers, like the Empire State Building and the Rockefeller Center. Ford established the assembly-line system of mass production through which the car industry emerged to become (and remain) America's major corporate business while simultaneously stimulating the whole of the economy. High tariffs led to huge budgetary surpluses that permitted massive tax cuts. Although they primarily benefited the rich, they also released a whole new level of spending power in the economy generally; cheap credit was available, which extended wealth to a large section of the population. During the period 1920–27, wages rose 26 percent in real terms and, to a certain extent, business and finance began to recognize the economic benefits to capitalism of a high-wage economy. Now "the symbol of American life was no longer to be a log cabin or a family farm, it was to be a gigantic cigar" (Brogan 1990, 505). The theme of American existence was to be consumption and "the belief in the possibility of happiness and a good time" which "led great numbers of people, perhaps especially the young, who now had money to spend in large amounts for the first time . . . to turn their backs on the struggle of work and politics as much as possible" (506). This was reinforced by the desire to forget the war and return to normal, which translated into an isolationist commitment to America and its own modern world. The world emerging had been developing since the 1890s. It now flowered after the First World War, with the motorcar playing a major part in breaking the town-country divide, shaping the basis of daily life, reorganizing the pattern of residential life in American cities, and precipitating a new migration from rural to urban America. A modern, large, and prosperous middle class had appeared with the carefree motorist as the celebrant epitome of its ideology and lifestyle.

Politically, this triumphant capitalism was matched by a politics of big business wedded to government with big businessmen in it (particularly Andrew Mellon, who was Secretary of the Treasury) and committed to supporting big business through high tariffs, low taxation, and deregulation. This it combined with isolationism and anti-immigration policies to protect and maintain its modern and successful capitalist world. Indeed, the American presidents of this era—Harding, Coolidge, and Hoover—were the very exemplification of modern capitalist America in both their backgrounds and rise to power, and unanimously espoused the political belief that the business of government was to "mind the store" nationally and promote a philosophy of "self-help" individually. This created a political ideology of particular appeal to the growing bourgeois world of America. Only rural America was left out of this (white) modern and capitalist American Dream based on industry and the city. Indeed, it was a last and final attempt by rural America to control the industrial transformation of America and its world that brought about the Prohibition—although the unintended effect was to add an extra dose of raciness to the hedonism of this world rather than curb it as intended.

Cultural commodification and materialization was part of the triumphal ascendancy of capitalist modernity. The 1920s saw the golden age of Tin-Pan Alley as radio, the gramophone, and cinema emerged to initially join forces with established forms of popular entertainment (see Goldberg [1961]). Broadway flourished because the cost of producing shows was relatively low; it had a virtual monopoly on star performers who were now transferring from vaudeville to the musical because the latter offered them better opportunities. The main requirement was songwriters and lyricists adept at creating self-sustaining songs that could be spotlighted—the experience of composing hit songs for Tin-Pan Alley had produced composers and lyricists who now entered the musical genre (see Green 1986). Tin-Pan Alley and showbiz were able to establish a symbiotic relationship with one another because, although the Tin-Pan Alley song is about the song with the widest commercial appeal (the hit) and the musical's song is about the show, show tunes could be designed to create a show that traded on hits. Moreover, hits could be served up as pop smashes for endless singers, performers, and recordings. More generally, Tin-Pan Alley and Broadway were inextricably entangled with one another in terms of popular culture because of the historical origins of the musical in all of the song-and-dance forms of American entertainment and its kinds of performers and stars. The musical and the revue acted as venues for Tin-Pan Alley to hawk its wares. At worst, this meant that the effect of Tin-Pan Alley on Broadway was to create musicals as commodities for the masses based on the lowest common denominator in the search of surefire success, but, at best, it prevented an avant-garde pretentiousness that made for a vernacular American theater that both reflected and was reflexive upon contemporary American society. Certainly it ensured that the Broadway musical was located in commerce and showbiz, and this is what it made of itself. Essentially the Broadway musical had to work as a show in order to be successful, and this functioned throughout its heyday as a rule that created a relation between author and producer that was success-oriented and dependent upon the musical gearing itself to audience taste. The result was that the form of the musical was one in which the artistry of the composer had to yield to the producer, star, audience, and profitability. But it also allowed the musical to develop artistically. The song-and-dance musicals of the 1920s particularly evince, indeed almost venerate, showbiz. The effect of this commercialization on these musicals was genuinely paradoxical. On the one hand, many of them were flimsy and formulaic mass entertainment; on the other hand, many exuded an exuberant populism that kept them vitally in touch with popular culture and the contemporary world of America. The further and also paradoxical consequence for our modern world is that while many of the songs of song-and-dance musicals remain as standards, the sheer contemporaneity of the shows themselves, in relation to their own very particular environments, has dated them and made these virtually impossible to revive, unlike book musicals.

Within this commercial framework and its heritage of popular and theatrical entertainment, Mordden (1983) argues that it was comedy, song, dance, and performer that come to be the basis for structuring the show. Its focus was essentially upon entertainment—this established its format in a number of specific ways. First of all, it was normally and deliberately composed as a vehicle for particular female stars. *Irene* (1919) was composed to show off the singing talent of Edith Day; *Sally* (1920) and *Sunny* (1925) were composed to show off the dancing talent of Marilyn Miller; *Lady Be Good* (1924) was composed to show off the dancing talent of the Astaires; and so on. The comedy, too, was star-orientated to figure star comedians sometimes as the male lead but always with a major place in the show. Finally, the dance was organized to bring in and to show off the girls of the chorus line, who were central to the show's *raison d'être* as entertainment. In this context, the book of such musicals rarely rose above the utilitarian demands placed upon it by the entertainment format, since the prime objectives were to feature the star qualities of its female star, accommodate the particular comic routines and shtick of its star comedian, and create the maximum opportunities for the chorus to show off their glamour and vigor in high-kicking hoofing routines. The song-and-dance musical was literally a comic song and dance show but, in this, it was tied to its era, expressive of the carnivalesque and hedonistic atmosphere of the 1920s and the new American world of consumption from which it stemmed. So the whole tone of the 1920s musicals was one of razzmatazz (thus the "opulent adornment"), but one in which comedy now took on a chic, knowing, and polished urbanity suitable to the growing bourgeois world that faced back on this with a sophisticated sybarite's grin. Music and dance deliberately took over black culture, particularly jazz, to use its expressive vitality to this purpose and make the song-and-dance musical truly modern in its total contemporaneity. As the hit song of *Lady Be Good* had it, a "Fascinating Rhythm" was not just at the center of this culture, but somehow at the center of the world it configured in such intoxicating ways.

All-black song-and-dance musicals appeared on Broadway too to share in this and enjoy a degree of success, by, as Southern (1997) suggests, being even jazzier than the jazz of white song-and-dance musicals. *Shuffle Along* (1921) inaugurated a whole series of such shows. But it was white composers who primarily established the jazz musical, with the Gershwins taking the lead—in *Lady Be Good*, *Tip-Toes* (1925), *Oh Kay* (1926), and *Funny Face* (1927)—to be followed up by all the major Broadway composers of the time: Berlin, Henderson, Rodgers and Hart, Tierney, Youmans, and so on.

However, if the libretto of the song-and-dance musical hardly constituted a book as such, certain common themes were dominant in these musicals that captured the American Dream in terms of both elements of continuity and the specific changes that were now reshaping its modernity. Continuous was the mythological element of America as a New World based upon democratic egalitarianism and the popular ideological sense of this as a "can-do" environment of individual opportunity and success. But the full precipitation of New World identity was contingent on the emergence of America as a capitalist bourgeois world that reconstituted the mythology and ideology and the social identities, relationships, and community around it. The primary structural foundation of this America was the success of the American capitalist economy and its transformation of the American world into one of increasing affluence and consumption. Particularly, it was the move toward consumption and the reconstruction of the American Dream to make consumption and its enjoyment the fruit of achievement and success that was crucial. In this context, the strict established bourgeois virtues and a morality of work, self-discipline, sexual respectability (especially for women), and societal segregation came to be modified. American middle-class men and women would still find their primary identities in work and the home respectively, but both genders became devoted to the new personal and more liberal styles that were the desired rewards of success. It was through these new personal styles that men and women articulated the assimilation of social progress to the terms of self-fulfillment. The new music and dance offered precisely the vehicle through which these new middle-class demands and values could find expression and fulfillment. Now, with this, youth came much more to the fore.

Most particularly, "new times" produced the "new" woman, and in this Irene Castle could be said to have played a major role through her "civilizing" (again in Elias's [1994] sense) of the new dance forms. The *Boston Traveler* insisted that she had created a new type of American girl who "dieted, exercised and practiced to become tall, dainty, slim and willowy" (quoted in Erenberg 1984, 167) as she sheared her locks and shortened her skirts. Castle embodied in her dancing the new and expressive woman who merged virgin with vamp to establish and legitimize newer kinds of behavior. She embodied a woman who could handle the troubles of passion by restraining herself as an elegant girl. She was exciting enough to attract yet innocent enough not to be associated with sinful sexuality. She could achieve a successful marriage but in a newly constructed way. Here the new wife signified an intriguing blend of leisure and work. Consequently the husband, attracted by this combination, spent more time with her, not out of duty but in the pursuit of fun and pleasure. So conventional marriage could be transformed into a much more romantic relationship. The song-and-dance musical seized upon this new middle-class world of self-expression, youth, fun, and romance to give it its contemporaneity, but often added a less innocent tone of naughtiness to it, as in a song like "Makin' Whoopee," which appealed to the inherent hedonism of the values of this new world. The audience could embrace it as dream and fantasy but not, ultimately, indulge it in reality beyond the boundaries of the conventional restraints of other aspects of middle-class respectability and normal routines of everyday existence.

The song-and-dance musical created this world by retaining the traditional American elements of love, romance, marriage, and community and, to that extent, sanctifying the American ideals of equality, sincerity, authenticity, goodness, and love, but now with a different expressive voice and worldly-wise sensibility. Here modern boy meets modern girl in an American world. The post-Enlightenment Jamesian "innocence of the New World" has been converted into success and prosperity as its virtuous expression. With this the Cinderella story, the staple diet of American musical comedy, finds a new lease of life. But this Cinderella is more likely to be a lower-middle-class immigrant woman with a white-collar job who meets, romances, and marries the boss's son as her prince. She has no need of a fairy godmother because she finds her suitor through her job—and it is her dynamism at work that brings them together. In their story they reflect the fulfillment of America as Promised Land. But the social context of this is widened further to accommodate the new urban and liberated social landscape of modern American society, allowing business, sport, college life, showbiz, the underworld, and high society of the time to enter. Youmans's *No, No Nanette* (1925) epitomizes the song-and-dance musical of the 1920s, and Green's synopsis captures its quintessential 1920s flavor:

Jimmy Smith [the hero]…a married bible publisher and guardian of the play's doubly admonished heroine…has been giving financial support to three comely young ladies living in three different cities. When the Smiths and their friends, including Lucille and Billy Early…—plus the three recipients of Jimmy's largesse and a sassy housemaid named Pauline…—all turn up at the Smith's Chickadee Cottage in Atlantic City, no end of comical embarrassments ensue. (1996, 47)

If this synopsis seems puzzling, it is precisely because there is little dramatic rhyme or reason to *No, No Nannette*, although it is coherent in the context of the carnivalistic atmosphere of the 1920s. Indeed, its frantic comedy, showstopping dancing, and star roles *are* its real structure, a structure punctuated by the necessary hit tunes, like "I Want to Be Happy."

Sunny (1925) was likewise entirely characteristic. Here the Cinderella story is told in terms of a wacky modern version of the immigrant dream of America. Sunny Peters, a spirited and adventurous bareback horserider working in a English circus has her heart stolen away by Tom Warren, an American tourist. In pursuit of this glittering prize, Sunny stows aboard the liner taking Tom back to the United States. Before she can land, however, Sunny must marry, and so she weds Tom's friend, Jim Denning, but once the agreed-to divorce has been granted, Sunny and Tom are happily reunited at a fashionable resort. *Sunny* has a kind of book (and a very American one), but basically this was less important than it being a star vehicle for Marilyn Miller. This, together with its comedy, dance, and song, is what it really hung on as a show. In this, it was a deliberate follow-up to a previous and similar hit show of Kern's (also for Marilyn Miller), *Sally* (1920).

Whoopee (1928), on the other hand, epitomizes the song-and-dance musical made for the comic (in this case Eddie Cantor), so comic shtick prevails. Here a hypochondriac, Henry Williams, in California for his health, becomes unwittingly involved with the daughter of a ranch owner, whom he helps to escape from the local sheriff. After a series of comic misadventures that involve hiding out in an Indian reservation and Henry (in blackface) posing as a singing waiter, the girl is united with her true love, an Indian half-breed who, "naturally" enough, turns out to be white. The America of this music comedy is typically a wacky place with a comic tale to match it. But *Whoopee*, too, had to have hit tunes—"Love Me or Leave Me" and "Makin' Whoopee"—at its center. Modernity was what it celebrated. It made the oddball almost its symbol of America, but it was the newness of the New World that it loved and sought to make its own as a life full of vitality in its carefree and careless exuberance. Perhaps the song "Good News," (from the show of the same name) with its celebration of the newest fad in dance, the "Varsity Drag," was most symptomatic of this embracing of everything modern.

The song-and-dance musical of the 1920s, then, was precisely redolent of the triumphant nature of the America of its era. That it celebrated and expressed this era as a "Jazz Age" is not surprising. It was an era that now founded itself on a reconstituted bourgeois American Dream of self-expression and consumption, which it used the song and dance of black culture to articulate. Lott (1993) is right to argue that black culture was purloined in this respect, but Gilroy (1993) shows why it had to turn here in search of expressive vitality (even if white American popular culture had a long song-and-dance history). Black culture, as Gilroy argues, is distinctive in its expressive character and the embodiment of this in song and dance. This comes not out of some essential blackness but through the countercultural response of the black community/communities to the racial oppression of a white modernity that both denied them access to and enslaved them through its cognitive and literate culture of reason. For the musical, the turn to black song and dance was a gain for its vernacularity and potentiality. Many of the shows of the 1920s were simply exploitative commodities produced by the American culture industry. But far from all were so. Many songs, too, from the 1920s song-and-dance musicals have stayed the course as fine examples of what popular culture can achieve in its own right, and many of the dances retain their vitality. It also remains true that this culture and theater industry, no matter its commercial nature, gave a place to composers to compose and institutional structures to support their lives, which ultimately allowed the musical to flourish as both popular art and entertainment.

NOTES

1. Berlin, Gershwin, Kern, and Rodgers, in particular, began their careers as composers of the musical by creating songs to be interpolated into operettas.

2. Both Rudolph Friml and Sigmund Romberg were academically trained—as was Victor Herbert—and also, in their earlier careers, composed serious concert music.

3. For a comprehensive account of specifically black musical theater, see Well (1989) and Hamon (2000).

CHAPTER 3

The Depression and the Broadway Musical

CONTEXTS

"Black Thursday," October 24, 1929, when the New York Stock Market spectacularly crashed, dramatically signaled a finale to the seemingly endless boom and bonanza of prosperity and consumption that fuelled the America of the 1920s—a time in which, as President Calvin Coolidge had precisely put it, "the business of America" had been "business." A few years later America was struck by the Depression, and it seemed as if the "whole fabric of modern, business, industrial America was unraveling" (Brogan 1990, 527). But it was President Herbert Hoover, not Coolidge, who would pay most dearly in political terms as the Depression gathered momentum and his government floundered in face of its disastrous effects, until he was replaced through the election of Franklin D. Roosevelt to the American presidency in 1933. The problem lay in the fact that Hoover was deeply committed not only to the capitalist reality and ideology of modern America, but also to the belief that its flowering represented the realization of the virtues and principles on which America and the American Dream was built—individualism, hard work, thrift, and personal honesty. He himself had risen from poor Iowa farm boy to millionaire. Consequently Hoover continued with the same Coolidge philosophy of government and economics, which was opposed to any form of federal government intervention and so unable to engage in any program of public expenditure that could maintain employment or stimulate demand. He subscribed to "the long Jeffersonian tradition [that] forbade the American government to use its power in that way" (Brogan 1990, 522).

Thus responsibility for finding a solution to the Depression was forced onto the private sector, and the economy slid further toward monumental disaster because American capitalist business was in no position to deal with it. Although some industrialists realized that the expansion and profitability of American economy in the 1920s was crucially dependent on high wages, low prices, and consumer demand, most industrialists understood America's economic success to be the product of the protectionist policy of the federal government and pressed for further such measures. This view was endorsed by the Smoot-Hartley Tariff of 1930, which produced an equivalent raising of tariff barriers against American exports by her foreign trading partners and an undermining of world trade. By the same token, industry actively and successfully undermined all attempts to further the trade union organization of labor and any increase in the wages of organized labor. But even more of a disaster lay in the state of the private American financial system. The banking system was based on thousands of entirely independent, disconnected, poorly managed, and underregulated local banks and brokerage houses, which constituted no real banking system at all. American high finance sought and found a profitable bonanza for its activities in the speculative financing of what in the end, as the Depression spread throughout the whole of the Western economy, turned out to be dubious and ultimately unredeemable investments in recovering post–World War I European economies. More ominously, in the late 1920s it began to invest the huge amount of profit and capital that it had initially accrued, but it was neither financing new industrial enterprises nor revitalizing the old. The strategy was simply to get its hands on a larger share of the profits of American business itself that accrued from economic expansion, low government business, and personal taxation. The result was to pump up the price of shares in what seemed to be a climate of the never-ending expansion of dividends. As the stock market rose in this way, it continued to offer, for all intents and purposes, effortlessly achieved and rich rewards for the investment of savings. The American Dream now suggestively presented itself as being on tap, and what looked like the very specific economic door to its entry was seemingly open to more than just the expert businessman and financier. So the well-heeled middle class that had emerged in modern America, seeing the riches beckoning and the seeming ease with which they could be acquired, took the plunge and entered the stock market. By late 1929, the year in which Hoover was inaugurated as President, there were nine million individual investors in the market.

The signs of a downturn in the economy had been present since 1926. The economic growth and prosperity of the 1920s was essentially a phenomenon of industrial and urban America, not of rural agricultural America. The boom in these sectors had begun to slacken after that year. But the stock-market bubble continued to grow without constraint until the point was reached at which it became evident that shares were changing hands at prices no dividends could justify. At the same time, warehouses were choked with unsold goods and factories began to diminish their output. Now, as the bubble burst, a situation in which cash and credit was in endless supply was totally reversed. Brogan shows the huge scale of this and its comprehensive effects. Industrial expansion had to be abandoned, but nobody was prepared to trust banks or brokerage houses or lend against the security of stocks and shares. Instead there was a desperate scramble for currency in order to keep ordinary business afloat while creditors insisted on collecting on their loans. This expanded immediately to the general population. Middle-class consumers were forced to cut back their consumption and sell off possessions to pay their debts, particularly the mortgages on their houses. But the whole working population of America was drawn in as industrialists now became unable to raise finance to run even their day-to-day business. Banks, many of which were in trouble because of their stock market speculations, refused to advance them either money or credit. A cycle set in where trade contracted and prices began to fall and, with them, profits and earnings, leading factories to lay off their workers. Hoover and the federal government responded. Hoover "was to act incessantly, doing more than any previous President had done in any previous economic crisis ... [but] ... what he did was never enough, so he seemed to be doing nothing" (Brogan 1990, 528). What he did, primarily, was to treat the situation as a crisis of business confidence and attempt to restore it by persuading the business community to agree not to lower wages or lay off workers.

Not only was there no recovery forthcoming in the American economy, it was now hit by a second massive blow—the spread of the Depression into the economies of Europe and Japan. Insofar as these foreign economies had recovered after the First World War, this had depended to a heavy extent on American investment propping them up. With the downturn of the American economy, that investment was now withdrawn. But worse, American industrialists and politicians argued that the policy of protectionism, always a central plank of American economic policy, should be reinforced. Congress passed the Smoot-Hartley Act in 1930 to produce the antagonistic and counterresponding raising of tariff barriers against American exports on the part of its foreign trading partners. This not only brought world trade to a virtual halt but also meant that these partners defaulted on their American debts. The crisis of the American economy was complete and out of control as Hoover and the federal government continued to refuse active intervention in the promotion of recovery, relying instead on optimistic reassurance and the ultimately equilibrating mechanisms of the market. All production was failing by this time, and this optimism not only fell flat but was greeted with total cynicism. "So it is not surprising that the industrialists soon forgot their undertakings and began, reluctantly, to cut wages and hours and give their workers the sack. Soon the only rising curve in the [economic] statistics was that of unemployment" (Brogan 1990, 530–31). Five million at the end of 1930, it became 9 million at the end of 1931 and 13 million at the end of 1932.

The effect on large sections of the population was brutal and extended into the middle class as well as its lower reaches and the working class. The 1920s was a period when more and more Americans began to achieve a degree of affluence where they could enjoy the inviting consumptory possibilities of a thriving capitalist economy. Now, even the necessities of life could no longer be taken for granted by huge numbers of them:

In their millions, they found themselves stripped of everything—jobs, possessions, housing—often unable to find a night's shelter for their families, or enough to eat…[But] bad as the hunger, weariness and cold…were the humiliation and despair. The descent came by stages: the loss of one's job; the search for another in the same line; the search, growing frantic, for work in any line; the first appearance at the bread-line, where astonishingly, you met dozens of other men who had kept the rules, worked hard and were now as low as professional bums. (Brogan 1990, 531)

Moreover, the unemployed were highly visible in the society through their numbers, the breadlines, the attempts to scrape together some cash through selling tiny items (paralleled by members of the middle class selling their possessions and homes), the begging, and most shockingly in the shantytowns ("Hoovervilles") that were established around major cities. This very visibility was a constant reminder to those in employment of the economic conditions with which their own security was threatened. It was this humiliation, despair, and visibility that now began to introduce a wholly new note into responses to the modern capitalist economic order, which had been ideologically formulated as the necessary foundation for the realization of the American Dream. Shock and fear over its collapse were the major responses, but critique began to find a voice too. If those who had committed themselves to the proclaimed virtues of the ideologized American system now found themselves threatened or literally thrown onto the scrap heap, so utterly cheated of the promised reward, what faith could be placed in the system?

Such responses were reinforced by the revelation of the scandals and malpractice that had gone on in the booming economic and financial frenzy prior to the crash and now began to see the light of day. But it was especially magnified by the whole antistatist American and philosophical tradition, which assumed that "the thrifty and diligent would never know real want; private charity was a duty, which would look after the unfortunate; the riffraff could be left to look after themselves" (Brogan 1990, 531).

The unfortunates of the Depression, however, were not riffraff. They ran into millions, and private charity and even localized state relief could not cope with poverty on this scale. It needed relief from the federal government, and the demand for this began to find an articulate political voice both popularly and among the media, intelligentsia, and progressive reformist politicians.

Most vocally the demand was that Hoover should at least give bread if he could not give work to his people. Hoover refused, clinging to the ideology of American individualism, which he saw as the essence of the American system and its achievement. He saw his own personal achievement as the very vindication of it, and "the system which had made such achievement possible must not be tampered with...it must be vigorously defended...[even against]...the economically and politically ignorant who wanted the state to take responsibilities which, in the American system, belonged exclusively to the individual" (Brogan 1990, 532). In disgust, the American people resolutely ousted Hoover in the election of 1932. But however critical of the system, they expressed a demand for remedy rather than rejection. Roosevelt and the Democrats were turned to for salvation. Socialism, except for a few radical voices, was not the popular demand, nor was socialism what Roosevelt proposed as his solution to the Depression. What he had recognized was "the bitter truth that American society was hopelessly ill-organized to cope" with the emergency of the Depression (531). His response, the "New Deal," was designed to save the American system and its modern capitalist order through a progressive modernism. This entailed the sense that capitalism itself needed to successfully transform the market to give it a larger and more effective purchase. The New Deal showed the way by developing a more interventionist federal state, establishing a degree of corporatism in industrial relations through trade union recognition and cooperative links with employers, and building up a proto-welfare system. The key here was to treat the Depression precisely as an emergency, one like that of war, and justify the New Deal in these terms. In his inauguration address, Roosevelt promulgated this policy:

Our greatest primary task is to put people to work. This is no unsolvable problem if we face it wisely and courageously. It can be accomplished in part by direct recruiting by the government itself, treating the task as we would an emergency of war, but at the same time, through this employment, accomplishing greatly needed projects to stimulate and reorganize the use of our natural resources. (quoted in Brogan 1990, 536)[1]

The New Deal was a policy of pragmatism, which accommodated itself to the political system and the capitalist economic order of modern America through acceptance and compromise as well as reform. And its reforms often proceeded in terms of political manipulation within this framework as well as through new legislation and public works and welfare programs. It was essentially a form of the piecemeal engineering of the American system and society, which would remain the political and economic philosophy of the American government into the 1960s. It worked its reforms in quite limited ways whatever the rhetoric attending them. The rhetoric was needed as well as the reforms, not least to guarantee Roosevelt's reelection in 1936. Economic hardship was still sufficient to provide a voice for cynicism and discontent about the American system, although never enough to radicalize the criticism into a significant demand to replace it entirely.

Throughout his second term as president Roosevelt had to confront conditions that fueled this voice of cynicism and discontent in terms of the failures and limitations of the New Deal policies. These were enacted in the face of a whole variety of financial scandals, traditional and corrupt forms of "pork-barrel" politics which had to be taken on board, and growing opposition from the business community. Die-hard conservative politicians, who held the balance of power in Congress; highly vocal demands for protectionism and isolationism; and, often most problematic, a Supreme Court intent on preserving a Jeffersonian sense of the American Constitution also made their opposition heard. But eventually discontent, and with it dissent, was brought to an end, in part because the New Deal succeeded in terms of Roosevelt's intent. At his inauguration for his first term as president (1933), "it seemed as if the entire economic structure which so many generations had labored to rear and improve had collapsed forever" (Brogan 1990, 534). By the end of his second term (1938), through a modernizing federal activism, he had "enabled the American government to assume the responsibility of safeguarding the welfare of the American people in a sense far more radical than that envisaged by the Founding Fathers, but not in a fashion inconsistent with what they most valued—republican government" (566). This he made possible by revitalizing America's capitalist economic order to promote and increase the forward movement of the processes of American modernization. World War II would complete this triumph and follow it through as postwar America entered into a global world that it would increasingly dominate and govern.

The economic effects of the Depression on Broadway were not immediate. In 1929–30, thirty-two musicals opened on Broadway, which was consistent with the number of shows opening each year during the previous decade. It was only from 1931 on that the Depression began to affect the production of musicals, with a large number of theaters going dark in the season 1933–34. Production reached its nadir in the season 1935–36, when only ten musicals were produced on Broadway and all of them lost money. The major reason was economic (see Lerner 1986).[2] The cost of the production of a typical musical of the 1920s was too large, and it was now difficult to find backers. It was not just the spectacle of the show and the cost of the artistes that had to be financed but the sheer length of time that was needed to prepare a show, including initial tryouts in other major cities outside New York, to get it right. Moreover, these costs had increased as the now unionized performers and technicians had finally won their fight for higher salaries against the small cartel of theatrical management companies that controlled Broadway and the touring groups that went out of New York to other cities. These rising costs had to be set against an audience that itself was finding itself in financial straits, meaning ticket prices had to be kept low in order to maintain it.

These conditions were exacerbated by a series of other important factors. First, as sound came to film, the musical lost the one advantage it had over the cinema, the media to which it had already lost a large section of its lower-class audience. To make it worse, not only was Hollywood not in the same degree of financial straits as the theater, because of the size and scope of the film industry, it also used sound to seize upon the musical as its own primary form of sound film. Eventually film would find a form of the musical that was cinematic (initially the back stage musical), but initially it simply attempted to copy the stage musical and transfer it on to film.[3] The effect of this was to draw off to the film not only the primary stars (both singers and comedians) on which Broadway traditionally depended as the mainstay and to large extent the *raison d'être* of the song-and-dance musical, but the composers of these musicals too. What Hollywood could offer were lavish salaries and a whole new career and kudos in a burgeoning entertainment industry that was already playing a major role in American popular culture—most of the major composers of musical (Berlin, the Gershwins, Cole Porter, Rodgers and Hart, and so on) went off in this direction at least for some time. That many also returned to Broadway, and some more quickly than others, had to do with their own sense of themselves as musicians and the musical as an artistic project, which was frustrated by their treatment, however lavish, as hired hands. In Hollywood they were subjected to the particular parameters of the industrial and commercial demands of cinema business and, indeed, the nature of film itself. Although Broadway was commercial theater, it was a commercial theater in which the form of the musical had taken shape and established a vehicle, with artistic provenance as well as entertainment value. But, finally, an entirely new temptation presented itself to Broadway theater managements in the economic situation of the Depression. Their theaters were properties in prime locations within the city, which forced up their rent to the point at which they could not be run profitably or it was more lucrative to sell them off—either way, many theaters were closed and knocked down as a result.

Most hard-hit on Broadway was operetta, which was already flagging badly in competition with musical comedy. But revue was also undermined. The period of the 1920s had been a period of economic inflation, and the revue, in this context (although it had a number of forms), had largely become more and more spectacular and thus increasingly expensive to mount. The cost of this kind of shows became far too prohibitive in the 1930s. In addition, it was faced with the competitive popularity of musical comedy, especially as this took a jazzy form which, with its new, sharp, cynical, witty, and sophisticated character, made the follies-type revue seem excessive, empty, and rather old-fashioned. At the same time, because of its relative popularity, many of the new artists and performers embraced musical comedy, leaving revue with the same old artistic personnel and a formula that was becoming increasingly stale. Certainly composers were choosing to withdraw from it in preference for the musical comedy, often because of their sense of the artistic possibilities that inhered in the developing form. Duke, Henderson, Rome, Schwartz, Youmans, and their collaborators created revues in the 1930s as they had in the 1920s, but Berlin, the Gershwins, Cole Porter, and Rodgers and Hart (very much the newer generation of composers, except for Berlin, and the leading edge in sustaining the musical and its development) now began to abandon the revue for musical comedy. Not just artistic reasons were responsible for this development. Financial factors were important as well. A revue usually has no afterlife much beyond its original production, whereas musical comedies could be and were revived and could be successfully toured. Revues could not be toured or performed by stock companies, because they needed specialized artistic resources. As always, on Broadway, commerce and art found itself reconciled. But yet another form of popular entertainment was faced as competition by the revue: the radio. This itself offered certain key elements of comic entertainment—singers, hit tunes, and dance crazes—that the revue had traded on. The effect of all this on the revue was to change its style away from the spectacular song-and-dance show to become, a new, intimate, and superior connoisseur show that traded on intelligent wit and humor but, most particularly, made use of the highly sophisticated form of the popular song that focused around extended melodic lines and burnished harmonics. "Crooning" had become the center of singing style. In a way, then, the new style of revue returned to the kind of cabaret entertainment so important in the development of middle-class nightlife from 1890 onward. One effect of this was to bring the revue nearer to the satirical kind of musical comedy that appeared with the Depression.

RESPONSES: ESCAPISM AND CRITIQUE

The response of the Broadway musical to the Depression was dual in character. On the one hand, the song-and-dance musical of the 1920s continued, but now in a spirit of entertainment deliberately designed to ensure that the audience could forget its troubles. On the other hand, a new kind of musical began to appear, which addressed the crisis of the Depression in terms of a satirical critique of the American economic and political system. Here the myth and ideology of the American Dream and the society it proclaimed was contrasted against the actuality of the American system and realities of life that it spawned. This (together with the economic cutbacks in the theater, which required a reduction in the costs of the show) led to the beginning of a change in the form of musical comedy. In the main, this took the form of the entry of the book to a position where it became the central part of the musico-dramatic structure of the work. It was precisely the biting and realistic content of the satirical musical comedy, addressing the economic failure and political corruption of American life and denting the optimistic enthusiasm for capitalism, that constituted the more sophisticated book. Now a musical comedy of real substance, as opposed to just wit, song, and dance (often no more than flippant, cotton-candy entertainment) began to be created. But more than this, there was a new degree of experiment with the form of musical comedy itself in terms of a self-conscious articulation of the heritage of the musical in relation to the development of other American forms of art both popular and high.

The Gershwins, following on from *Strike Up the Band* (1930), created musical comedies in *Of Thee I Sing* (1931) and *Let Them Eat Cake* (1933) that utilized extended musical forms of song, recitative and ensemble, specifically drawing on this element in Gilbert and Sullivan's satirical operettas to fuse with their own American musical invention. Similarly, Rodgers and Hart, through a series of works—*Jumbo* (1935), *On Your Toes* (1936), *Babes in Arms* (1937), *I'd Rather Be Right* (1937), *I Married an Angel* (1938), *The Boys from Syracuse* (1938), *Too Many Girls* (1939)—extended song-and-dance into forms of narrative and comedy more sophisticated than just showbiz and entertainment. In *Pal Joey* (1940), they reached the point of creating a true musical comedy drama—one that Rodgers himself liked to call "the first musical comedy in long pants" (Rodgers 1975, 202). En route, Rodgers and Hart were the first of the composers of musicals to incorporate dance into the musical as a narrative part of its dramatic structure, which they did with *On Your Toes*, using Balanchine as the choreographer. *Pal Joey* was also innovative dramatically in a second sense: its dramatic structure eliminated showstopping tunes and grand musical finales in a favor of a musical narrative that wove in and out of the drama in a continuous way. This was essentially cinematic rather than melodramatic, as had been the case with the musical narrative of musical comedy up until then (see Engel 1972; Mates 1987; Swain 1990).

The musicals of Cole Porter were quintessential examples of the first kind of response to the Depression, the "forget your troubles" type of musical comedy. He composed a prolific series of hit shows—*Gay Divorce*

(1932); *Anything Goes* (1934); *Jubilee* (1935); *Red, Hot, and Blue* (1936); *Leave It to Me* (1938); *Du Barry Was a Lady* (1939); and *Panama Hattie* (1940)—that essentially repeated the format of the star- and hit-tune–based song-and-dance musical. These continued the spirit of the 1920s. The lyrics of the song "Anything Goes," with their evocation of a crazy and libertine, if rather shocked, world, would be precisely illustrative here. They are representative of an upside-down culture where formally stable moral categories (of good and bad, for example), or even of perception (of the colors black and white, for instance), are reversed, but for all this upheaval— indeed, in some ways because of it—the world of "Anything Goes" remains decidedly exciting and engaging.

However rooted in the 1920s, the songs reach a different level of musical sophistication and maturity that is the essence of Cole Porter's art and basis of his high stature as a popular composer. Many of them have become standards and have a canonical stature in the history of American popular music. Nevertheless, his musical comedies of this period are thematically of a piece, and *Anything Goes*—the fourth-longest-running musical of the decade—illustrates their character most exactly. It portrays a society composed of a wealthy, high-living haute bourgeoisie and its louche friends that finds its cultural embodiment in a hedonistic and sophisticated ideological and moral world. This context sets the tone of its wit, comedy, and narrative. Here the American Dream and its aspirational realization as the American Way of Life become portrayed as a kind of "style" and "party-time," suitably concretized by the fact that the action takes place on board a luxury liner symbolizing wealth and high living. This allows Porter to give comic invention to the musical by playing on the classic symbol of the ship as "ship of fools," but in a way that also keeps faith with basic American values. The story and action of the party-time ends with the familiar romantic happy ending in which sex becomes love and love finds its true realization in marriage.

The story concerns a nightclub singer (Reno Sweeney) and her best friend, Snake Eyes Johnson (Billy Cracker), who is posing as the celebrity criminal and who has stowed away on the ship in order to be near to and continue his pursuit of the debutante he loves (Hope Harcourt). But also on board is Moon-Face Mooney, who, because of his status as Public Enemy Number 13, is disguised as a clergyman in order to escape the FBI. Sir Evelyn Oakleigh, a rich English aristocrat to whom Hope Harcourt is engaged, completes the main cast.

The comic narrative concerns the fact that Reno has long had a romantic, but unrequited, love interest in Billy. Billy, however, although he worships Reno as a friend, is desperate to win Hope for himself. To that end, he draws upon his relationship with Reno to get her to seduce Sir Evelyn Oakleigh, which she does. To her and the Englishman's surprise, they find themselves well suited: he because she restores his masculinity both sexually and in terms of rekindling his capacity for endeavor, and she because she is enchanted by his quaint Englishness and his foreign and comic lack of command of American style. But especially, she is taken with him because his wealth promises to give her the lifestyle to which she aspires. Meanwhile Billy attracts Hope as she realizes simultaneously that a life married to Sir Evelyn would have been an unhappy mistake. Hope appreciates Billy's get-up-and-go and steadfast pursuit, which brings out the romance and liveliness in her. But she will only accept Billy if he abandons his criminal disguise for a respectable use of his energy, which he is prepared to do. He starts by announcing his stowaway status, only to be shunned in consequence by the rest of the passengers on the ship and placed under arrest. Moon Face Mooney moves in and out of the action between these main characters as a kind of comic turn. So indeed anything does "go" in this modern America and happily. In this sense the show continues to fulfill the American Dream by combining pleasure with endeavor; individual self-expression and happiness with wealth and success; and sex with love, romance, and relationship. The songs convey all of this: we see the mutual admiration between Reno and Billy ("I Get a Kick Out of You" and "You're the Tops"); Hope and Billy's relationship is sealed as he brings out the gypsy in her ("The Gypsy in Me"); Sir Evelyn's masculinity is rekindled through a relationship cemented by Reno's sexy American star style ("Blow, Gabriel, Blow"); and she gets her man on her terms ("Buddy Beware"). The comedy twists and turns louchely and romantically as *Anything Goes* takes place "All through the Night."

Yet there is a darker side presented in this American Dream in *Anything Goes*. It is an effect of the new popular attitudes generated toward the American world and way of life by the Depression. This lies in the considerable quality of cynicism that the "anything goes" morality contains: what happens if anything goes? For some commentators, the show exposes the wrongheadedness of disguises and pretenses of various kinds and the unthinking attraction that common folk have for celebrities, even celebrity criminals; more cynically still, the central dramatic moral of *Anything Goes* suggests that sexual attraction and the desire for wealth exert a power superior to friendship and camaraderie in determining long-term partnerships (see, for example, Block 1997, 53). Perhaps this is the truth of the modern American Dream and what it really offers despite its ideological guise.

The new satirical form of musical comedy confronted and exposed precisely and more directly the flaws in this ideology. The Gershwins led the way with *Of Thee I Sing*, the third-longest-running musical of the 1930s and winner of the Pulitzer Prize, and *Let Them Eat Cake*, but they were substantially joined by Berlin's *Face the Music* (1932), Rome's *Pins and Needles* (1937), and Blitzstein's *The Cradle Will Rock* (1938). As Green, puts it, *Of Thee I Sing* "sharply and deftly skewered...such institutions as political conventions and campaigns, beauty pageants, marriage, the Vice Presidency, the Supreme Court, foreign affairs and motherhood" (1996, 78).

The hero, John P. Wintergreen, is persuaded to run for the office of president by his cynical and corrupt political supporters on the slogan of love, because it is both entirely meaningless and vacuous in terms of content and implementation yet deeply held as a value by the populace and so will guarantee election. Thus in this show love is cynically ideologized as a syncretic force, binding all members of society and sweeping the country, making passion a kind of national emblem. The running mate for vice president, Alexander Throttlebottom, has been chosen because he is a totally innocuous nonentity without any political position or common sense. He himself realizes this fact as he tries to participate in the presidential campaign only to be either asked who he is (he is such a nonentity that the politicians campaigning for the presidency can't remember who they chose for vice president) or told to shut up and stay out of the way as is the proper duty of the vice president. A major political campaigner is a prominent Southern ideologue who constantly boasts of both his own honesty and integrity and that of American democracy. In fact both he and his political practices are a living example of the opposite. The political campaign dreamed up by the campaigners in support of the slogan of love and the vindication of its truth consists of holding a beauty contest in which the prize for the winner will be marriage to the president himself. He, however, has fallen in love with the heroine of the show, the administrator of the beauty contest (Mary Turner), because he has a passion for that favorite dish of America, apple pie, and she bakes the best apple pies in America. The beauty contest is won by a spectacularly stereotypical and sexually overblown Southern belle (Diana Devereux). Wintergreen wins the election, but he refuses to hand himself over in marriage as the prize. Diana Devereux appeals to the Supreme Court to impeach him, but Mary Turner appeals to them too, asking whether the decision of the president to marry her on the basis of her all-American apple-pie baking skills should be set aside for mere Constitutional rules. Devereux insists that they must uphold the rules of the Constitution and, with it, the law of the land. After weighty deliberation, however, the Court unanimously votes for apple pie. In despair, Diana Devereux turns to her French heritage as a Southern belle and approaches the French ambassador to America. He discovers that she is the illegitimate daughter of the illegitimate son of an illegitimate nephew of Napoleon. Consequently he insists that Wintergreen's refusal to marry her places the honor of France at stake, and France will declare war on America if he does not relent. Wintergreen persists and America is thrown into a quandary in which his impeachment is re-demanded, but Mary Turner saves the situation again to prevent this by giving birth to twins. Thus that other great virtue of America, motherhood, must be given its proper due and the president defended in its name. But war remains in the cards, and this dilemma is finally resolved only when Wintergreen decides to resign so, following the requirements of the American Constitution, the vice president can now take over the office, since it provides for this when the president is unable to fulfill his duties. Now as president, Alexander Throttlebottom agrees to marry Diana Devereux and all is resolved, leaving John P. Wintergreen and Mary Turner to go off and live their happy married lives together in private and realize the anthem song of the musical, "Of Thee I Sing Baby," as against "Wintergreen for President."

The satire of *Of Thee I Sing*, with its denting of a faith in the conventional cultural and moral values of America and its new political system, was followed up (but not as successfully) by the Gershwins with *Let Them Eat Cake*. This was altogether more acerbic. It handled the possibilities of dictatorship arising out of the American political system. In a similar vein, but now linking politics and economics, *Face the Music* explored the corrupt relationships of New York's financial and business social elite with New York politicians and the police force. In it the depredations of the Depression are now fully exposed and critiqued through a comic tale of an attempt by the wife of a police sergeant (Mrs. Martin Von Buren Meshbesher) to launder and lose his ill-gotten gains by backing a tasteless Broadway show. To her surprise it becomes a hit, but she avoids the cops being exposed through this by contributing the profits to New York City's now depleted treasury—a financial rescue, but hardly one in accordance with the supposed virtues of capitalism or the values and practices of the democratic American political system. With *Pins and Needles*, a musical comedy originally written to be presented at the Labor Stage by and for the Ladies Garment Worker Unions, Harold Rome followed this economic and political connection. The success of this show led it to being transferred professionally onto Broadway to become the longest-running show of the era (and indeed of Broadway up to this point altogether). Its stance was that of a pro-union liberalism that explored the exploitation involved in contemporary factory work conditions, but it also attacked the ideology of Americanness as enunciated by warmongers, bigots, and reactionaries of various hues. Its attitude, however, was "generally good-humored" (Green 1996, 100) and ultimately supportive of America in terms of a progressive liberalism. It attacked, as well as conservative American ideology, communism and fascism as contemporary and alternative evils. Much more genuinely critical was Blitzstein's *The Cradle Will Rock*. This was so much so that its government sponsorship was withdrawn and its original theater producers banned it, padlocking the theater in which it was to be performed. It was moved to another theater in which, to meet the letter but not the spirit of the ban, it was performed to an invited audience by a cast positioned within the audience and accompanied by a piano. Eventually it did move on to Broadway to enjoy a certain degree of success and some critical acclaim for its originality—sufficient for it to be the first musical ever to be recorded with its original Broadway cast. Blitzstein was a committed socialist and followed Brecht in his belief in a proletarian music theater. Indeed, he consulted Brecht about *The Cradle Will Rock* as he composed it. Brecht insisted that he "write a piece about all kinds of prostitution—the press, the church, the courts, the arts, the whole system" (quoted in Lederman 1983, 67), which is precisely what Blitzstein did. The action is set in Steeltown, U.S.A., on the night of a union drive led by Larry Foreman, who battles against the power and corruption of Mr. Mister. The latter owns everything and virtually everybody in Steeltown. He is attempting to bust the union, but Larry eventually wins the battle. It is not just the economic reality of capitalist work and business that is critiqued here, however, but also the institutional and cultural world of the American society spawned by it. These other issues are tackled through such characters as Junior and Sister Miss, the son and daughter of Mr. Mister, typified as classic examples of the idle rich. The popular song and dance to which they are committed is critiqued as vapid. The art-for-art's-sake modernist philosophy of Mr. Dauber, a painter, and Yasha, a violinist, is presented as a philosophy without social conscience, and they have sold out to Mr. Mister's patronage. Editor Daily, the editor of the local newspaper, simply massages the news on behalf of Mr. Mister's interests. All of them are presented as cynically engaged, under the banner of modern America, in what are, in practice, forms of prostitution. By comparison, the only real prostitute in the musical, Moll, will not sell her body to Mr. Mister. In this respect, she is conjoined with Larry Foreman as the only other incorruptible figure in the show.

But in the end, the didactic and sociopolitical critique of *The Cradle Will Rock* went beyond the limits of what musical comedy could popularly sustain. Not only was this kind of satirical musical competing against the well-established "forget your troubles" musical and also many of the films of the time of a similar ilk, it also failed to recognize that the troubled and cynical mood that had arisen in the American population during the Depression was reformist rather than revolutionary in character. What was demanded was a renewal of the American economic and political system in order to revive the American Dream. The original optimism had been badly damaged by the loss of hope that came with the Depression, but Roosevelt and the New Deal managed to reform the American system sufficiently successfully to recover that hope and once again to allow America to proceed with confidence. Most satirical musical comedies moved within an essentially liberal framework, basing their satire on a sociopolitical critique that imagined change in terms of reform. And once reform had taken place, as seemed to be the case for Americans by the late 1930s, the satirical musical comedy no longer had an audience constituency to appeal to and faded from Broadway with only small echoes throughout the 1940s, 1950s, and 1960s. It had, however, left a legacy in the form of the strengthening of the book in the musical, and demanded some degree of reflexive thought in the sensibility of its audience. This led the way for a more substantial theatrical version of the musical as music drama. The Depression had had an effect to the point where it was possible for musical theater to recognize that not all was rosy in American life even if, basically, it was the best way of life.

Pal Joey shows how musical comedy could develop as music drama through this with its story of another darker underbelly to American life, but one woven out of some of the same materials as the optimistic version (the individual pursuit of freedom, success, and wealth). "With its heel for a hero, its smoky nightclub ambience and its true-to-life, untrue-to-anyone characters" (Green 1996, 112), it was indeed as Rodgers thought it—a musical in long pants for adults.

NOTES

1. See also Major (1963) and Mitchell (1955) for useful accounts of the New Deal.

2. For an account of the shows that were produced in this period, see Green (1971).

3. For an account of the musical film, see Barrios (1995).

CHAPTER 4

Broadway: The Book Musical and the End of Ideology

AMERICA TRIUMPHANT AND THE END OF IDEOLOGY

With the end of the Depression and America's entry into the Second World War, the earthquake that had potentially threatened to destroy the faith and self-confidence of Americans in the American system settled instead into the New Deal. What was forged over the next decade was a revised national destiny that transformed "America" into an international mission on behalf of a vision of capitalism, modernity, and democracy. This centered on America's now established economic and political supremacy on the global stage and was fought out in opposition to the alternative of communism and socialism, which the USSR as the only rival world superpower was perceived to represent and sponsor.

Almost all the elements in this position were new. Throughout the 1920s and 1930s, following the effects of its participation in the First World War, America had pursued a policy of isolationism. It sought to rely upon and live within its own existing economic, political, and geographic boundaries. In political terms, this isolationism created an ideology of pacifism, which was reinforced by memories of the trenches and the brutalities of modern warfare as well as a belief that financiers and the pursuit of profit had drawn America into the Great War. The Depression helped to confirm this sense that it was not democracy or legality that brought America to war. In terms of policy, it created a commitment to nationalism where the pursuit of American nationalism was defined as the need for America to be entirely itself and a free agent. But the isolationism also had an economic correlate in the form of the rejection and end of immigration to America.

Immigration was now no longer seen as the primary pump through which to propel the dynamic of American capitalist modernization, but rather as an economic threat to social and economic order and prosperity. The Depression could only reinforce this perception and drove the subsequent changes in immigration policy. America, then, initially greeted the rise of fascism in Europe in terms of this isolationist stance. Roosevelt may have recognized that the isolationist response to fascism would not, in the end, be possible, because fascism represented a serious threat to both American economic and political interests, as well as an ideological threat to all America stood for as a modern society. He had begun to prepare for conflict both economically and ideologically. But he could not act until a decisive threat to American economic and political interests and its territorial integrity was invoked by Japan's entry into the Second World War. At that point, America embarked on its an official crusade to make the world safe for democracy. It now saw itself, and led its allied partners, in a fight on behalf of the future of Western civilization against fascist barbarism.

Central to this mission became America's self-definition in relation to the idealized position that it created for itself as a superpower on the global stage. It stood as the model of contemporary civil society and the embodiment of the Enlightenment ideals that lay at the heart of modernity in the West. *Oklahoma,* a musical first produced in 1942, was not simply the paradigmatic example of the book musical but a triumphant celebration of this formulation. Its status as a classic Broadway show was in part a matter of form but also of a content tied to the status America had achieved through the New Deal and its emerging political and economic supremacy on the global stage. As America entered the Second World War, Roosevelt provided the basis through which this tie would be woven: "We are going to win and we are going to win the peace that follows" (quoted in Brogan 1990, 584).

The New Deal constituted a new basis for modern capitalist America here. It produced a vision of America and its destiny in terms that were both progressive—inasmuch as they visualized a cooperative and unified nation creating a new activist, democratic state—and yet traditional. New Deal government remained firmly located within the republican framework of the American Constitution, conceptualized in terms of the separation of powers as preserved by the Supreme Court and established by the Founding Fathers. Thus, as Brogan argues, it did not produce a utopia but it did preserve the American system through adaptation and, in this, Roosevelt and his administration understood precisely what the intention had been: to vindicate "American democracy in a darkening world, [rescuing] the 'profit system' and [bringing] succour to the millions of his desperate fellow-citizens" (1990, 561). It was a deal based upon piecemeal engineering as its form of governmental activism, using the traditional "logrolling" of American politics, which established the American political system, now, as a modern corporate liberal state uniting business and labor in its organization of the economy and society. This was not done, as in Europe, through bureaucratic centralism but through federalist pluralism, interest group coalition, effective antitrust laws, the extensive legal regulation of business and political deals, and media participation. In this respect, "it cultivated individualism, liberalism and popular anti-elitism, shared by both the Left and Right" (Crook, Pakulski, and Waters 1992, 90) as the form of corporatism entailed in its sense of America as a cooperative and unified nation. It gave birth to an ideology through which America now envisaged its own national identity and international mission as an "end of ideology" (see Bell 1960; Lipset 1960; Shils 1955—the primary proponents of this ideology as enunciated by the American liberal intelligentsia). Here was a positive value judgement upon the modern American political and social order as one in which ideological politics had ended because America had reached or was well on the way to reaching the "good" society. Ideology became a corrupting force that would only serve to hinder the process of completion. The reformist politics of this end of ideology became, then, an empirical politics of social engineering, bringing solutions to economic and social problems in which no different conception of human nature or society was envisaged other than that embedded in the originary liberal individualism of the Founding Fathers. Equipped with this, and utilizing the apparatuses of modern science and technology harnessed to the needs of the capitalist economy, such engineering had produced America as the good society, the epitome of enlightenment and modernity. Its engineers were enabled and trained to be value-free and objective in constructing the policies and practices in which the general welfare of the nation could be achieved within a community based upon democratic participation, assent, and the reconciliation of individual and sectional interest (see Waxman 1969).

Oklahoma presents the ideal of the community (albeit rural) that was envisaged in this original liberal and individualist conception of the good society. The New Deal enlarged on it, and Eisenhower, working on the formula that what is good for the United States is good for General Motors and vice versa, would capture it in practice for the America of the 1950s and 1960s. Also embodied in this ideology, and this is what the book musical would evoke and encapsulate so decisively, was a particular kind of optimism central to the American Dream and stemming, again, from Enlightenment ideals and the progressive vision of liberal individualism extended to fund the good of this "good" society. Still, in this, it carried a snub to the Old World of Europe, expressively delivered in the lyrics of Cole Porter's song "Brush Up Your Shakespeare" from *Kiss Me Kate*. Here

Shakespeare is taken over for America by annexing his gallery of comic characters on behalf of America's hoodlum gangsters, who enunciate the benefits of Shakespeare for sexual conquest. The lyrics evoke

two cultural milieux and two appropriate modes of action. They are deliberately constructed so as to be in conflict. The more obvious cultural milieu is American. It is strongly masculinist and domineering...It is conveyed in the vernacular of the street, emphasized by rhymes which draw on dialect...or which work only through perversion of received pronunciation...The other cultural milieu is English in origin and feminine...This time [the rhymes constitute a perversion which] is a parody of the language of the English aristocracy, represented abroad by officials of the British Diplomatic Service ... [but now] ... Shakespeare can be used, not just by the wives of British Ambassadors, nor just by the British, but by everyone. His works exist in both a universal and a superior realm. In consequence they unite the two milieux. They allow the American street to make contact with and dominate the British Embassy. (Lawson-Peebles 1996, 89–90)

Shakespeare's potency as not only the prime figure of English drama, but also a dramatist of universal significance who is our contemporary, makes him available to a large audience and therefore capable of the modernization and democratization realized through America. In this sense, truly, great art not only reflects life but is also an aid to its successful and effective accomplishment. The end of ideology, and the optimism it embodies, is precisely this myth of success that is the modern American Dream yet co-terminus with its originary Enlightenment foundation.

The economic success of post–Second World War America was palpable. The New Deal was ultimately secured through America being put on a war footing that dynamically extended and increased the economy, in part through the extension of the Taylorist/Fordist system of production. This, in turn, finally rescued the unemployed and funded a new wave of social mobility. The result was a massive economic boom that went way beyond the affluence and social mobility experienced in the 1920s. Disposable income rose by 17 percent between 1947 and 1956 and finally established America as a primarily middle-class society, particularly as, after the war, production was turned toward consumption and, very specifically, the production of automobiles resumed. This emergent middle class of "middle America" was quite distinct from the older liberal bourgeois, characterized as the "chattering" class. It established itself through the great internal migration by the American population, which was the reflection of the new processes of bourgeoisification, so there were geographic and sociogeographic dimensions to its formulation. Geographically, the internal migration was to the West (and particularly California), but sociogeographically the general movement was a movement out of the cities and into suburbia. The major act of the Eisenhower government, the Interstate Highway Act of 1956, finalized this latter movement as it reinforced the ascendancy of the car over any form of passenger trans-portation (while reinforcing the geographic movement by making conti-nental buses fully competitive with the declining railway system) and by boosting truck transportation. This gave a huge lift to the automobile, building, and engineering industries, which formed the basis of the pros-perity of the late 1950s and 1960s. It stimulated, through the car civili-zation that it created, the growth of America as a vast suburbia in which work, leisure, and all other facilities were located (see McShane 1994).

The population of this migration formed middle America, and it became the popular locus of the American Dream now fixed in the ideol-ogy and mythology of the end of ideology—a belief in the American sys-tem and what it could do. The good society that it embodied was essentially a middle-class suburban dream of affluence and consumerism but combined with the work ethic. It based itself evaluatively around a sentimental and traditionalist morality of love, marriage, and the family, within which women were expected to play out the stereotype of good wife and mother and men the role of provider. Crucially, at the end of ide-ology, liberalism and conservatism could cohabit the same world as two intertwined variants, specifically brought together in the book musical.

America's entry on to the global stage as a superpower that charged itself with the task of saving the world on behalf of a campaign to give American values universal acceptance reinforced this popular middle America. In the more sophisticated progressive liberal form of end-of-ideology ideology, the Pax Americana that America sought to enforce after the Second World War was woven into the charter of the United Nations and preserved through the construction of the Security Council within it. The charter enunciated four basic aims and freedoms that it would be its task to establish: the right to self-determination, the right to democratic self-government, the preservation of free trade, and the achievement of universal disarmament. In practice the Cold War transformed these as the USSR became the problem in America's attempt to establish a world order in its own image. The Pax Americana that America had initially estab-lished and secured during the Second World War through its leadership of the allies in collaboration with the USSR (and which the UN Charter enshrined) had been produced by focusing the ideological defense of the War upon the fight for democracy against fascism. Here the USSR was treated as a champion of democracy too. Now America faced, in the USSR and communism, a vision, whether practiced by the USSR or not, of a democratic society and world order that stood in complete opposition to its aim. In the face of this, the Cold War turned Americanism into a mili-taristic, conservative, self-righteous, and crusading faith that was anxious to "liberate" the peoples of the world; desperate to expose and confuse its enemies; and committed to forestalling any ideology or revolution that threatened the continuance of a liberal, capitalist, individualist, system as the basis of the world order. Both progressive and conservative end-of-ideology thinking was united in this. Communism now came to be defined as essentially subversive and was assumed to be as expansionist as Americanism. This was reinforced as the USSR acquired the atomic and hydrogen bombs and took a lead in the space race. Now Americanism turned into a religion as opposed to a variety of realpolitik and this became very particularly how middle America embraced it. Reinforced at home by the affluence that sustained it, Americanism gave rise politically to a generalized conservative quietism that tended to induce a political lethargy (putting the Republicans in government). At worst, it fuelled the demagoguery of McCarthy, seeking to create a fear of "reds under the bed" and became effectively institutionalized on a popular basis as the Cold War conjoined with modern national government and the modern media. Together with the powerful economic foundation, this made for a much more seemingly socially homogenous population with a homogeneous culture formulating middle America. In many ways, America seemed to become Marcuse's "one-dimensional society" (1964).

Post–Second World War America was fusing into an Americanism that saw the form of the good society as now complete and needing only to be kept in order. This was to be done at home through the end of ideology and worldwide though the active spreading of Americanism as an ideology of the end of ideology. The ability of Americanism to spread in this way took its success from military and economic might and the affluence that made America seem the wonder of the world, which other societies would became eager to copy. The book musical is, in a whole series of ways, a complex and reflexive engagement with this end-of-ideology Americanism in a mainly celebratory fashion, reconciling the liberal version of social engineering with the conservative quietist manifestation of this ideology. Perhaps somewhat paradoxically, this constitutes an artistic development in terms of the theatrical, dramatic, and musical sophistication of the musical as a popular form of art that comes to steer itself within and around the ideological and mythological boundaries of post–Second World War America.

This artistic development also has an aesthetic trajectory that comes from within the musical itself as a genre. Hamm (1983) argues that despite the clear commercial underpinnings of the musical and its emergence as part of the development of the culture industry that tied it to the American music business, the songs and music from the musical were always distinguishable from the pure hit tunes of Tin-Pan Alley. This was because they were written for the theater and so shaped by that theatricality. Against Adorno's claim for the total homogenization of popular culture, he argues that the major result has been the establishment of a popular musical tradition that lends itself to a high degree of subtlety and creativity. One need simply witness the many composers who have worked within its framework. In the realm of the musical, which was a primary commercial and compositional home for American popular composers, the theater created the basis of an aesthetic through which the musical could be established as an art form (albeit a popular one) in which the central ideal was the theatrical realization of the musical as music drama. *Oklahoma* is the paradigmatic exemplar of the realization of such music in the book musical for a variety of reasons, not the least of which is that it enforced the format that virtually all Broadway musicals would have to and did follow for the next 25 years. But it was not the original book musical.

AMERICANA: *SHOW BOAT* AND *OKLAHOMA*

The original book musical is Kern's *Show Boat,* and it is in no sense adventitious that Kern should have originated the book musical (and it was Kern who had first proposed to turn *Green Grow the Lilacs*, the book on which *Oklahoma* was based, into a musical). He established a position for himself in the 1920s, which extended into the 1930s, as the doyen of the Broadway musical. This stemmed from the early pre–World War I stage of his career in London and then in New York as a composer of songs interpolated into Broadway operettas and musical comedies, through to the Princess Theatre musical comedies that bridged the period following the First World War, into the 1920s, and then on into his successful musical comedies of the 1920s and 1930s. He was committed to an aesthetic of the musical that was concerned with forging its music as drama, stating his view in *The Dramatic Mirror* (1922), that "musical numbers should carry on the action of the play, and should be representative of the personalities of the characters who sing them. In other words, songs must be suited to the action and mood of the play" (Bordman 1980, 149–50). His work as a composer for operetta had given him a sense of the character of operetta as a form of musical play but, since he had converted to and believed in specifically American forms of popular music theater, his sense of musical drama found its first full expression in the Princess Theatre musicals of 1915–20. Here the comedy sprang from the plot, situation, and character; the music was specifically tailored to this and the words were colloquial. *Show Boat* however, is much more. It is, and seeks to be, a serious and integrated music drama that both panoptically captures and reflexively manifests a vision of America through making the showboat, its characters, and the world through which it sails the emblematic vehicle for this. And it does it in a whole series of ways that nativize the musical as American music drama. The music is entirely American and draws on almost the complete range of its native forms, as do the lyrics and dialogue, which are utterly and colloquially American. Crucially, it is American in its attitudes, rejecting both the sensibility and morality of Europe for the life, ideas, and ideals of American society and the conflicts that are generated within their context. It tackles the American world through a serious engagement, of racial conflict in particular. The exploitation and degradation of black America is clearly established both musically and dramatically, and the racism that creates it is explored in the tragic interracial relation between Julie and Steve. This engagement is both historical and contemporary and moves through polyvalent moods of romance, sentiment, fatalism, and pessimism to end, however, with that essential American mood of optimism, achievement, and success presented as the liberal and individualist birthright of the inhabitants of the New World. In *Show Boat* this is expressed nationalistically through the scenes of the World Trade Fair in St. Louis in 1906 (where, symbolically, America triumphantly came of age as modernity and futurity) and narratively through the final reunion of the hero Gaylord Ravenal and the heroine Magnolia (after a long saga of tragedy and separation). But *Show Boat* also remains, and this is key to the musical as a genre, entirely within the theatrical traditions of American popular entertainment with its size, spectacle, tunes, and stars. That it is a showboat in this musical that is the emblem of America is, of course, highly significant here.

Show Boat was not immediately followed up by other book musicals of a similar nature, probably more due to the Depression that anything else. Certainly the aesthetic of music drama that it expressed was not an isolated one to which Kern alone was committed. His younger contemporaries—particularly the Gershwins and Rodgers and Hart—were imbued with a similar aesthetic that they partly realized in their musicals of the 1930s. This aesthetic was, again, specifically reinforced and taken up by the satirical Depression musicals, and Kurt Weill, on his translation to America and Broadway, would also embrace this aesthetic, arguing insistently that Broadway properly evinced the theatrical ideal that was the basis of his European popular music-theater collaborations with Brecht (see Block 1997, 135–36).

In its deliberate, self-conscious, and positive commitment to Americana, *Show Boat* displayed the ideology and mythology that would continuously fuel the book musicals that eventually followed. They, too, posited themselves as essentially American, exploring their postwar America within the new framework of aesthetic integrity permitted to them through the book as both popular art and entertainment. The musicals of Rodgers and Hammerstein clinched the ascendancy of the book musical beginning with *Oklahoma*, which established the paradigmatic form of this kind of musical. From 1943 to their final collaboration, *The Sound of Music* (1959), their later musicals extended the book musical to the point where it achieved an almost dominant position on Broadway. A classic shape was given to the Broadway musicals of the 1940s, 1950s, and 1960s where the characteristics of the musical became those of a music drama—that is, a complete musico-dramatic integration of the work on the basis of a play constructed and expressed in terms of popular music and dance. As such, it eschewed vocal pyrotechnics for smoky chromatics and harmonies. The waltz was brought back as a vehicle of romantic feeling but now also as a vehicle for the purposes of jubilation. The chorus was transformed from a collection of hoofers engaged in set song-and-dance routines into a dramatic protagonist of the action as the people or community. Their songs and dances became the manifestations of the group life within which the lives and story of the leading characters were located and shaped. And, finally, theatrical ballet and modern dance were integrated into the music and play to carry the drama instead of being the freestanding tap-dancing routines of the chorus line. At the same time, the musical and theatrical realization of the musical took on itself some of the now established (as the primary form of popular entertainment) characteristics of the cinema. The crossover borrowing from film lay in the partial exchange of mere showstopping tunes, of extended concerted musical passages and grand finales, for a musical narrative that wove in and out of the drama on a continuous basis. However, the commitment to showbiz was retained, that essential marriage of commerce and art that characterized the Broadway musical. The musical moved, as Block (1997) argues, from "opulent adornment" to "textual realism" but within the parameters of a popular format in which song and music remained memorable (if not now autonomous) and performance required the "star," but was not simply a vehicle created around and for the particular persona of a specific star to shine.[1] The book musical located itself within the popular musical and theatrical culture of America to construct itself as a tradition, but now one that through its aestheticization as music drama raised the genre to a form of art within that culture. In this art as popular entertainment, where once the audience took away only the hit tunes, they were now required, as Steyn comments, to take away the whole show (1997, 116).

The fusion of commerce, popular culture, and aesthetics became the structural embrace through which the musical's ideological and mythological Americana was established as an essential expression of society, even when the musical came to seemingly and actually address other societies as the substance of its drama. This was because the Broadway musical of this period carried a specific American cultural outlook, formulating a social and institutional picture of American society (and its others) and expressing a version of its roots and life. This varied in depth as it maneuvered between the liberal progressive and quietist conservative senses of the end of ideology embraced by respectively the "chattering" middle class of America and middle America. But it was united by its fundamental outlook—an attitude and mood of optimism that was itself established in terms of a moveable and pragmatic mixture of conservatism and liberalism. On the one hand, the liberalism figured as an Enlightenment commitment to a civil democratic society with a right to happiness, opportunity, and equality. On the other hand, the conservatism was reflected in the fact that this commitment was typically seen in terms of an organic community (even within the city) harmonized and civilized through the traditional values of love, romance, marriage, and the family. The whole cultural package was bourgeoisified in many musicals to create a particular tie between work, achievement, love, marriage, affluence, and consumption, thus ensuring that it incorporated the new middle America of suburbia. Above all, though, it was optimism that characterized the musicals of this time and that took a particular form. As Steyn (1997) argues, this configuration was essential for musicals to retain a mass audience, with "heart" becoming the real key: the optimism, which was a combination of sentiment, sentimentality, hope, enthusiasm, and determination and which is still understood as being particularly American. This was mightily evinced by the Broadway book musical and found perfect expression in the key song of *Damn Yankees* (1955), "You Gotta Have Heart."

Assimilating both liberal and conservative tones, then, the end-of-ideology book musical indulged in a utopian but workaday vision of a New World social and cultural order, stemming from an originary revolutionary and constitutional foundation, passing through an immigrant and frontier history to finally flourish in its largely urban (suburban) and modern form. The unity of this form of the musical was reproduced in relation to an implied united audience.

The musicals of Rodgers and Hammerstein are crucial in this respect, because they marry perfectly the form of the book musical to end-of-ideology America. Their musicals are deliberately and self-consciously reflexive about American history and society while ideologically committed to its values and way of life. They embrace a liberal progressive commitment in the sense that character, story, and outlook are taken up in terms of social and moral issues and anxieties that emerge within an American context of society and culture.

Oklahoma, for instance, is wedded to and celebrates the ideology and politics of liberal democracy, where differences of political interest can be reconciled through cooperation and coexistence rather than resolved through conflict. It is an idealized statement about community as American community. Its dramatic world might seem to be quite parochial, in the sense that its primary narrative is about the romance and love between Laurey and Curley and the obstacles that get in their way. Indeed, in one sense the whole drama hinges on nothing more than who shall take Laurey to the box social. But this is set in the context of the simple rural and domestic lives of these characters, from their kith and kin, neighbors, and friends to the wider ambit of farmers and con men. This environment is more than backdrop. It constitutes a gallery of rural North American types, in terms of class, psychology, and morality. Thus the seemingly modest and homely world that *Oklahoma* represents takes on a much grander signification as the musical unfolds. It symbolizes the American Dream of a social world that embodies the best in modern human life; it presents America as the promised "land of the free" wrought by the individual and collective labor of its inhabitants. When the show opens with Aunt Eller churning milk to make butter and Curly singing "Oh What a Beautiful Morning," it sets before the audience a hymn to America as the new Garden of Eden. It is, indeed, both God's own country and the first nation-state. The box social constellates all this. Its purpose is the collective funding of the roof for the community school, and so the dance becomes a celebration of a collectivity and of its form as a democratic association. As the musical progresses, with Oklahoma gaining statehood and entering the American political federation to the tune of "You're Doing Fine Oklahoma! Oklahoma O.K.," the sense of community takes on its widest meaning.

The time of *Oklahoma*'s composition and production was crucial to this ideological stance. "Pioneers carving a new state out of what has been called Indian territory and setting up a community which embodied the values of North American paternalism constituted an idealized, utopian context in which to place anxieties for the future of the U.S.A., having emerged from a crippling depression, [and] confronted the consequence of involvement in World War II" (Filmer, Rimmer, and Walsh 1999, 385). At the same time, Roosevelt's Federal Arts Project (1939–43), part of the New Deal program, had created an art agenda based around American themes and focused on the idea of the artist's responsibility to American society. *Oklahoma* resonates with such notions, but, even more strongly, it represents its time in the sense that the year of its composition and production coincided with America joining the struggle against fascism. This conflict was already ideologized by the allies, rightly, as the fight for freedom and civilization against barbarism, where the very nature of human civil society was at stake. *Oklahoma* enters this conflict in 1943 through its thorough vindication of the American idea of folk in opposition to the *volk* of fascism. It celebrates the humane practices of civilizing nature against regression into a primal, instinctual, and reductive naturalism of race, blood, and soil. While fascism rejected reason and the intellect to honor the nation as an organic community based on racial solidarity, *Oklahoma* applauds the Enlightenment values that underpinned an America based on freedom and harmony, where members are differentiated by interest but united by democratic association—a world of civilization.

In this world of civilization, as Laurey's dream sequence suggests, the challenge to the integrity of order comes in the form of primordial instinct. In terms of the outside fascist world that America was fighting, this is the dehumanized atavism and aggression of the fascist masses. In terms of *Oklahoma*'s internal world, it is configured largely by Jud Frye. Neither a farmer nor a cowman but a hired hand, Jud pursues Laurey out of crude carnal desire. A lascivious bully, he lives, surrounded by pictures of semi-naked women, in a smokehouse. He is outside the community and represents a disruptive decadence, but he is also representative of a potential wider threat to the community. Laurey's ballet scene—a great innovation in the musical, since dance could now become part of the narrative construction of the musical—works this anxiety out as a dream sequence. As dream it offers an intelligibility to the audience without threatening the official values celebrated by the musical. Here all uncontrolled sexual desire, including Laurey's desire for Curley, becomes indicative of a force that threatens to exceed the regulatory social order.

The new Garden of Eden must be protected from this negative sexual instinct, in part through the regulation of desire through marriage. Jud is beyond the pale, because regulation is not possible for him. He is condemned as savage, both from the point of view of reason and American puritanism.[2] He represents, of course, a serious problem in America as Garden of Eden, both as a disruptive force but also in terms of how he got there and the issue of why, in *Oklahoma* at least, he cannot be saved. It is important for the development of the musical that it can encompass an evil character like Jud, but the utopianism of the musical makes this difficult, which may in part account for why *Oklahoma* stumbles here. It has no response to Jud's salvation. It will take a further development, exemplified by a show like *Carousel*, to offer a different approach to the problem of evil, where destructive and destabilizing forces can be understood in terms of psychology and resolved in terms of the "American" way of life by a combination of romance, pragmatism, and the potential of democratic social engineering.

IN PURSUIT OF THE GOOD: *CAROUSEL* AND *GUYS AND DOLLS*

It is this kind of encompassing resolution that extends the capacity of the Rodgers and Hammerstein musical for maintaining plenty of heart, to the point, according to Kislan (1980), of sickliness. In the world of Rodgers and Hammerstein, ultimately love conquers all; virtue triumphs and dreams come true (Hammerstein was frankly unabashed by this point of view and happy to tackle critics of it). The dramatic intensity of something like "When You Walk through a Storm," from *Carousel*, precisely captures this tone, and its potential power.

Carousel crucially exemplifies the particular marriage of structural form and ideological and mythological content that the Broadway book musical entails. It was, for Rodgers, the favorite of all of his musicals, and artistically he had good reason for this view. Both Block (1997) and Swain (1990) have pointed to its essential musical sophistication. It begins not with an overture that is a medley of the songs to follow but a single piece, the "Carousel Waltz." Rodgers himself explained the intention: "in this way we...gave the audience an emotional feeling for the characters in the story and helped to establish the mood for the entire play" (Rodgers 1975, 238). As Swain argues, this implies a complex advance on the more usual musical overture. "The 'Carousel Waltz' has an extraordinary relationship with the songs in the musical play. Like a classical overture, it sets the musical terms of the entire composition and is the main source of musical material, not tunes so much as basic musical elements and procedures" (1990, 100). As the show develops, its music is set to a complex drama where protagonists are a combination of subtle contradictions. This is part of the basis of its sophistication, for Swain:

dramatic action occurs not just between characters...but within them, and this action is the more important one...Such complexity demands an equivalent complexity of musical expression, and Rodgers and Hammerstein respond to the demand with a number of musical resources. There is much more [dramatic] use of melodrama, which means that characters speak over music from the orchestra. There is also a large amount of sung music which has a freedom of organization, the absence of repetition, and the melodic and rhythmic flexibility of recitative, although the sense of meter never quite disappears. These techniques make transitions from spoken dialogue to song much more gradual and smooth. The musical play therefore seems more serious because one is much less aware of the seams of operatic convention. (1990, 104–5)

The moral dilemma that is dramatized through its hero—Billy Bigelow—also represents a growing sophistication, a serious treatment of good and evil and the struggle between them. *Oklahoma*, it is true, had done something similar. It was almost unique in placing a truly evil character in the musical as a major dramatic protagonist. But Jud Frye's evil, as we have seen, is hugely problematic from the point of view of *Oklahoma's* portrait of an idealized American society. He represents the threat, in his brutal animalism, that this society cannot accommodate. How and why he comes to be a presence in the New World is never explained, nor is whether his nature may or may not be endemic to this world—Jud Frye becomes, simply and somehow, the inhuman other of the Enlightenment.

The evil in Billy Bigelow, however, is presented as endemic, and humanized in a particular American way to fit in with Americana. The play that *Carousel* adapts is Ferenc Molnar's *Lilliom*—a moral fantasy—first staged in Hungary in 1909 and brought to America in 1921. In the play, the antiheroic Lilliom is a ne'er-do-well and braggart dreamer, a vicious and primitive person yet full of finer feelings. He meets and marries Julie, an unselfish and taciturn woman of sense and endurance who loves him undemandingly, despite her realistic sense of his true nature, a nature that he will not and cannot comprehend. He fathers a child, a girl, and in his desire to support her engages in a crime in which he is killed. Unregretful of his actions, he is doomed to purgatory and then required to return to earth and atone for his sins. Here, disguised as a beggar, he meets up with his daughter and slaps her when she refuses the star he has stolen from Heaven and wishes to give her. He sends her away and the play ends pessimistically on this failure of atonement, presented as the inevitable consequence, despite the offer of redemption, of the flawed character of Lilliom. Lilliom, now translated into Billy Bigelow, and his story are transformed in *Carousel*, not just by its resetting in a nineteenth-century New England coastal mill town, but by making it an American moral fable. Billy is still the mixture of arrogant braggart and finer dreamer, aiming for a better life but actually living the life of a drifter on the margins of American society as a barker for the carousel of a fair. Here he meets Julie Jordan, a mill-hand, who retains the same characteristics of Molnar's heroine. He falls in love with Julie but cannot properly acknowledge his true feelings for her, although she recognizes and understands them, until he marries and fathers a girl with her and realizes the need to act responsibly on behalf of their, and particularly the child's, support. But, as a drifter, he knows only one life, that of crime, and plans a burglary through which to achieve the wealth needed. In this he is killed and goes to Heaven. He is sent back to atone for his sin and this time succeeds by helping his "little girl," Louise (although he initially slaps her for not realizing the help he is able to offer), to overcome her misery and loneliness at her graduation. So, "Louise finds the courage to live, Julie realizes her marriage... was worth the pain ... [and] Billy redeems his soul" (Block 1997, 161). Positioned against this narrative is a subtext of a worthy responsible American couple, Carrie Pipperidge and Enoch Snow, who inhabit the traditional everyday moral world, falling in love, which rightly (from this perspective) leads to marriage, a family, and dreams of a better world for themselves. These are realized through Enoch Snow's entrepreneurial achievement of moving from work as lone fisherman to the creation of a fish business based on a fishing fleet.

The Americanization of Lilliom by *Carousel*, in its story of good and evil, focuses largely on Billy, his nature and predicament, and the consequences that follow from it. Marginalized from the conventional American society represented by Julie, Carrie, and Enoch, his self-deluded sense of himself is presented as a product of his outsider status. His "good" side, however, and its dreams and aspirations, embody a desire to be a participant in the American Dream. He is, then, characterized as socially maladjusted rather than genuinely evil and thus presents, through social exclusion, a personality problem of a false-self and self-image. Through her undemanding love, Julia offers marriage and family, the possibility of the redemption from exclusion, and an entry into the American world that he desires. But this achievement lies in self-knowledge, reform, commitment, and responsibility to their love relationship and marriage. In the "soliloquy"—the dramatic heart of *Carousel*—Billy realizes this, but his maladjusted and marginalized "bad" half can only practically envisage its accomplishment financially in terms of crime. So this, with its inevitable consequences, is how he acts. Julie, understanding the true nature of her man, but also the true (un)demands of love, accepts the pain and tragedy that follows from it. It is Louise, however, the daughter, who takes the fall for her father's crime. The community, as evinced by Carrie and particularly Mr. Snow, refuse to accept her because of her father. Having failed to pass the first test on earth, Billy must return a second time, and this time secure the possibility of redemption that was always in him and, with it, redeem and validate the love of Julie and the marriage and family life he created with her and Louise. Particularly, he must do this by securing the future happiness of Louise and justifying the love of Julie. With this, Billy is redeemed and American ideals and faith become renewed through it and the form it takes—the optimistic individual realization of the "civilized" and the "good" in oneself through the transforming powers of a morality of responsibility and relationship within community. *Carousel* becomes, then, a story of American characters engaged in an American moral struggle, which American enlightenment resolves, and thus it ends—and this too is the American New World—happily.

The crucial thing about *Carousel* is, again, its Americana. *Carousel* is a morality musical that places its issues of good and evil within American values of optimism that are homespun and sentimental. Yet there is a degree of complexity about it that saves *Carousel* from a merely simplistic commitment to Americana (and the liberal progressive formulation of it). The American Dream must be played out in terms of confronting the problems of human nature. *Carousel* also insists upon a need for a change in utterly traditional conventions. Enoch Snow, the epitome of conventional American morality in many ways, is also, in his rejection of Louise, sexist. Even more damning is the negative conventionality of his complacency in opposition to Billy, who struggles. The "good" are not just the successful but also those who do their best, and Billy is shown to be better in this respect than Enoch Snow. But to participate in the American Dream fully and become "civilized," Billy must give up his image of himself and his braggadocio to love Julie honestly and recognize his own dependence on her. He must come to terms with himself and become affectionate, and this he can only do by seeing himself as married and as a parent, because only this can make him responsible. He sees and wants this, but his social exclusion and maladjustment perverts it into providing for his daughter through robbery rather than proper labor and endeavor. In Heaven, he is given one more chance to reform and learn to love by returning to help his daughter. But he must also love in the context of community, and this is where the American conservatism of *Carousel* lies. As in *Oklahoma*, the organic community is treated as the center of American life and society, and *Carousel* celebrates it in a central scene, that of the clambake, where the community incarnates itself and its traditions. *Carousel* is, of course, sentimental in its ideologized and mythologized utopian world, but maybe it is American in another and more positive or, at least, different sense. It possesses an unsubtle and unabashed sentimentality that favors the potential for good in everyone in a very American dream of self-improvement and homeliness. Love will conquer; marriage will civilize; hope will be repaid, people have the capacity to be good, and the right conditions can produce the good. *Carousel* also keeps its popular enter-tainment value as drama while presenting drama as song-and-dance. Per-haps only the most cynical (and, additionally, hard-hearted) critics of America would refuse to be moved by any of it.

Similarly, only a startling lack of *joie de vivre*, and an utter refusal to accept American culture, could lead to a total rejection of *Guys and Dolls*, although it makes an equal investment in Americana. It is, as Green puts it, "the high-minded lowlifes and spunky do-gooders of Damon Runyon's world come colorfully alive" (1996, 148), and in this it perfects the Ameri-can musical comedy through its book. This is an entirely vernacular, idiomatic, and sophisticated comedy based upon the play of comic con-tradictions. What it presents is an American community, but one that is an eclectic melting pot of ethnic types situated in the lowlife urban world of America. Here "community" is crucially characterized by the social prob-lems that exercised the progressives and reformers as "modernity," where the immigrant city becomes characterized as the ousting of healthy work and pursuits by hedonism and entertainment. But lowlife in this show, though constituting a world of illegality, exactly mirrors the straight world in its essential attitudes and values. For example, the pursuit of suc-cess and wealth through the maximization of opportunities available in America is the primary interest of its central characters: it is just that here crime is the vehicle for achievement, and the hope that sustains it becomes a superstitious entreaty for success ("Luck Be a Lady Tonight") rather than an ethical ideal. The *Guys and Dolls* narrative is essentially that of the mythology, ideology, and ideals of America. The characters may be lowlife, but their stories are stories of love and obstacles that fall in its way, and they lead to marriage as the inevitable conclusion. The gambling hero Sky Masterson is morally reformed by, and marries, his pure Salvation Army sweetheart (Sarah Brown); Nathan Detroit finally makes an honest woman out of Miss Adelaide in the same way. The narrative, then, is one in which resolution comes through the redemption of American religion, morality, and values. The conclusion to *Guys and Dolls* is precisely the desired end for America as pursued by the progressives and reformers, and an embodiment of the liberal end of ideology. This may be a simple, even folksy, ending, but that should not obscure the fact that *Guys and*

Dolls is a masterpiece musical that clearly shows the growing sophistication of the form. If it is about America as a juicy melting pot, the music
matches this through its use of a whole variety of American popular song
and the use of counterpoint to create its musico-dramatic organization. Its
achieves its "musical power and unity from the rhythms associated with
specific characters. The 'guys' and 'dolls,' even when singing their so-
called 'fugues,' display a conspicuous amount of syncopation and the
half-note and quarter-note triplet rhythms work against the metrical
grain" (Block 1997, 202). This level of integration is mirrored in the vernacular wisecracking dialogue that introduces a delicious note of irony
into a lowlife world.

FROM *LIEBESTOD* TO MELTING POT: *WEST SIDE STORY* AND AFTER

In *West Side Story* (1957) American liberalism became almost a mani-
festo. Bernstein was a self-conscious liberal spokesman of the artistic intelligentsia positioned within the "chattering classes" of the America of his
time (a fact that Tom Wolfe mercilessly lampoons in *Radical Chic*—see
Wolfe 1971). As an artist, he sought to give liberalism aesthetic expression
in his compositions both serious and popular. At the same time, *West Side
Story* represented a major advance in the book musical in several ways.
Musically, Bernstein drew upon his academic training and experiences as
a musician to construct a "complex score rich in organicism...and other
musical techniques associated with the nineteenth-century European
operatic ideal" (Block 1997, 246). This was combined with a "peculiar
brand of popular eclecticism" to create "an accessible musical interaction
the like of which Broadway had never heard" (Swain 1990, 208). For all
this innovation, however, *West Side Story* was still essentially Broadway. It
remained, and essentially was intended to be, a musical—Bernstein stated
that his goal and that of his collaborators was to compose "a musical that
[told] a tragic story in musical-comedy terms," never falling into the
"operatic trap," a show that would not depend on "stars" but must live or
die by the success of its collaborations (quoted in Block 1997, 260). And
chief collaborator was Jerome Robbins. More than any other musical up
until this point, *West Side Story* relied on dance and movement to convey
the dramatic action. As Walter Kerr put it, in his *New York Herald Tribune*
review (27 September 1957), this was "the show that could have danced all
night, and nearly did." Most of all, it created, in the form of the musical, a
music drama that was a genuine tragedy (see Swain 1990, 205–7).

Notwithstanding the eclectic range of these and other aesthetic agen-
das, *West Side Story* remains, of course, fundamentally American. Thus as
a tragedy it operates very much within the American ideological mold of
the book musical. This is especially evident in the particular way that it

adapts Shakespeare's *Romeo and Juliet* to provide the book. *West Side Story* becomes, not a *liebestod,* as is Shakespeare's play, but a social document. The tale of *West Side Story* is still one of youthful passion, obstacle, and death, but the crucial shift is to make the war between the Montagues and Capulets, transmuted into the urban and gang warfare in contemporary New York, primary in determining the course of the romance. It is, then, the modern urban world of America that *West Side Story* inhabits. The tragedy lies in this social, rather than personal, world of Tony and Maria— a world of racial hatred and prejudice that fires the dramatic and tragic gang warfare between the Sharks and the Jets and one that ultimately has an economic foundation (echoing the basis of the new American rejection of immigration to the United States). The tragedy is finally precipitated not by a poisonous filter, but by the racial prejudice and harassment Anita receives from the Jets as she tries to deliver Maria's message to Tony that Chino is looking for him. Instead, because she is so provoked, Anita tells the vital lie that Maria has been killed by Chino. This, of course, leads directly to Tony exposing himself as he looks for revenge. The cure *West Side Story* offers for the tragedy produced by the social problem of this conflict essentially draws upon the liberal sense of the ideal of the end of ideology. It asserts a sense of America as a "melting pot." Difference lies at its core, but so does the imperative for assimilation, and assimilation that relies on the American Way. Here rational understanding is seen to depend on the authority of democratic association. Together they are the weapons of community in opposition to might and violence. But in *West Side Story* this attitude is one in which the rights of youth are particularly honored, because youth constantly carries and guarantees in itself the spirit of the "newness" of the New World. Authority is not even notionally vested in the elders in *West Side Story,* but in the authoritativeness of the troubles youth faces in society and must overcome. So although *West Side Story* is a tragedy, its message is one of hope in the ultimate victory of the American Way, and heart is still seen to be central to this way. The tragedy is resolved in terms of the power of love as it finds expression in under-standing to ally itself with reason, so love here has a social as well as a per-sonal basis. Thus the song "America" celebrates the idea of America and its community as a melting pot and land of opportunity; "Gee, Officer Kruppke" comically captures the social problems faced by young people seeking assimilation in it, and "Somewhere" expresses the hope and opti-mism of the good life that is ultimately possible as the American ideal of tolerance. The latter also confirms the power of a mythologized romantic love and marriage to preserve this "good," however much the full fruition may still lie ahead.

It is not the personal tragedy of Maria and Tony that is registered as the final note of *West Side Story,* but rather the unfinished business of Ameri-can society, which only the full realization of its particular sense of community can complete. Maria's speech at the end, as she begs the two warring gangs to unite and carry Tony's body away in recognition that they share responsibility for the tragedy of his death, is entirely consistent with such reading and gives the "American Way" a poignant advocacy. In all, then, *West Side Story*, despite its basis in Shakespeare, is a story of American characters in a modern American context where the personal tragedy of passionate love is placed socially and culturally in the American world. In this world the personal tragedy is not one of fate but of character and society and one that only social understanding, love, and reconciliation can resolve. It is important that Maria should carry this message at the end. Two things are American about her and in marked contrast to Shakespeare's Juliet. Unlike Juliet, she is allowed to live and enunciate the drama's message as a protagonist (and not through its statement as a postscript) so that American optimism shines through in the end. Second, as in *Oklahoma* and the vernacular tradition it enshrines, it is given to her, as the feminine figure, to enunciate the message as the vehicle of romantic love and its civilizing character.

THE FINALE OF THE CLASSIC BROADWAY MUSICAL

My Fair Lady (1956) also takes up issues of gender, power and love in an American way. It does so by reconstructing Shaw's *Pygmalion* as a story of romantic love (the one thing Shaw insisted it was not) and in terms of the Cinderella theme that typified the early Broadway musical comedy. It continues with the book musical tradition, deploying music that "for the most part accurately serves most of Shaw's textual ideas. Additionally, the songs themselves, which are carefully prepared and advance the action in the Rodgers and Hammerstein tradition, convey the dramatic meaning that underlies [the] action" (Block 1997, 242). It starts off by faithfully following the classic myth (which Shaw had updated) of man as the sculptor and women as the block and the traditional power gendering of male-female relationships that this entails. But, in providing the story with a happy ending in the marriage of Henry Higgins and Eliza Doolittle, it twists this toward the American by positioning *Pygmalion* as really the story of a modern Cinderella. So, in *My Fair Lady*, Higgins is required to question his misogyny by reflecting on how Eliza might be feeling about what he is doing to her, and Eliza is presented as altogether less crude than Shaw presents her. But, most important, she is given strength and independence as a person, which, as a result, reverses the relation of power between the protagonists after the Embassy Ball to give Eliza the upper hand. In a song like "Just You Wait 'Enry 'Iggins," it is Eliza, then, who signals her determination to leave Higgins high and dry. Crucially, it is because Eliza becomes the power that she and Higgins can marry. Her transformation allows Higgins to reform himself by recognizing his need for her ("I've Grown Accustomed to Her Face") and so establishes a love relationship between them, and not just one of master and servant. So, whereas it is still true that *My Fair Lady* is a story of love and romance, traditionally American in this respect and in its gender mythologizing, it is also the case that gender relationships have been subjected to a limited and modern reorganization at the level of power, and class relationships considered from a more democratic point of view. At least, and unlike much of opera, musicals do not usually punish their heroines as part of the myth of romantic love, but rather enshrine the idea that they will live happily ever after once the true end of romance, marriage, has been achieved.

My Fair Lady also displays a central feature of the aesthetic and artistic development of the musical into music drama, in that it demonstrates how it was venturing further afield in terms of what it sought to dramatize. More and more it engaged in "the practice, ubiquitous after *Oklahoma* of adapting a literary source for the musical stage" (Block 1997, 10). Thus the stories of a large number of "serious" writers became assimilated by the musical: O'Hara (*Pal Joey*), Molnar (*Carousel*), Landon (*The King and I*), Knoblock (*Kismet*), Michener (*South Pacific*), Runyon (*Guys and Dolls*), Hart (*Lady in the Dark*), Gerstacker (*Brigadoon*), Voltaire (*Candide*), Shakespeare (*Kiss Me Kate, West Side Story*), Shaw (*My Fair Lady*), Howard (*The Most Happy Fella*), Aleichem (*Fiddler on the Roof*), and so on. But, always, the adaptations entailed reconstitution in terms of Americana and the end of ideology, even when the drama moved outside of America itself. And, of course, in itself, this aesthetic and artistic transformation constituted at attempt to authenticate the musical in new ways, bringing it to term and vindicating further it as American popular art.

Man of La Mancha (1965) is a classic illustration of these dynamics. The artistic ambition is considerable—nothing less than the transformation of Cervantes's *Don Quixote* into a musical through the adaptation of Dale Waserman's television play *I, Don Quixote*. The Americana contextualization is total. Thus the musical follows the story of the Don's worship of the serving woman Aldonza, as the perceived original and eternal feminine Dulcinea and for whom he constantly seeks to engage in valiant battle against all odds in order to be worthy of knighthood. Aldonza scorns the Don as essentially a fool, but eventually she, too, is won over to a belief in his dream. The Don is indeed presented as the "dauntless, demented Quixote [proclaiming] his quest to dream the impossible dream" (Green 1996, 215), but the pursuit of this is effectively transformed into a metaphor for the American quest for the "newfound land," as the song "To Dream the Impossible Dream," with its dramatic urging to overcome all odds in search of fulfillment, signifies so dramatically. The Don's dream is positively endorsed and pointed toward fulfillment when Aldonza is won over to it, becoming in the process truly Dulcinea as the saving "civilizing" agent who embodies the mission of the dream. Don Quixote's nobility is given American definition, then, as a nobility of spirit created by a heart that can indeed ennoble a seemingly foolish heroic quest for a better world and turn it into realization. In this quest, he is indeed a true knight, but a knight in New World terms.

As the end of ideology book musical took charge of the Broadway stage, the old song-and-dance musical, dependent on stars, the chorus, and spectacle, also made a reentry, but now one reformed by the book. In this came pure manifestations of heart—*Call Me Madame* (1950) with Ethel Merman, for instance, as well as *Can-Can* (1953) with Lilo, *Bells Are Ringing* (1956) with Judy Holliday, *Gypsy* (1959) with Ethel Merman again, *Hello Dolly* (1964) with Carol Channing, *Mame* (1966) with Angela Lansbury, and so on. *Hello Dolly* is the most archetypal of these because of the showcase nature of its central part for a grande dame of the theatrical world (on Broadway alone played by such figures as Pearl Bailey, Carol Channing, Bette Grable, Ethel Merman, Martha Raye, and Ginger Rogers, and, in film, Barbra Streisand). But *Gypsy* is probably the more literate and sophisticated. It is the story of a driven stage mother pushing her children into showbiz (particularly her elder daughter, the less-talented Louise, who becomes the burlesque stripper Gypsy Rose Lee). Louise becomes successful, and in this finally throws off her mother, as she no longer needs her. But in both the mother's pushing and Louise's success, it is the American dream of achievement and success that is being celebrated. Mama Rose is the dreadful pushy would-be showbiz mom negatively gripped by it while Louise is its true realization, as it is she who genuinely possesses heart. *Hello Dolly* is heart as American kitsch in its tale of Dolly Gallagher Levi, a New York matchmaker, who eventually makes a match for herself with the merchant Horace Vandergelder, who has originally hired her to find him a match. Its central scene is utter Broadway as Dolly makes a grand entrance into the high-class restaurant that is her favorite haunt to trigger a rousing and high-kicking reception of her by its waiters. As they sing "Welcome Back Dolly," it comes apparent that this is not just a welcoming of Dolly; Broadway itself and its showbiz traditions are being welcomed home here. It was within this latter context of a salute to Broadway that the revue began to flourish again, both cannibalizing and celebrating, through reconstitution or tribute, musical entertainment of Broadway (see Bordman 1985).

But this apotheosis would not last. Already, the theatrical culture industry was feeling the sheer cost of mounting the Broadway book musical. This made the search for the surefire success even more imperative, as runs had to be longer for a profit to be made. Yet the generation of composers who could be relied upon to create such musicals were beginning to die or had ceased to compose. The fostering of new compositional talent to replace them, moreover, had become too risky to be tried out on

Broadway itself. Moreover, popular music was moving away from the musical culture espoused by the musical to that of rock and roll, which focused on a new and youthful generation. Even more important, however, the consensual end-of-ideology America was beginning to come apart at the seams. The election of President Kennedy in 1960 promised a renewal of the national and international mission of America, and the resolution of the Cuba crisis seemed to confirm America's global might as a superpower. But the triumph was short-lived. The assassination of Kennedy, the rise of the voice of the dispossessed against end-of-ideology America in the civil rights movements, the race riots of the 1960s, and the opposition of the middle classes and youth culture to the Vietnam War— all produced serious conflicts with and about middle America and its dreams. To dream the impossible dream had now begun to seem not merely impossible but delusional. Perhaps Lerner and Loewe's *Camelot* (1960) was more prescient than it seemed as it began the era of the 1960s. The dying King Arthur may, at the end of *Camelot*, optimistically urge a young boy to recount the glories of his kingdom (read *America*) to keep its vision alive. But the tale the musical tells is one where Camelot begins as a heaven on earth, only to become eventually ruined through conflict, treachery, and a breakdown of trust and loyalty—a destruction primarily wrought by romantic love itself. The musical would go on in America, but now it would be reshaped by a more changing and problematic American world than Broadway had hitherto envisioned.

NOTES

1. The relationship between Rodgers and Hammerstein and Mary Martin is a good example of this new kind of relationship between the star performer and the book musical. More generally on this issue, see Gottfried (1979).

2. This excellent point that the figure of Jud also allows for the exercise of puritanical sexual ethics was made in private correspondence with the authors by Stephen Banfield.

CHAPTER 5

Broadway and After: The Transformation of the Musical

THE FRAGMENTED MUSICAL AND THE POSTMODERN WORLD

Steyn has argued that the musical is now dead. For him the "Broadway babies" have said goodnight and the curtain has rung down on the musical as a genuinely vital form of popular musical theater. What has destroyed it is that it has "broke faith with the peculiar amalgam of art and commerce that R & H [Rodgers and Hammerstein] represent" (1997, 145). Now it has become uncommercial high art (e.g., Sondheim), commercial schlock without artistry (e.g., Herman), or mere spectacle in which music and lyrics have been replaced with the technological extravaganza of a show musically mouthed through a *Reader's Digest* version of opera (e.g., Boublil and Schönberg). What Broadway brought to the musical to make it its own and best as a musical theater genre is gone—the wit of musical comedy, but in a "unique form of literate slang—specific, quirky allusions couched in a rich, urban vernacular set to the rhythms of the day" (231); the music and lyrics where character, song, and dramatic impulse are entirely synchronized; the dancing, which advances the show by revealing something about character or developing the narrative; the mythic and emblematic themes and characters that allow the musical to address the wider world outside itself; and the real stars that were made and made themselves in the musical, "those men and women who aren't merely players" (250) and whose "stellar qualities" as musical theatricals are necessary to enact the larger-than-life characters who people the musical (241). Instead of these ingredients, so constitutive of the musical for Steyn, what has now occurred is its fragmentation to make it either self-referential or geared restrictively to specific audiences. The result is musicals that are either "too good" for the "average man" or so undistinguished musically and dramatically that they are good only for the average man and his matronly blue-rinsed consort. In both, the musical has experienced the death of its "theatrical culture and its metaphorical power" (211) through the loss of its Broadway tradition, which entailed an appeal to "Everyman" and not just to one group or the lowest common denominator of an "anybody." Now it is either art and unpopular or popular but lacking artistry.

But why has this fragmentation occurred, and does it really constitute the death of the musical as Steyn argues? Is it not, instead, a transformation of it? As popular theater, the musical is inevitably tied to the world of its production and particularly the American world. This American world is a globalizing, late-modern world led by an America undergoing social and political changes that have reconstituted everyday life within it. The changing nature of the musical, as a popular form, has become reenvisioned and reconstructed in terms of its engagement. Steyn's argument depends on a highly specific conception of the musical that irrevocably ties it to the tradition of Broadway. What he is bemoaning as the death of the musical in terms of art and artistry is the loss of "heart." But, as chapter 4 has argued, the equation of art with heart as the nature of the musical belongs to a specific period of American history, society, and popular culture in which the musical was an expression of an American supremacist and consensual ideology of the end of ideology. It is the end of this period that explains the dearth of the old kind of Broadway musical, but this is not the end of the musical as such; it has changed its form in response to a changing world. Steyn has a case about the condition of the new musical, but it may not be the loss of heart that is the problem. Rather it may be, as Burston argues, that the musical has increasingly lost the active, interpretative, organic creativity and dialogical authenticity that are essential to and distinguish live theater—a loss brought about by the rise of the "megamusical" (see Burston 1998a, 1998b) and discussed in chapter 6.

The consensual ideology of the new postwar America and the harmonizing unity of American society that the musical proposed and celebrated both disguised and suppressed the reality of the structural inequalities within. In particular it obscured the position of black Americans within America and the imperialist aims that were engendered in America's foreign policy, where a world power was now understanding itself as the leader of the "Free World." In this latter, freedom and the American system were equated with one another. This system was essentially that of a capitalist society now in the process of transforming itself, through the internal dynamics of its profit and market mechanisms, into a global system to which the American concept of freedom was inextricably bound. America's world mission, then, was a mission on behalf of capitalism. But this very capitalism produced both inequality and implicated change in its character as it transformed from a system of production to a system of consumption. Here new forms of social, political, and cultural organization began to emerge to create heterogeneity within an essentially bourgeois edifice.

A central reality suppressed by the ideology of the end of ideology was racism as the actual and continuing exclusion of black Americans from the "good" society. As Brogan puts it, "the bland smile of American democracy displayed a rotten tooth, or rather two rotten teeth: the plight of the South and that of the American Negro" (1990, 634). The two were interrelated because the South, too, shaped the conditions of tl.˷ ʰlack population in the North. The trap for the black population of the South, as Brogan says, was the "Jim Crow edifice...[in which] the region stood supreme in disease, poverty, ignorance, sloth, hunger and cruelty [and where, in Southern politics] the old order of corruption, demagogy and reaction, cemented by hatred of the Negro, persisted, it seemed, unchanged" (634). The First World War and the decade following it revived the fortunes of the South as the demand for its traditional agricultural produce (cotton and tobacco) was boosted and Northern financiers and industrialists poured capital into it to realize what they saw as the other investment opportunities that it held—the exploitation of oil, coal, and timber, and, above all, cheap labor. This, in turn, began to create a new industrial, business, and financial class in the South and produced a new measure of prosperity for its poor population, both black and white. Yet it was a prosperity that only marginally trickled down to the former, for whom federal and state poor relief was still necessary to existence. The Depression hit the South just as badly as it hit the North, but, again, the economic fortunes of the South rose with the Second World War and the postwar boom that followed it. Still, the black population that remained in the South was trapped in its racist structure. A primary response of the black population of the South, then, to the prosperous economic conditions produced by the two world wars and the postwar booms that followed was to migrate to the North and attempt to develop their fortunes through the enormous demand for unskilled labor there. This demand was further boosted as the anti-immigration policy of America during this period eliminated the traditional historical source of such labor.

In both the North and South, the experience of segregated service in the American army of the world wars, the racist violence practiced toward black Americans, and the economic and social inequalities forced upon them had now begun to give them a sense of the profound injustice to which they were subjected. Now, very specifically, this sense began to be politicized in ideological and organizational terms. The start lay in both the separatist Marcus Garvey and his United Negro Improvement Association with its emphasis on black pride and Africanist program, and the more liberal W. E. B. Du Bois and his National Association for the Advancement of Colored People. The NAACP was arguably the more successful of the two pressure groups, operating an integrationist ideology and scoring certain Supreme Court victories on behalf of black Americans in the interwar years. However, it was essentially committed to the pursuit of political liberties for blacks rather than the transformation of their economic conditions. This remained the case following the Second World War, but the NAACP managed to achieve particular success in 1954 when the Supreme Court overthrew segregated education on the grounds of the NAACP claim that separation could not mean true equality. More generally, the policy of the NAACP was persuasive enough for both the Democratic and Republican parties to officially espouse and commit themselves to "racial equality" (the federal governments of both Truman and Eisenhower enunciated this as policy). But this was not pursued with any real sense of urgency or active legislation on the part of either government, since, ultimately, both were dependent on the support of southern politicians, who resisted such legislation. Moreover, even in the case of desegregation, the federal government was unable to put policy into effective practice in the South in the face of white Citizen Councils, dedicated to the intimidation of blacks, and state governments and their law enforcement agencies, which were committed to the maintenance of the "Old South" and, indeed, controlled by its traditional power structure.

The NAACP persevered in its attempt at legislative changes in the face of determined Southern resistance, but now came a different response from other black movements, who rejected its conservative pathway to legislative change in favor of direct action. So, beginning with the boycott on the bus company in Montgomery, Alabama, in 1955, "the demands of the Southern blacks [began] spreading out to touch every aspect of segregation" (Brogan 1990, 649) through direct action. This included the enforcement of the right of black schoolchildren to enter Little Rock High School, Alabama, in 1957; the sit-in at the whites-only lunch counter in a restaurant in Greensboro, North Carolina, in 1960; and the Freedom Rides of 1961. Moreover, this policy of direct action pursued through various black movements now developed a thorough political stance and strategy under the leadership of Martin Luther King Jr. with the adoption, through him, of Gandhi's philosophy of *Satyagraha* (nonviolent confrontation). The response of the federal government was to pass the Civil Rights Acts of 1957 and then of 1960, important statements however limited they may have been in real terms. Kennedy inherited this rising situation of black activism and the open racial conflict it was now precipitating. He committed himself to a legislative program for the creation of civil rights for blacks, but attached little urgency to it for a variety of reasons. He was primarily engaged in Cold War politics and specifically with the issue of confronting Russian communism (now perceived as being actively engaged in a policy of expansionism against America under Kruschev's USSR). Moreover, Kennedy needed the support of a southern-dominated Congress in order to govern. Finally, he held the primary aim of channeling the activity of black civil rights movements into the peaceful and orderly pursuit of voting rights. That this would not be enough was made clear when, in 1963, King and his movement mounted a huge campaign with the NAACP to free the black citizens of America starting in Birmingham, Alabama. Thus began a whole series of convulsions throughout the South as its unreconstructed white structures battled it out against black demonstrators. What this induced was a state of near riot in a whole series of towns and cities. Kennedy now recognized that civil rights was a top priority and sent a comprehensive civil rights bill to Congress in 1963. This was conjoined to the "March on Washington for Jobs and Freedom," which combined black and white supporters and whose leaders Kennedy met in the White House. But white southern politicians resisted all attempts to enact the bill and, in November 1963, Kennedy was assassinated. Ironically enough, it was this that gave Johnson the opportunity to push the bill through in 1964. Not only did he actively seek to inherit the mantle of Kennedy, but also he needed to assert himself with Kennedy's constituency. This, together with the shattered moral and national mood of mourning and reassessment throughout America, accompanied by a need to reassess the state of the nation and the fact that his opponent (Barry Goldwater) represented the extreme right wing of the Republican Party, secured Johnson the presidency in 1964. It gave him the power to enact Kennedy's original bill and, later, in 1965, a second civil rights bill to deal with southern resistance. The South continued to resist, but its politicians finally gave in with President Carter in 1976, especially as they now knew they would have to gain black votes to remain in office. Formally, then, civil rights had been established at this point and now specifically in the South. This emancipated blacks by giving them full political rights, but, and here was its whole weakness, it did not alter the economic and social structural conditions that were the primary foundation of their unequal position in American society.

It was the latter that was the primary trap of racism into which the northern black population had fallen (and which would afflict the South in its own way too). The successful expansion of capitalism that had brought black Americans to the North was a period of abundance that had taken white Americans out of the city and into suburbia, the new social space of its life of wealth, work, and consumption. From this space blacks were actively excluded by the white population (often directly through discriminatory clauses in the sale and renting of housing, although such discrimination was outlawed by Johnson's Open Housing Act in 1968). Blacks discovered, as they had moved north, particularly after the Second

World War, "that there was work for most of them (not all), but not the best work; housing, but only the worst; education, but not what they needed" (Brogan 1990, 658). Moreover, the move to suburbia was a movement of the economy out of the city. "The blacks would not inherit a going concern... Instead, they would fall heir to a vast area of decaying housing, with decaying services and no prospects except of indefinite reliance on welfare" (662). Increasingly these city areas became wildernesses in which poverty, exploitation, and crime were all entwined in a downward spiral. In this context, the active black political response began to turn away from the civil rights movement (especially after King's assassination) to radical versions of black power and now, even more threatening for American society, race riots (notably in Harlem in 1963 and Watts in 1965, to be followed by similar events in numerous cities throughout America in 1966). King's last attempt to bring Gandhian tactics to the problems of the North was through the "March on Chicago," which proceeded through its white suburbs and secured little support from the city administration and active and violent opposition from the white population. As Brogan argues, Mayor Daley knew the black movement was split and Washington was relatively inactive. But, most of all, Daley needed the votes of the white population to stay in office. The assassination of King in 1968 precipitated a vast and open rebellion in the black population with riots in 125 cities but, apart from bringing it under control, the federal and state governments made no concerted effort to change the conditions that were the source of its discontent: poverty and racism. The neoliberal economic policies that were to follow under Reagan's presidency, in addition to the new welfare-to-work policies under Clinton's, while creating a small and growing black middle class and providing certain kinds of jobs for the rest of the black population (albeit badly paid and insecure), still leaves half living on or below the poverty line as a destitute underclass. Through this, the American social order is under threat internally as a capitalist system and racism join hands, with the former economically institutionalizing the latter, whatever ideological proclamations are made about the "goodness" of its good society and the free and affluent life it can produce for all its members. For the majority of blacks, inequality remains first reality. As Thurgood Marshall, the first black justice of the Supreme Court, put it in 1978: "Be careful of people who say, 'You've got it made. Take it easy. You don't need any more help.' Today we have reached the point where people say, 'You've come a long way.' But so have other people come a long way. Has the gap been getting smaller? No. It's getting bigger. People say we're better off today. Better off than what... Don't listen to that myth that [inequality] can be solved... or that it has already been solved. Take it from me, it has not been solved" (quoted in Brogan 1990, 665).

The penetration of black music and dance into American popular culture and the success of black performers is not, then, an index of structural advance by America's black population, but, in many ways, a closure for their aspirations that is culturally incorporative (like sport) but structurally constraining in terms of that advance within American society. The musical *Dreamgirls* (1981) explores this in the context of the rise of Diana Ross and the Supremes in the world of pop music of the 1960s and 1970s, showing how it is a world structured by racism.

But a second major source of the fragmentation came from the role that America now adopted as a world power, locked in Cold War conflict with Russia and China and crucially shaped by Kennedy's determination to assume the mantle of the defender of the "Free World." By the *Free World*, America meant the American world and the capitalist system in terms of which it was organized. Thus the American government treated communism as essentially its enemy (ideologically it was presented as the enemy of freedom). Every move on the part of Russia or China, and any movement in any part of the world that was seen to smack of socialism (defined as not adopting the capitalist system), was regarded as part of a conspiracy against America. In this context American foreign policy became frankly imperialistic. In all, "it rested on a deep unwillingness to accept the world was never going to dance to Uncle Sam's every whim or share his every prejudice" (Brogan 1990, 668), with the corollary that it could be made to. From this perspective, Indochina represented a particular threat to America, which had long had a concern with the Pacific border and the East as its own specific area of commerce and trade. As the French were forced to abandon their Indochina empire, America took over the French message that the nationalist movement in Indochina was part of an internationalist Communist conspiracy. America developed this understanding into a domino theory. If one part of Indochina were to fall, then the rest would follow. Consequently America committed itself to the support of South Vietnam and entered into the Vietnamese war, its commitment being sustained by the near "hot" war that the Cuba crisis brought on in 1961. Johnson, and then Nixon, adopted precisely this same American stance to vigorously pursue the Vietnam War. But America was pursuing a war it could not hope to win. All the elements of a civil society had been destroyed in South Vietnam, and President Diem and his successors were far from having a legitimate claim for their rule. The Vietcong, by contrast, did have legitimacy. Moreover, the pouring of American money and resources into South Vietnam, as part of the war effort, undermined its economic and social stability even further. The means by which America fought this war (such as spraying the jungle with poisonous defoliants) destroyed the one essential and indigenous economic resource that South Vietnam possessed. In this respect, too, as well as tactically, America's decision to fight the war in terms of its military technology, which was unsuited to and could not defeat the guerrilla tactics of the Vietcong, was disastrous.

But much more than this, Johnson and then Nixon had misjudged the seemingly original commitment of the America population to the war. There remained not only the isolationist strain to foreign ventures in American society, but Johnson had forgotten, too, that the most popular deed of Kennedy's presidency had been the Nuclear Test Treaty in 1963 and that he (Johnson) had won the presidency against Barry Goldwater because he was seen as the peace candidate. This began to come home as American casualties started to mount, making the war very unpopular. Moreover, the Vietnam War was a highly mediatized war, both intensively and extensively covered and recorded by TV and the press. This brought home the full horror of events on a day-to-day basis and in highly critical terms (which was reinforced by the international criticism of its pursuit). A central part of the horror that emerged in this (represented in particular by the My Lai massacre of 1968) was the recognition of the deeply corrupting effect on the America army.

The army was largely composed of black enlisted men, who had joined to escape poverty and prejudice [but] their white officers gave them most of the nastiest and most dangerous work to do. Hostility spread: by the end of the war the practice of "fragging" was fairly widespread—the murder of officers by their men. Hard and soft drugs were plentiful in Saigon...addiction became a major problem. Violence, venereal disease, theft and petty crime were commonplace. Morale and discipline came near to collapse, in large part because the men of the army could see no sense in the war and were disgusted by its cruelty [and, in all]...relations between men and officers remained poor and notions of how to fight remained rigid. (Brogan 1990, 677)

But the Vietnam War now produced another and new situation of conflict within American society, because it reached its peak when "the age group most affected by it came together in what was...a formidable political movement" (678). Nourished and fostered during the post–Second World War boom by the economic might and abundance of America, youth had become a differentiated social group within it, possessed of its own economic power and cultural identity. This had found expression in the virtual annexation of popular music to a huge youth market. But, also, this was a highly educated generation. It had espoused the idealism of the "New Camelot" that Kennedy proclaimed as the aim of his presidency. It used this as an ideology for empowerment, pursuing in this that Enlightenment vision of the American Dream as producing the "new" and "better" world in which the torch was to be handed on from one generation and on to another as part of the mechanism of the path of progress. The death of Kennedy, and the pursuit of the Vietnam War, brought this dream to an end, and the idealism located within it turned now into an alienated and critical attack on the American system itself, mounted in terms of radical politics and direct forms of political action, protest, and rebellion (particularly against the draft). The Vietnam War became, for youth, the very symbol of the corrupt nature of the American system and its structures of power to which, at another (particularly American) level, peace, love, freedom, and equality were proclaimed as the alternative. *Hair* (1968) was the musical that particularly attempted to capture and present this. To the older generation of middle-class America, and certainly to the America government, this appeared as entirely revolutionary and un-American, so it split the umbrella of "consensual America" into a battle between liberal and conservative.

1968 saw the peak of the forces of fragmentation within American society break it into component conflicting parts. "It was a year in which everyone was protesting, it seemed: the South against the North, the blacks against whites, the young against the war, the Northern working class against the young, and the 70% of Democrats who remained faithful to their party against Richard Nixon" (Brogan 1990, 682).[1] But Nixon had won presidential office in 1968 on a promised plan to end the Vietnam War with honor and satisfaction for America, which gathered up the opposition to Vietnam and solidified the antiliberal forces, who saw the peace movement as antipatriotic. In fact, Nixon prolonged the war, but mounting casualties and the realization that the South Vietnamese government was near collapse were alienating even his Republican supporters, and this led to a change of tack. Nixon made an official visit to China and finally signed a peace treaty in 1972. This, in turn, brought him overwhelming victory in the 1972 presidential election. But he also carried into that presidency a Manichean sense of his own power, which led him not to cooperate with the forces of Congress but to override them in terms of his own power and designs. A central ambition here was the crushing of all opposition and especially that of what he saw as "liberal intellectuals," particularly those who inhabited the press. The result was fatal, leading to the Watergate Affair of 1972. The office of the psychiatrist David Ellsberg, who had leaked the Pentagon Papers to the *New York Times* (laying out in detail the whole sorry and sordid business of America's involvement in the Vietnam War), was broken into on the orders of Nixon, the aim being to find incriminating evidence against Ellsberg. Also the offices of the Democratic National Committee in the Watergate Building in Washington were entered in an attempt at bugging. Nixon's agents (posing as plumbers) were caught and, as the 1972 election approached, a whole process of cover-up and exposure began. The culmination here, in many respects, was the announcement by the president's counsel, John Dean, that the deception could not be continued. Dean's confession to the FBI led the Senate to set up a special committee to investigate the affair. Nixon continued to fight it out, but Congress decided there was sufficient evidence to begin impeachment proceedings against Nixon for conspiring to pervert the course of justice. Nixon finally gave in and resigned in 1974, never accepting that he had acted unconstitutionally but, rather, regarding himself as the victim of vindictive enemies.

The Watergate Affair had simply increased the tensions within American society. Nixon's "countrymen, dismayed by defeat in war, violent social conflict and now by betrayal of democracy at the very heart of their political system, wondered if they could ever trust any President, or politician or voter" (Brogan 1990, 688). Ford, who was Nixon's replacement through his vice presidency, now sought to repair the damage by pursuing a policy of limited presidential office and enunciating the constitutional principle of democratic government—that is, the argument that government in America was a government of laws and not men. This brought the situation back into the constitutional status quo, where separated powers and the pragmatic compromise was identified as the modus operandi.

But this pragmatism was beginning to be shaped in new terms as it became associated with the new emerging forces of differentiation produced by the transformation of the capitalist economic system into a global system of consumption, one in which consumption had moved from the material to the ideistic. The result has been a restructuring of the market through the enculturation of production. Mass production based on mechanical means of production has been replaced, to a large and increasing extent, by flexible and niche production based on media, communication, and informational technologies and systems using intensive advertising and focused marketing to maintain a continuous and innovatory relation to consumer tastes and demands. With this post-Fordist capitalism a bourgeoisie has emerged whose position is based upon labor, which entails the possession of knowledge and its use (and an underclass of manual laborers who are unemployed, casually employed, or service this bourgeois world). This bourgeoisie increasingly defines itself socially in terms of a consumptory and lifestyle identity that is simultaneously one of the differentiated community. Within this world, the enfranchisement of the population and the extension of civil rights has produced a better education and state guardianship, but also stronger demands in terms of human rights to freedom, personal development, and quality of life. Moreover, it is not just the educated and informed who articulate such political demands. Politically marginalized groups have become empowered. As Crook, Pakulski, and Waters argue (1992), pressure-group activism has replaced class politics to a large extent, operating partly through a constitutional system that allows political activity to proceed more readily through legal challenge and partly though the media.

To some degree this kind of decentered mobilizing has developed from the 1960s and 1970s. With the civil rights movement, the student movements, the anti–Vietnam War protests, and so on, the basis was laid for an even wider range of groups to begin demanding specific rights for themselves and their constituencies. Most especially, the feminist movement in America has effectively been able to challenge much of the traditional and unequal gendering of social structure and organization within it. What has emerged in America, then, is a cultural politics in which political forces are increasingly focused around issues, rights, and social movements and that engage in strategies for mass representation and political activism using the media as their major instrument, both as a means of mobilization and a vehicle for action. In this way consumption has produced differentiated communities, and popular culture has increasingly framed itself around these differentiations. But this is not entirely a cultural phenomenon. Below it lies the structural reorganization of capitalism around ideistic consumption and the reconstitution of the life chances, as well as the lifestyles, of consumers. Differentiated culture has increasingly produced a differentiated market for capitalist accumulation to sustain itself in terms of the commodity as sign. Nor is this entirely divorced from traditional forms of mass production to sustain the global market. It is in this context that the aestheticization of everyday life through consumption, and the cultural politics of identity, can and have conjoined to preserve a capitalism in terms of new neoliberal consensus among the large majority of beneficiaries within America (and now outside).

This configuration found its initial representation in Reagan's two presidencies but has continued in that of Clinton—economic conservatism combined with an antistatism that espouses the market as the pragmatic guarantor of wealth, freedom, and order. What becomes visualized here is a society whose unity begins to approximate more that of a mosaic than a homogeneous entity. How far this process has gone is a matter of considerable dispute. Certainly the protagonists of the arguments for the advent of a postmodern society are convinced of the emergence of a qualitatively different world. Its radical and liberal critics are faced with the problem of how precisely to characterize the dynamics of its global capitalist economic structure, especially with the death of socialism. But they are united in the search for a political economy of its nature that argues for "real" structural and not just cultural processes at work in the production of the world.

FROM SOCIAL REALISM TO CONCEPT IN THE MUSICAL

We have seen that one way of conceptualizing aesthetic development in the Broadway musical is in terms of Block's movement from "opulent adornment" to "textual realism." The result is that the musical becomes integrated not just by the song and dance but, crucially, by the book, which turns it into musical drama. It is a music drama that typically takes the form of realism and, specifically, of "social realism," the classic form of bourgeois tragedy as Raymond Williams (1966) defines it. The essentially realist character of the book resides in the fact that it establishes the drama in terms of a specific narrative. This entails a linear plot in which the sequential organization of the plot constitutes a drama brought about by and given meaning through the motivations, tensions, actions, and interactions of the protagonists as they live out their lives in the world constructed by the book. Centrally, as social realist drama, the book musical sets out to be a drama of "real" characters with real motives living in a real world. It seeks to be a correspondent representation of the world that it sets out to inquire into. This involves a particular structuring of song-and-dance that must help to convey the "reality" of the drama, to give it believability. Musical numbers must carry the action of the drama, expressing the personalities of the characters who sing them and representing the mood of the play. It is for this reason that vocal pyrotechnics are displaced by musical characterization. Song-and-dance becomes the manifestation of the group or community life within which the lives and story of the leading characters are located and shaped. Increasingly, too, cinematic techniques come to be adopted, where the musical narrative weaves in and out of the drama on a continuous basis rather than on the more opera or operetta-like melodramatic basis of formal song and speech structure.

Crucial in this, and here we come to the central issue of the link between the social realist aesthetics of the book musical and its nature as a popular form of art, is the social nature of the "reality" maintained. Herein lies the essential character of the book musical as a manifest expression of American popular culture. As is the case with all social-realist forms of drama, however, it becomes apparent that the realistic basis of the drama involves a conception of the nature of the reality that is ideological and mythological, as well as culturally specific. In the context of the book musical, this conception is an indigenous and popular Americana conception of the reality of America.

The ideology stems, as we have seen, from the establishment of America as the first new and modern post-Enlightenment world. This ideology visualized America as a particular kind of community—one in which freedom and harmony were integrated, whose members were differentiated by interest but united through democratic association to create an emancipated world wrought by reason and understanding. From this grew distinctive culture forged in terms of a particular mythology that legitimated the aspirational American Dream. The preamble to the America Constitution set the foundation of this Dream in terms of the right to liberty, property, and happiness, which modernity translated into the "American Way of Life." Here individual ambition, effort, and work find success in a world of equality and social mobility. So a myth was created of a society where self-development could be achieved within the wholeness of an organic community rooted in and maintained through the civilizing agents of love, romance, and marriage. The American Dream was guaranteed by modern capitalism—indeed, the two become synonymous. By the 1960s, it had reached a kind of apotheosis to which the end-of-ideology book musical gave reflexive expression at the level of an art form of popular culture.

The mid-to-late 1960s, however, cracks began appearing in the "reality" of the world that the book musical had espoused and expressed as America. The American Dream it enacted became overshadowed and subject to a disabling interrogation of status. One major artistic response within the Broadway musical was the continuation of the aesthetic trajectory of the social realism of the book musical. Now, though, it engaged in a reflexive encounter with this new American world of fragmentation, deepening its address upon America in terms of the problems this was beginning to raise for it. Burston has articulated something of this development:

stylistic traditions of Broadway helped create shows that often subverted Broadway's own established conventions to ironic effect, and additionally, toward expanding social consciousness on the musical stage. In many...hit shows...Broadway composers employed their traditional musical languages, often inflected with musical connotations of social difference (chromaticism from the Yiddish theatre, dropped sevenths from African-American music), toward identifiably progressive ends. *Cabaret* is set against the backdrop of encroaching fascism in Weimar Germany. *A Chorus Line* earnestly examines the working lives of Broadway gypsies and presents the first out gay character in a hit musical. *Dreamgirls* retells the story of Diana Ross and the Supremes, and offers a brilliant analysis of structural racism in the American popular music industry. (1998b, 74)

Kander and Ebb's *Chicago* (1975) is also instructive here, challenging and exposing the ideology and myth of the American Dream from a critical social realist perspective. It revisits American history by setting itself in the 1920s, not in order to confirm identity but, rather, to establish "a scathing indictment of American huckstering, vulgarity and decadence" (Green 1996, 244). It does it in terms of a portrait of the American justice system that it sees as little more than another branch of the American pursuit of fame and celebrity (the American Dream *in reductio ad absurdum*). Roxie Hart and Velma Kelly, the heroines of the show, are presented as two of the essentially merry murderesses who largely make up the population of County Cook Jail. They are represented by Billy Flynn, a completely amoral but charismatic lawyer who, through his razzle-dazzle way of relating to his clients and his showbiz manner of legal representation, turns their crimes into the stuff of pop culture. The aim here is not only to get them off but also to win them new careers as vaudeville entertainers. Murder becomes, then, the very means of a life of fame and fortune. So Roxie happily realizes the American Dream in these terms. She sings about becoming a celebrity, somebody who is universally known through the bizarre process that turns life into art. Velma's rehearsal of her court appearance visualizes the legal process in the same terms of performance, media representation, and the cult of celebrity status. She imagines herself quite literally as an actress, eyeing up the jury in preparation, teasing them through her sexuality, acting out the role of defenseless womanhood, and appealing to their protective instincts as she strategically falters and asks dramatically for a glass of water. According to *Chicago*, even life and death in America is just another kind of entertainment, and justice is just another branch of showbiz, with its own impresarios, theaters, star system, and reporters, who are really little more than reviewers. Theater critics of the London revival of *Chicago* in 1997 have pointed out how pertinent this view of the American justice system remains today, when the TV trials of O. J. Simpson, Louise Woodward, and others have become a new entertainment in the living room, to make the process of justice—supported by the official argument that justice be not just done but seen to be done—an actual subversion of justice.

However, in *Chicago*, just as in Kander and Ebb's earlier *Cabaret*, a new form of Broadway musical has also begun to appear that shifts away from social realism to "concept" as the integrative principle of musico-dramatic structure and organization. In this the Broadway musical engages with modernism to raise the issue of the relationship between representation and reality, not just in terms of what and whose reality but on the basis of an existential questioning of the basis of reality itself. Here the modern musical joins hands with modernism. It images a world "confronted... with [an] overwhelming sense of fragmentation, ephemerality and chaotic change" (Harvey 1990, 11). It also places a special responsibility on the artist, whose role it becomes to define "the essence of humanity" (19), by finding a representation of it that challenges realism, with its now redundant sense of an absolute correspondence between art and reality.

On Broadway, the emergence of the conceptual musical has realized the issue of the relation between representation and reality through a central concern with its own form, with theater and theatricality itself. Illusion becomes a target of this exploration. *Cabaret*, *Chicago*, and *A Chorus Line* offer particular cases in point as they theatricalize music drama to recall the traditions of music theater, deconstructing them while reassembling them in new and experimental ways. In *Cabaret*, for instance, a sleazy Berlin nightclub is turned into a metaphor for the decadent world of Weimar Germany, with the floor show numbers being used as commentaries on situations in the plot. The Master of Ceremonies here constitutes the unifying element of *Cabaret* as a musical but also of its representation of the world, which it portrays as cabaret. In the same way, the musico-dramatic form of this show takes the form of cabaret turns, with the audience coming to the musical to find itself confronted with a *mise-en-scène* on stage (with curtains already up) and being invited by the siren song of

Sally Bowles to come to the Cabaret. The stage is designed as a cabaret on which there is already an "internal" audience. The audience for the musical is required to become part of this and so be treated (as one with the internal audience) to the show. The whole issue of the reality and illusion of fascism and Nazi Germany is paralleled by the way *Cabaret* trades off the reality and illusion of theater. In *Cabaret*, art and life can merge through theater under the sway of the truly dramatic nature of the reflexivity of metaphor and in a critical engagement with the world.

Chicago is also reflexive in its presentation of music drama. Its theme of American justice as just another branch of showbiz is established by creating a musical vaudeville with a Master of Ceremonies introducing each number as if it was a variety "turn." The characters act out their lives in pursuit of the American Dream like theatrical performers engaged in song-and-dance acts. Again, theater provides the drama through its potential as metaphor. The American Dream is merely song-and-dance, but, even more than this, it is completely tacky, since it is vaudeville song-and-dance, and with this the critique is deepened.

A Chorus Line is more realist but similarly deconstructive. It attempts to capture the experience of that unsung backbone of the Broadway musical, the chorus line. In this it challenges that classic version of theater itself as a vehicle of the American Dream, the one where the chorus girl, who for one reason or another has to replace the star, goes out onto the stage as a chorus girl and comes back as a star herself. Thus the show sets out to dramatize the hopes, fears, and insecurities of a group of dancers auditioning for the chorus line. But the audition, which is the concept through which the musical is organized as a music drama, is treated as a larger image of American life and, particularly, the life of the ordinary person. This is, at one level, a critique of American success and achievement where the chorus line becomes metonymic of all who have to stand in line and be judged. Or, more neutrally, the musical conveys the experience of anyone who has ever stood in line in an effort to present "his or her qualifications for a job" (Green 1996, 243). Using the audition as a framing device, *A Chorus Line* allows the chorus gypsies to step out of the line and produce their autobiographies (to create a series of miniature dramas) at the behest of Zach, the producer, as part of the process through which he is selecting them for the show he is staging. Each applicant reveals truths that, supposedly, will help the director to make his final decisions:

Among those auditioning are Cassie...a former featured dancer now down on her luck...the street-smart but vulnerable Sheila...who recalls how she had been attracted to dancing because "everything was beautiful at the ballet"; the still-hopeful Diana...who had once failed a method acting class; the voluptuous Val...who uses silicon to enlarge her talent; and the pathetic Paul...who relates his humiliating experience as a drag queen. (Green 1996, 243)

A Chorus Line ends with the appearance of these characters as the immaculate chorus in the show that is being produced, singing and dancing "One" as a triumphant demonstration of that perfect unity of action that is the essence of the chorus line. Very much like the film *Backstage Musical*, *A Chorus Line* humanizes the theater in terms of the life-dramas and work behind the production of a show, except, in this case, no member of the chorus goes out as a chorus gypsy and comes back a star. Indeed this theater myth is deconstructed—"once a chorus gypsy, always a chorus gypsy" is its message about showbiz. So the end for the chorus gypsy, then, is not to be an individual at all (as "One" demonstrates) but essentially to submerge his or her individuality in the chorus line as the performing entity. This is reinforced specifically in terms of Cassie—a onetime lead singer and dancer who is trying to remake her career on Broadway through humbly seeking entry into the chorus line but who is constantly admonished by Zach for the "starlike" individualistic qualities that make her stand out. She is finally chosen to appear in the show when she has eliminated such qualities.

For all these in-house revelations, however, *A Chorus Line* is structured not by local narrative but by larger metaphor. The humanity of the chorus gypsies and the sympathy that *A Chorus Line* shows for their predicament trawls the "is" of American life in relation to the myth of the American Dream. Waiting in line, uniformity, mediocrity, and failure, rather than success and stardom, are the more usual conditions of its pursuit.

The concept musical, then, has a modernist character. In it the idea or concept replaces the narrative of the now traditional book. The point of song-and-dance is to ensure that all aspects of the vision/concept/metaphor are fully explored and worked out, and in this the manner, as well as the matter, of the drama becomes equally crucial. A result of this has been to give the role of the director a more central position in the creation of the musical, as the rise and consolidation of Hal Prince's career on Broadway illustrates (see Hirsch 1989; Ilson 1989). What is essentially at stake in the concept musical is the meaning and understanding it produces as music drama, not in a representational correspondence with the world but as a consciously critical engagement with reality that addresses where reality and representation meet. Both representation and reality feed off one another and hopefully discover a larger and new sensibility as the contribution and value of theater. But it does this still with the essential dimensions of the popular song-and-dance musical. The problem is how and whether this degree of sophistication can be combined with a continuing popular appeal. *Cabaret*, *Chicago*, and *A Chorus Line* manage to do this by holding onto the traditional forms of Broadway's songs and dances and tying metaphor clearly to American history and modernity both nationally and globally.

The conceptual musical, however, did not entirely replace the traditional book musical with its constitutive Americana on Broadway. Herman continued to write, as Steyn puts it, "warm-hearted ... and big-lady-on-staircase numbers" (1997, 201) in a royal succession of shows like *Hello Dolly, Mame,* and *La Cage aux Folles* (1983). The latter was derived from a French film and concerns a homosexual couple, one conservative (George) and the other flamboyantly camp (Albin), who run a transvestite night-club of which the latter is the drag-star highlight. But the arrival of George's son from a long-past heterosexual phase in George's life upsets the settled homosexual relationship and status quo of George and Albin as the son plans to marry the daughter of the local moral crusader (Edouard Dindon). George, in order for his son to get married, now has to present himself to his future father-in-law as an upstanding citizen, which means putting Albin back in the closet. This is achieved by persuading Albin to use drag to pose as George's wife. He agrees, but additionally, in this guise, blackmails Edouard into permitting the marriage to proceed by semi-seducing Edouard with his "female" charms and threatening to reveal all. But, as Steyn states, this story does no more than to recognize that "Dolly and Mame and the other caricature broads had been drag queens all along, [the only difference in this case being that] the lady on the staircase [is] a guy in a frock" (1997, 201), a point reinforced perhaps when Danny La Rue, the drag artist, played Dolly in a revival of *Hello Dolly* in Britain in the 1980s. That Albin insistently sings "I Am What I Am" (the disco version of which, by Gloria Gaynor, would later become a gay anthem) does not make *La Cage aux Folles* a paean to gay liberation. Herman made sure that on no account were the two principals to kiss (according to its director, Arthur Laurents, that would have driven half the audience out of the theater). It was, in this and other respects, traditional musical theater, essentially in the Broadway tradition, complete with a glamorous chorus line.

As an alternative, but still within the Broadway tradition, was Strouse and Charnin's *Annie* (1977). This took the comic strip figure of Little Orphan Annie, an eleven-year-old foundling at the municipal orphanage during the Depression who yearns to be rescued from its monstrous matron (Miss Harrigan), and finds herself saved by the billionaire (Daddy Warbucks) who adopts her. So "Tomorrow" literally becomes a day away, as Annie hopes in this song of yearning in the orphanage, and the pro-claimed message of the musical is fulfilled—Annie is a metonymic figure, standing for decency, courage, and optimism against hard times and despair. In this *Annie* follows in the long line of Cinderella shows that punctuate the history of Broadway musical comedy and include *Mlle Modiste* (1905)—hat-shop girl becomes prima donna; *Irene* (1919)—uphol-sterer's assistant becomes assistant to society belle; *Sally* (1920)—dish-washer becomes Ziegfeld star; *Peggy Ann* (1926)—small-town drudge becomes adventuress; *Lady in the Dark* (1941)—austere career woman becomes imagined femme fatale; *Annie Get Your Gun* (1946)—illiterate hillbilly becomes world-famous sharpshooter; *Silk Stockings* (1955)—drab communist becomes vivacious beauty; *My Fair Lady* (1956)—cockney flower-seller becomes belle of the ball; *Gypsy* (1959)—talentless vaudeville trouper becomes burlesque headliner; and *Funny Girl* (1964)—ugly duckling becomes Ziegfeld star. But in the world of 1977 outside of the American Broadway tradition, one might wonder if the adoption of an eleven- year-old girl by an elderly billionaire man (which *Annie* portrays) might not have suggested something rather darker than the American Dream fulfilled.

La Cage aux Folles brought virtually the end of this kind of Broadway musical insofar as new works were concerned. What largely replaced them as indigenous American productions on Broadway were revivals of "classic" musicals that belonged to this tradition. An audience was still there for them. But now, with the door of opportunity opened to it by the dearth of the local product, the Brits victoriously entered Broadway to steal away this audience for themselves through the "megamusical," which specifically targeted it. The conceptual musical continued in various forms, including specifically feminist and gay works, although these did not usually play on Broadway.

STEPHEN SONDHEIM AND THE DECONSTRUCTION
OF "HAPPY EVER AFTER"

The dominant figure on Broadway, creatively but not commercially, from the 1970s to the present has been Stephen Sondheim, and, as Banfield (1993) argues, the modernism that is inherent in the "conceptual" musical finds its fullest flowering in Sondheim's Broadway musicals. Banfield finds that Sondheim's philosophy has an intrinsic relationship to the modernist apprehension of Hegel and Kierkegaard. He quotes from Bradbury and McFarlane's account of the centrality of these thinkers to the modernist mind and finds here a powerful resonance of the central Sondheim position:

[T]he modernist mind . . . seems to want to approve [Kierkegaard's] concept of "either/or" in the place of the Hegalian "boWand." "Either/or," Kierkegaard claimed, should not be considered as disjunctive conjunctions...their unique function is to bring life's contours into the most intimate relationship with each other, whilst at the same time presenting the validity of the contradiction between them. It is then as though the modernist purpose ought to be defined as the resolution of Hegel with Kierkegaard; committing oneself neither wholly to the notion of "both/and" nor wholly to the notion of "either/or" but (as it were) to both and to neither. Dauntingly, then, the modernist formula becomes "both/and" and/or "either/or". (Bradbury and McFarlane 1976, 88)

Sondheim notably established himself first on Broadway as lyricist, particularly for *West Side Story* and *Gypsy*, but came to prominence as composer-lyricist with *A Funny Thing Happened on the Way to the Forum* (1962). This worked well within the formula of a book musical comedy, although it already took a particular modernist delight in exploring the nature of its genre (farce) in order to fulfill one of Sondheim's particular rules for a musical: "to define the type, understand its parameters and excel at it" (Banfield 1993, 91). Certainly *A Funny Thing Happened on the Way to the Forum* was a considerable success—only *A Little Night Music* (1973) would give Sondheim a comparable degree of commercial success on Broadway. But it was with *Company* (1970) that Sondheim established the form and nature of his conceptual musical, or, better, the integrative organization in terms of which his musicals could deconstruct the traditional Broadway musical (both structurally and thematically) to reconstitute it in a modernist form. In this musical and those that followed Sondheim turned to American life itself—the ideology and mythology of the American Dream and the American Way—as both the subject and object of his modernist deconstruction.

Their illusory nature is revealed through a critical address. Thus in *Company* the romantic ideal of love and marriage comes under scrutiny as an American myth that cannot sustain relationship. The setting is New York, representing the quintessence of the new encultured capitalism and defining a society based on social relationships forged through an aestheticized consumptory lifestyle. Here the American Dream has been materially fulfilled but, as Sondheim presents it, at the cost of an emotionally deprived and narcissistically driven existence. This gives marital relationships a psychological dimension saturated by conflict, tension, and ambiguous feelings. In this way *Company* targets the ideal of marriage, treating its substitution for reality as a destructive fallacy—indeed, marriage becomes characterized by the contradiction of the myth preventing the commitment that relationship actually demands. Bobby's (the hero's) predicament is how to confront and address this issue. He has accepted the bourgeois ideal of marriage, but approaches it with all the narcissism built into modern America culture. Crucially in this psychological conflict, he enshrines Sondheim's sense of the modern individual as the neurotic figure. His bourgeois world, although a world filled with relationships, is the society of Riesman's (1950) "lonely crowd." It entails an outer-directed and conventional society that forms a cocoon of friendship. This obscures the inner neurotic and narcissistic selves of its participants and the wary interdependence that is established between them because it substitutes projection for inner-directedness. Bobby is surrounded with married friends who deliberately but unconsciously both use and support him to maintain their own ambiguous marital relationships, as he, in turn, uses them to support his own life. But it is this ambiguity that creates the problem for Bobby. Ultimately, he is an outsider looking in on their relationships as a friend who is never privy to their internal dynamics except when they vouchsafe what it suits them to vouchsafe. So he is puzzled by the ambiguity and put off marriage as a result. Left only with the ideal of marriage and the contrast between it and his friends' marriages, Bobby does not know whether marriage is a prison for which he cannot sacrifice his autonomy, or his autonomy is a prison of unrelatedness in which he can never achieve emotional satisfaction since this would demand commitment. But what is the reality of this commitment? Sondheim's position is that a real commitment to marital life is about compromising the ideal to embrace ambiguity as the essence of marriage. But there is no value in approaching contradiction and ambiguity in the spirit of narcissistic game playing. Thus Bobby is hampered by the fact that his friends displace the ambiguities of their marriages as they wax and wane onto Bobby in the name of friendship. At the same time he must stop displacing his anxieties about marriage onto *their* marital lives to arrive at an inner-directed choice for himself. What is needed, then, is more consciousness at the expense of convention, and whether either Bobby or his friends are genuinely capable of such growth gives *Company* its critical edge. His friends have compromised with marriage, but in terms of a huge amount of projection and avoidance. The question over whether Bobby actually comes to terms with marriage in the end, or merely imagines he has, is a part of Sondheim's deconstructive technique. Sondheim produced four possible endings to the musical in terms of four different songs. "Marry Me a Little" suggests Bobby makes a half compromise between marriage and autonomy, "Multitudes of Amys" sees Bobby arrive at a straightforward romantic decision to marry, and "Happily Ever After" entails a refusal to marry because it leads to imprisonment. But "Being Alive" (the song finally chosen for the finished version of the musical) presents Bobby as accepting marriage as a compromise and embracing an ambivalent happiness. This is accompanied by pain yet involves joy, embodying a fundamental contradiction that the autonomy of a single life could never attain. But we cannot be sure whether, ultimately, it is Bobby and the musical that produces this seemingly happy ending (is it real or simply more projection on his part?) or the audience at the musical who decides this is indeed the proper resolution and goes home thinking that a happy ending has occurred. *Company* appraises the romantic American ideal of love and marriage and treats it as an illusory version of the commitment that marriage implicates (it is not happy ever after). In this it adopts a cynical tone, but the cynicism is reserved for the ideal and not for marriage itself. Marriage is valued here, but only when its reality is embraced. The illusion is to refuse the ambiguities, tensions, and conflicts that make a reality of its commitment, but this entails a consciousness that rejects both narcissism and idealism for a genuine and interdependent relationship of human value and possibility.

Into the Woods (1987) enlarges on the theme of the necessity of interdependence for human existence, both in term of community and generational relationships. This show, as Gordon (1992) points out,[2] substantiates Donne's claim that "No man is an island" and becomes a paean to the brotherhood of man. In this sense, it reiterates the very ideological foundation on which America was built as a new post-Enlightenment society. But it deconstructs this foundation by exposing the transformation of the ideal into a world of egotistical and selfish individualism organized by the promise and pursuit of mere and gross material needs and desires.

Into the Woods is constructed in terms of a fairy tale in which four traditional stories—*Red Riding Hood, Cinderella, Jack and the Beanstalk,* and *Rapunzel*—are woven together by an original plot. This controlling story is of a childless couple (a baker and his wife) who have been cursed with barrenness by their neighbor, a witch, for the ruin of her garden by the baker's father. In order to break the spell, the baker and his wife must now set out on a quest. This is what brings them into and intrudes upon the stories of the four fairy tales in the musical. They have to get hold of Red Riding Hood's cape, Cinderella's slippers, Jack's cow, and Rapunzel's hair. Sondheim uses the format of the fairy tale as one of a quest to fulfill a desire. The subtlety of the musical is how the story of the baker and his wife weaves in and through the similar quests for fulfillment by each of the chief characters in the four fairy tales. For all, the quest entails being subjected to the dangers of its pursuit. This teaches them a lesson about themselves and their desires. So each story, including the original one that frames them, becomes a rite of passage through which insight and maturity are achieved, although this is not to say that fulfillment of desire matches expectation in these stories. On the contrary, the characters come to recognize the ambivalence of desire and the problems that follow from its satisfaction. With this they learn to compromise.

The wood they must enter to pursue their quest is the dark and dangerous wood of their inner desires, and constitutes a rite of passage. The figures learn, as they exit from the wood after having successfully completed their quest, that achievement does not produce happy ever after. This is how each character in the musical reaches maturity as innocence is replaced by truth. So Red Riding Hood learns both the thrills *and* terrors of indulgence. Jack must be taught a similar lesson, and he also has to compromise his moral code to achieve his goals. His melancholic farewell to his cow has its sentimentality undercut by the concluding hope that when he finally sees the cow again it will not be on a plate. Cinderella, despite her experience of family rejection and her ultimate triumph in marrying the prince, has come down to earth. Replying to the baker's questioning of what happened at the ball, she ecstatically recalls the triumph of her grand entrance. But when asked about the prince she can only say how "nice" he is and the mundane fact that he is tall. There is a similar deflation for Rapunzel, who is forced down from her tower. Similarly, the baker and his wife, in their struggle to wrest the articles from their rightful owners, must face certain painful choices. In the first place the baker discovers that he must breach his male instinct for autonomy and independence and recognize the need for love and understanding and the value of cooperation. Moreover, the couple must face the uncomfortable fact that in their overwhelming desire to obtain their wish they have lied and cheated. This has unfortunate consequences that must ultimately be confronted.

The baker and his wife's quest, and its entanglement with all the other quests, is used by Sondheim as a paradigm of contemporary America and the pursuit of modern American Dream. The desires of the characters are the desires of its bourgeois capitalist form: the entanglement and its consequences are the social world that the pursuit of this dream produces. The wood through which the social world is lived out becomes the psychological undercurrent. It images the desires and conflicts sets up in society's members, motivating their relations with one another at a largely unconscious level. Sondheim chose the fairy tale for the basis of his musical because of its deeply allegorical, anthropological, and psychological layers of meaning; he had a particular interest in Bettelheim's interpretation of fairy tales (Bettelheim 1978). But much more important to Sondheim is the ethical content of fairy tales and the way in which this allows him to artistically construct the American world of desire and behavior to make his own point in the musical. In the fairy tale world, the individual is liberated by his own choices and behavior; in the real world we are "more dependent on each other... the real world is about being part of a whole" (quoted in Banfield 1993, 383–84). It is this point that the second half of the musical drives home.

In the first half of *Into the Woods,* the characters exit from the wood with their goal achieved but their integrity compromised in the process. They are no longer sure that happy-ever-after has been wrought by their quest. In the second half, they find out that life is far from perfect as a result. But, more, they find out that the problems of the individual are only of minor importance compared with the necessity of preserving community. This is precipitated by the new danger that confronts all the characters—the wife of the giant killed by Jack, who returns to seek revenge. As Green points out, this communal threat has been variously interpreted by critics to represent forces as diverse as "nuclear proliferation, AIDS and the deranged individualism of Reaganomics" (1986, 311). Most likely, it figures a sense of the more general combination of gross materialism and self-centered individualism as an inherently constitutive part of the American Dream: the major force, in fact, that militates against the communal responsibility necessary to preserve society. The confrontation of individualism requires an ethical sense, as opposed to the pursuit of a desire for psychological self-fulfillment. "Understanding ethical distinctions, or the distinction between ethical and psychological fulfillment, means choosing between them" (Banfield 1993, 387). But, in the contemporary world, values are ambivalent and choice is difficult. Thus "in *Into the Woods*, not only does choosing matter, but making the right choice. The dynamics of choice are not self-sustaining...but lead to fruitful or damaging consequences for the whole community. Self-interest is a liability, and once wronged, the giant returns and must be appeased or destroyed" (388–89). In this new and very subtle kind of show, judgments are generally hard to make, especially when they have implications outside of the single individual. It is not, then, as the characters of the fairy tales so insist as they pursue the wish fulfillment expressed by the contemporary American Dream, that the journey into the woods can be followed by happy-ever-after. This fairy tale ending is an illusion, and the society created by individualism is hollowed out by its irresponsibility. The American world is indeed one of individuality and choice, but it is not a wonderland where wish fertilizes contentment and satisfaction to produce a perfect world: only a child dreams of this as real.

Sondheim doesn't advocate an alternative counsel of perfection on which to create a community through a brotherhood of man. What is advocated is sufficient self-understanding and moral sense to recognize the consequences of choice and pursuit of desire and, through such personal maturity, to see the necessity of compromise. Such is the *sine qua non* for a mature communal American society to exist in the complex conditions of the contemporary world. It is a world in which we must individually choose, but wisdom and responsibility and not wish fulfillment are required to make it humane and livable in together.

In *Follies* (1971), America and the American Dream are engaged by Sondheim in a musical that is the very quintessence of his modernist art. It is "about time and memory, illusion and reality, dreams and desires, fantasy and truth...themes explored through one all-encompassing metaphor: the American musical theatre" (Gordon 1992, 76). But this is set within the larger metaphor implied by the title itself—folly. As many critics have argued, the community presented by its characters, and their relations, are a metaphor of contemporary America. Their dreams have broken down because they could not come true, and this is symbolized in the closed and decayed theater of Ziegfeld renown, which is about to be knocked down and in which the characters are brought together for a reunion. The drama made out of this is represented through the format and use of the Broadway musical (in its various historical forms), deconstructed and despoiled in its Americana. In this, Sondheim deploys Broadway to examine,

employ, and exploit the connotative values of the structures underlying the American musical theatre and to reveal their relationships to predominant social attitudes and presuppositions. Realizing that each age has its own particular style, its own unique structures that reflect its beliefs, truths and assumptions, Sondheim uses these patterns both to suggest and to comment upon different social and aesthetic milieux. No style is "innocent," for a choice of style is a choice of a particular reality and system of values. (77)

The reunion brings together two couples and former friends, Sally and Buddy and Phyllis and Ben. The women, when they were young, both danced with the Follies. The romantic Sally had been rejected by Ben and married Buddy on the rebound, but Ben remains the romantic hero of her dreams. Buddy, her husband, is a brash businessman and has become an insecure womanizer because of his doubts about his wife's love. Ben and Phyllis are altogether a more affluent couple, but their marriage is also brittle and desperate. As they meet, the past is reawakened and the false frivolity of this is reenacted by four alter egos who represent their younger selves. The result is the dramatization of a clash between past and present in which the characters come to recognize the psychological malaise in which each of them finds themselves. The conflict between past and present is created through them entering a follies-like show in which they sing a typical type of Broadway song, revealing their psychological state. They find the experience of this self-examination shattering and, as they leave at dawn, the audience is left with the hope that it has proved to be a catharsis for them through which they now may be able to find happiness at last. In this, their particular drama is articulated through Broadway. Theater is seen in a state of degeneration and decline, but this has a much wider signification. "The gloss and artificial glamor, the false values and insecurities are peeling away; ugly crevices have appeared in the shiny surface of the American Dream" (82).

What *Follies* presents is characters who have based their lives and choices on an illusory past and suffered the consequences of this as their memories have suppressed the ugliness, the cruelty, and the boredom it has produced in the present. They have distorted their lives until they are lived in terms of a nostalgic myth of themselves and their past that acknowledges only what is agreeably acceptable to them. The reality surfaces all too openly in the reunion between them. But this is America too— a world living in a past that is as illusory as the future: a utopia in reverse. "Utopianism, whether it looks backward or forward, robs the present of its impact and significance" (Gordon 1992, 78). The Broadway musical is presented as fostering this as popular art, in another form of nostalgic foolishness. Sondheim uses its forms, tradition, and history in *Follies*, but to critical effect in terms of his own theme. In its "many-leveled uses of theatricality, as a profession, a state of mind, and a cultural milieu" *Follies* reveals, according to Gordon, a "profound truth about the American psyche" (78). It demonstrates a loss of faith in the American Dream as a nostalgic illusion that can no longer be perpetuated unless one chooses to love what has completely decayed. It insists instead that a true sense of America, and existence within it, can only be achieved by embracing the complex truths of its modern society. *Follies*, then, is about folly in all its many layers of meaning and is played out in terms of the tragedy and cruelty of self-delusion. The personal folly is essentially one of self-dramatization, where no one comes to see him or herself objectively. It is a folly that makes the past more glorious than the present, because this is the only way that reality can be withstood. The show is about growing old and the selective memory of nostalgia and myth that prevents the acceptance of the truth. The general folly is trying to live over and over again entrenched in fantasies where the past is mythologized because it promotes a sweet fantasy and happiness, however unreal. Such folly is the American Dream, but America must surmount this to have a genuine life again in the present. This is the message of *Follies*, with the corollary that the musical too must, as an art tied to culture, do the same if it is to remain vital and relevant.

In *Pacific Overtures* (1976), Sondheim turns from the internal landscape of America to its foreign relationships. The musical shows how this America was essentially engaged in an imperialist adventure, with the gunboat being deployed to enforce its will. Here the popular reading of America's foreign policy as a Pax Americana on behalf of the good of the world is deconstructed by the recognition that America's entry and intervention on the world stage represents the globalizing trajectory of its successfully developing capitalist modernity. Indeed, the musical reveals that the American mission is a capitalist one, and, in the specific context of Japan, it explores the consequences. Ultimately, the musical suggests that the effect of American intervention in Japan was to corrupt Japanese civilization and increasingly replace it with the "tacky" materialist consumption characteristic of America. Together with recognition of America's aggression in its overseas mission, this sense of corruption makes American foreign intervention the occasion for the exercise of guilt rather than triumphalism. In this respect, as Banfield (1993) argues, Sondheim adopts a different position from the Orientalism through which the East has largely come to be constructed in the West, especially in its music theater. Here the Orient has been traditionally represented in terms of "the allure of the exotic [which is] pre-eminently a matter of color, titillation and escapism" or used to "construct cultural parables, most often comedies or tragedies of conflicting manners" (253). Instead, Sondheim seeks to approach the confrontation and culture clash from both points of view. The drama of this is held together narratively in terms of a narrator, selected portrayals of episodes in the American Japanese relationship between 1853 and 1865, and comparative stories of two Japanese characters and friends in terms of their response to the historical situation. One, Manjiro, a humble fisherman, begins by appreciating America but eventually rejects it because of the upheaval it creates for Japanese culture. His response is to retreat further into the traditional Japan. The other, Kayama, a samurai and minor official, is increasingly intimidated by things American, but eventually embraces the American in terms of a shrewd and manipulative usage that entails rejecting the traditional forms and patterns of Japanese civilization. Manjiro eventually confronts and kills Kayama, but, despite the celebration this produces in the traditionalists, they know in reality that all is lost. So Sondheim does not put forward, "a linear perspective of historical narrative [but] a much more kaleidoscopic one" (254). This, in turn, leads Sondheim to organize *Pacific Overtures* structurally and musically in terms of utilizing the resources of Japanese musical theater (specifically Kabuki) in a marriage with the resources of American musical theater. The result is to create what Sondheim calls a "documentary Vaudeville" that simultaneously keeps the lyrics haiku-like. The point for Sondheim was to develop a musical theater that was genuinely Japanese in its music and form and not a Western musical with an Eastern flavor, but to do so within a total framework that accommodated many of the tonal characteristics of Western music, particularly as they surface in Western music theater. A central part of the subtlety with which he does this consists in a gradual Westernizing of the music of *Pacific Overtures* as Japan, in the dramatic narrative, becomes more Westernized. What emerges then is a musical that is "undoubtedly anti-imperialist and consequently, anti-West" (Gordon 1992, 177). This finds its apotheosis in the show's final number, where the ultimate outcome of Japan's commercial conquest and corruption is dramatized as a thoroughgoing assimilation of the materialism of the West.

A distinctly critical message for America is delivered, too, in the two musicals where Sondheim moves out of the American context altogether for settings. In both *A Little Night Music* (1973) and *Sweeney Todd* (1979), the issue of class is examined in relation to the most sacred of American values: individualism, freedom, and choice. In *A Little Night Music*, the characters inhabit the world of turn-of-the-twentieth-century Swedish aristocracy. The drama concerns their intricate romantic relationships with one another and the eventual outcomes of these (the musical, appropriately enough, takes the form of an operetta). But the luxurious way in which these characters can indulge their pursuit of the entanglements of romance and spin their lives around them is a product of their privileged position. Their attitudes spring from the mores of an aristocratic world and display little demotic sense of love and romance. Consequently, in the dance of life that is portrayed in their love lives, to surrender to love truly can only end in social death. In *Sweeney Todd*, the class-structured modern world is similarly shown to be a determinant of Sweeney's character and his revengeful actions. He is a member of the exploited working class. Revenge is his solution to his disempowerment. He lives in a world in which there are only two choices available to its inhabitants—to eat or be eaten.

The themes of American imperialism (in *Pacific Overtures*), the American Dream (in *Company, Follies,* and *Into the Woods*) and class (in *A Little Night Music* and *Sweeney Todd*) come together in *Assassins* (1990), a musical Sondheim created for off-Broadway. Composed at a time when the Gulf War was brewing and the first President Bush was whipping up patriotic fervor to support another bout of gunboat diplomacy, it not only dramatized the destructive power of the gun, but placed this in a wider cultural context, again conducting a thorough examination of the lies implicit in the American Dream. Its drama focuses upon the nature and motivations of those Americans who have either assassinated or attempted to assassinate the various presidents of America and presents it, again, in the form of "documentary Vaudeville." It shows essentially the fictional character of the American Dream, presenting the assassins as those who, committed to the dream, have had their desires thwarted and hopes blasted by their systematic stratified exclusion from the modern capitalist American world. Thus they take their revenge, through the gun. But it is not, for Sondheim, merely the reality of stratification that is the major problem. There is also the fact that the American Dream is a fool's paradise to begin with that cannot be delivered. So the American Dream must always carry the shadow side of its ambition as a destructive accompaniment that furnishes a constant underlife of aggression and violence that can never be eliminated as long as the dream remains intact. At its most perverse, the dream itself can happily take on a pathological form—assassination can come to be seen as an achievement and stardom (as it is for some of the assassins in *Assassins*). Here the gun becomes, then, a wonder of modern civilization that has the very special quality of delivering power to its user, for whoever has a gun commands attention. In this way *Assassins* questions "the very assumptions upon which the edifice of American idealism is based [by dramatizing] the...thesis that the most notorious killers in our culture are as much a product of that culture as the famous leaders they attempted to kill" (Gordon 1992, 317–18).

It should be emphasized that it is not just in terms of theme that Sondheim's musicals are modernist. The principle of integration in Sondheim, in terms of which his musicals are constructed as music drama, comes out of this modernism too. Content determines form here in a particular way. Each of Sondheim's musicals is given a particular form in terms of this principle but also grounded in what Banfield calls its general *melapoesis*. Banfield coins this term to distinguish the particular character of the art of songwriting in the musical, where vernacular song becomes more than just interplay between the verbal and musical elements. He describes a complete integration between lines of verse and lines of music that becomes the essence of the vernacular (see above, Introduction). For Banfield, Sondheim is the absolute master of melapoetics, at both the local level of the song and the wider structure of the whole show. He revels in the forms of meaning and communication that melapoetics can achieve. In Gordon's view, this causes Sondheim to find a new lyrical, musical, and theatrical language for each of his musicals. In each show, musical and lyrical nuances are perfectly complemented by the appropriate character and the particular situation. In this way, music, lyric, character, and plot are interwoven to form a symbiotic whole (see Gordon 1992, 7). Moreover, the register of language used essentially matches the character so characterization in lyric and music establishes the whole fabric of the character. But, as Banfield points out, Sondheim takes such practices even further by making particular use of diegetic song for dramatic purposes:

> a diegetic song…as music, lyric and gesture…is not just engaged as an artificial means of conveying a point to the theatre audience or highlighting it for their benefit…the song is actually happening on stage as part of the real-life story…it is an item in the narrative plot…It is sung by a character who knows that she is singing, and it implies that the other characters onstage know it too…Song as part of the narrative is an entirely different concern from that of the "integrated" [or book] musical…The integrated musical aims to highlight or simply show what a character is going through by musical…means: in real life emotions, reactions, or decisions would occur either silently and motionlessly, in the mind, or accompanied by talked or whispered or shouted conversation and gesture and movement, perhaps with laughter or tears or even…a certain amount of soliloquy…To add music to them may convey their nature and truth in an unambiguous or even profound way, but it is a highly artificial way…Diegetic song does not so much reverse this approach as cut across it. It implies a different attitude to musical significance and even style…what matters is that it is actually *there*…[because of this] the recognition of musical and lyric style actually becomes an issue in the plot…[and] through the very practicality of its usage it takes on a heavily symbolic role. (Banfield 1993, 184–86)

Diegetic in Sondheim's musicals, first put to use comprehensively in *Follies*, has the same role as it does in film. Whole new layers of dramatic meaning can be conveyed through its use in and in combination with narrative song. Particularly it allows songs to reveal character to the audience although the character does not have enough self-knowledge to describe himself in these terms. So the psychological depth and turmoil in the character can be revealed. This, as we have seen, ties in with the dramatic structure that Sondheim brings to his musicals. They do not have a linear plot. For example, *Company* consists of episodes and cross-sections, and often other characters are no more than Bobby's projections; *Merrily We Roll Along* (1981) goes backwards; *Follies* recounts the first half of its story in flashback and the second half in terms of progress; and *Pacific Overtures* offers a kaleidoscopic presentation of history. There is always a kind of narrative, but it is more the kind of narrative that characterizes cinema and one that is symbolic and at most neorealist. Similarly, there is always character development in Sondheim and invariably characterization of some psychological depth. However, this depth is always achieved in terms of the complex and dense texture of lyric and music and never through reprise.

Finally, there is one further facet of Sondheim's work that is unique. He utilizes the forms and patterns of theater music in a self-reflective way where it comments upon itself (see Gordon 1992, 9). In this, theater music, in addition to conveying emotion, becomes a second-order language:

Certain musical styles are definitely associated in an audience's mind with certain eras, certain emotions, certain truths. Sondheim takes these...musical forms and places them in antithetical situations. Lyric and character are thus at odds with the musical suggestion. Such dislocations of style and content achieves a number of interesting...results, as the audience is forced into examining the truth of the lyric and the contrasting emotional implications of the musical structure. The psychological gestalt of audience expectation is placed in ironic relief. (9)

In all of this Sondheim remains a modernist and not a postmodernist. Certainly his musicals are highly reflexive, but they are not a commitment to deconstruction per se. They are about relativities but are not, finally, relativistic. They remain about the "and" and "either/or" of the world, but they do not reduce it to "just a." He deconstructs the American Dream, but in order to reveal it as an illusion. This does not entail complete rejection of America. Structurally, he deconstructs the musical (partly as part of this thematic deconstruction), but he does not entirely reject the traditions of Broadway. In fact, he argues that his musicals represent the developing trajectory of that tradition—they represent what this development is about and what it responds to. Block (1997) argues suggestively that Sondheim essentially continues the tradition of musical theater but offers a new principle of integration for the musical. In other words, he reveals precisely that other side of modernism, rejected by postmodernism, that is to find the eternal verities in the fleeting and transient modern world (see Harvey 1990). The constant theme of all Sondheim's musicals is ethical—how to establish significant values. His answer is always that of compromise—a compromise that can only be brought about by facing up to realities and abandoning the nostalgia, illusions, delusions, and lies of the American Dream as it has been ideologically and mythically woven into American society and culture. What Sondheim offers in the end, then, is a modernism that entails critical realism as opposed to postmodernism.

One might ask, then, if his musicals are Brechtian, which is sometimes argued by both his supporters and critics. Sondheim himself rejects Brecht because Brecht puts politics entirely before character, whereas character is central for Sondheim. Certainly his musicals make a major appeal to the intellect rather than the emotions and often they are cynical if not pessimistic, and they are highly politicized. Moreover, the music is more dissonant and less tonal and the characters more neurotic. Critics of Sondheim go further and call his musicals cold and bloodless, insisting that he is out of reach and out of touch with the audience for musicals except for the most sophisticated. He is too reflexive, too knowing, too indirect, and too lacking in passion. Some have argued that he is perhaps too novel and experimental for the ordinary audience of the musical. Steyn (1997), however, goes further. Sondheim, he writes, takes pride in embedding his score in the drama, giving no thought to memorable take-home tunes. "His fans seem happiest to hear the songs without book, staging and design, not only on the cast album but also on innumerable recital albums by self-consciously cerebral *chanteuses*" (1997, 135). For Steyn, Sondheim has replaced heart by scowling, emotion by intellect, and minority interests for the interests of a majority, and he is tuneless to boot. Thus he cites Sondheim's *Passion* (1994) as a musical that is the very antithesis of its title.

He has, at one level, a point in that Sondheim's musicals have not proved to be a commercial success on the whole, and probably some of these criticisms of Sondheim's work explain this. But whether it is possible to put heart back in the musical in Steyn's sense, if it means reverting to an old and simplistic Americana to do so, is doubtful. As to the issue of whether his work is emotionless, this is more arguable. Certainly his audiences do not see it as so, although they do recognize that Sondheim is caviar for the general rather than a staple diet for the masses. In many ways, Sondheim's effect on the musical *has* been to create a musical for connoisseurs, and this may be not so problematic in itself. What does become problematic for the form of the musical pioneered by Sondheim (which is very rich in an aesthetic sense) is if it becomes, as is often the case with Sondheim's musicals in Europe, a musical to be found only in state-subsidized theaters and opera houses and not in commercial theater. Historically the musical has been produced by commercial theater. It may be a tribute to the musical as a form to find itself in the cultural realm of state-subsidized art, but this distances it from popular culture. It is given, through such theatrical institutionalization, the characteristics of "high" culture. Neither popular culture nor the musical could be seen to gain from this in the end, because it would encourage an artifice that loses contact with the organic. More specifically, the musical may lose its ability to entertain. This is central to its nature as popular theater, however critical and didactic it may wish to be, and legitimately so unless one insists on treating art and popular culture as antithetical—always the fault of the Frankfurt School and Critical Theory as well as the conservative hegemonic art-culture denounced by the former. The critical and didactic have to be sensitive to the entertaining—a point that Kurt Weill clearly recognized in making his own contribution to the Broadway musical, and one that, as he saw it, entailed a continuity with and not a break from his earlier collaborations with Brecht.[3]

THE ROCK MUSICAL

The advent of rock and roll significantly altered the American music business but not the musical to begin with, except in a way that excluded it from the transformation of American popular music and culture effected by rock and roll. Emerging, as it did, with youth self-consciously establishing itself as a generation in "association with a growing affluence that permitted a market for [rock and roll] to be established...it reshaped the music business and split the music market" (Shaw 1985, 15). Now the older generation bought albums of recordings by the old and established artists while the younger generation bought rock-and-roll singles. These constituted the expression of this youth culture and were central to its development to the point where the single eventually became the central basis of American popular music itself. The musical originally held out against the rock-and-roll revolution, partly because of its audience, which consisted of the older generation. This effectively painted the musical into a corner by making it stand aloof, conservative and middle-aged, and thus something for parents. More importantly, perhaps, the musical's very position in relation to traditional forms of popular music had made theater song seem unassailable as popular culture. In fact Broadway lost out in the transformation of popular music, first as the singles chart came to consist almost solely of rock-and-roll music, then as the album chart began to take the same form, and finally as the film musical (which consisted of the translation of Broadway musicals into film as well as original film musicals) came to a close. One result of this was to force Broadway to live more in its past, which, in turn, cut it off from treating the transformations taking place in contemporary culture. This was reinforced by the essential principle that accompanied rock and roll itself—that its music be authentic and not a form of bourgeois exploitation. That it was far from free of the latter, in terms of its rapid market consolidation and organization by the American music industry, in part explains how Broadway (as itself a commercial enterprise) gave it entry to the musical. Broadway could not afford to lose the audience for rock music and simply rely on its middle-aged audience, particularly as the latter could only consign the musical to an appalling law of diminishing returns. But the entry of rock into Broadway required the musical to find terms that could marry youth culture and its concerns to the dramatic purposes of the Broadway stage. Particularly, how was Broadway to maintain the idea of the authenticity of rock music, which was necessary to draw in a new generation audience?

The answer was not simply a cynical exploitation of rock. Part of the transformative claims of rock popular music and culture was one of experiment, making this an important part of the politicization of youth in the late 1960s in America. Experiment was to be a means of political representation, and by definition theater could become part of this politics and experimentation. But in the name of this ideology of authenticity, most early rock musicals would reach Broadway not as Broadway productions but as experimental productions mounted off-Broadway. Only through their success there did they go on to be restaged on Broadway. Here, however, they came to be subjected to an annexing process of commercialization that sold them in terms of Broadway's own form of audience management and production.

Galt McDermot's *Hair* (1967) was the first major appearance of a rock musical on Broadway. It took as its aim the defiant definition of the mores and beliefs of a politicized and socially rebellious youth culture and positioned these in a critical relation to established middle-class capitalist America. In one sense it was a conceptual musical based around the politics and lifestyle that it proclaimed and represented through a new alternative form of social organization of life that it advocated—the tribe. In this context, *Hair* grew out of the emotional turmoil of the Vietnam War, which generated an antiestablishment politics that promoted dropping out as a reconstitutive political program. With very little in the way of narrative story line, this loosely structured musical celebrated the lifestyle of hippies and flower children, who greeted the dawning of the age of Aquarius by opposing the Vietnam War and the draft, and bourgeois values and standards of behavior and dress. Its transformation from off-Broadway to Broadway entailed a commercial makeover that strengthened what narrative it contained to create a more recognizable drama (focusing on the "hero," Walker Daniels, as a draftee who spends his last civilian hours with a tribe of hippies). It also played up the show's sensational character to achieve hit status. Thus the Broadway *Hair* was made more outspoken in dialogue as well as redesigned to make it wilder and bolder. Famously, it ended the last act in semidarkness, with its entire cast advancing forward to the front of the stage in the nude.

Schwartz's *Godspell* (1971), too, emerges out of this same ostensibly hippie context. It seeks to create a Christian religious message on which to found its idealistic conception of love, but one that matches the social and political demands of a progressive youth culture. Thus Christ becomes an antiestablishment representative. Like *Hair*, *Godspell* first appeared as a conceptual and experimental workshop production at Café La Mama, to be later turned into an off-Broadway musical and then transferred to Broadway. Schwartz saw in Christianity a true and legitimate wellspring for the idealism at the heart of the new youth movement, but argued that it required a new theological image of Christ himself for its reinstitution. Cox, writing of this new youth movement, captures precisely how *Godspell* effects such a transformation:

Christ has come to previous generations in various guises, as teacher, as judge, as healer. In to-day's world these traditional images of Christ have lost much of their power. Now in a new, or really an old but recaptured guise, Christ has made an unexpected entrance on the stage of modern secular life. Enter Christ the harlequin: the personification of festivity and fantasy in an age that has lost both. Coming now in greasepaint and halo, this Christ is able to touch our faded modern consciousness as other images of Christ cannot. (1969, 139)

This is just how *Godspell* establishes a modern Christ and the message of Christianity. It retells the last seven days of Christ with Christ himself in clownish makeup and emblazoned with a Superman *S* on his shirt. His disciples are flower children, and the Gospel becomes enacted in a youthful, contemporary manner. Such transformation allows Schwartz not only to make use of a variety of rock-music forms to structure the musical but also to draw upon the conventions of the various genres of the tradition of the Broadway musical itself (and so make it transferable to Broadway). The idea behind *Godspell* is to weave God's spell over the audience, and it works this out conceptually in terms of the metaphor and experience of conversion—that is, a turning to the divine. This conversion concept is essential to the show's ability to work dramatically for a contemporary world and to do it through the form of the musical. Swain (1990) has argued that traditional forms of musical religious drama, the Passion and the oratorio, already assume a religious experience, which they simply deepen or reinvigorate, but a modern audience is largely secular and so requires conversion. First, in this transformation, they must abandon the source of secularization. So *Godspell* begins with all its characters wearing shirts with the names of the philosophers that have intellectually helped to produce and define the secular society—Socrates, Gibbon, Nietzsche, Sartre, and so on—as they sing simultaneously about an Ivory Tower of Babel. Silenced by a *shofar* (the ram's horn of Jewish ritual), the cast is confronted by John the Baptist, who enters to sing "Prepare Ye the Way of the Lord." Now Christ enters, dressed as a clown—the fool in its very traditional opposition to the philosopher. This, in turn, is designed to identify him with youth culture and the rock festivals of love of the late 1960s. The drama follows from the theme of conversion, which is established through the characters being drawn generally and given first names to make them anonymous figures of the people. This permits the development of an idea that stresses that Christian conversion exalts but does not subvert the individual; this dramatically allows for solo conversions, but also the expression of a range of conversions within the framework of traditional forms. Using different idioms of rock music, each form of conversion is taken up—supplication ("Day by Day"), intercession ("Save the People"), and thanksgiving ("Bless the Lord" and "All Good Things"). These conversions are playful in nature, but intellectual weight is given to the proceedings by using the Gospel of Matthew in its King James version for the lyrics. Finally conversion in Act I proceeds into a kind of Passion Play with

Christ's death in Act 2 as a symbol of a world fallen into agony through the refusal of God to intervene. *Godspell*, then, is a rock musical with a religious message, but it is not simply and only a Christian one. It is about the formation of a community in which mutual understanding and support is its very cement. In this it seeks to capture the idealism of the youth movement. Paradoxically, and like *Hair*, the idealism of *Godspell* can locate itself very much within the humanist philosophical roots of the founding of America, if not in the specific bias of Enlightenment rationalism.

Once established on Broadway, and with youth culture turning away from political revolt to become deflected and institutionalized in consumptory lifestyles, the rock musical was able to make itself a Broadway offshoot as part of the entertainment business's encroachment. Broadway rock musicals began to appear that were commercial products of this catering-to-audience in terms of a conventionalized generationality of lifestyle and social identity. Jacobs and Casey's *Grease* (1972) is particularly apposite in this respect, and again it began off-Broadway (as befits the generational pull of its audience and their world) before moving to Broadway.

Grease is pure entertainment, but it is by no means entirely unsubtle in its musico-dramatic hold on youth culture and its reproduction of the social world. It sets itself within the American High School (Rydell High) of the 1950s and takes an ironic view of the lifestyle of teenagers at the beginning of the rock-and-roll era. In narrative terms it is simple, the chief concern being the attraction between ostensibly "cool" greaser Danny Zuko and a prim and proper Sandy Dumbrowski, who "eventually learns there is little virtue in virtue" (Green 1996, 234). She eventually joins forces both romantically with Danny and socially with the world in which he possesses heroic status as its masculine embodiment. The musical is conventional in the sense of how it produces a view of youth as generation. It chronicles a world of teenage triumphs and emotional angst, largely induced by the calflike nature of their romantic and sexual entanglements, in a world in which the young have "little on their minds excepting hanging out and making out" (234). In this the characters could be seen in highly critical terms as foul-mouthed, self-indulgent, and self-pitying. They mock individuality, celebrate conformity, defend illegitimacy, and undergo every pubescent trauma that is possible, clothing it in complete sentimentality. The tone the musical takes toward them, however while it may be anti-sentimental, is only gently mocking—these are, after all, adolescents, and that is how the musical presents them. It achieves these tonal qualities very effectively in rock-and-roll terms by mobilizing a range of its various styles—energetic, lachrymose, mooning, romantic, aggressive, celebratory, self-pitying, and so on—to achieve its dramatization of the life, society, and characters of the adolescent world of Rydell High School without any pompous moralizing. Rydell and its community becomes a world that is funny rather than reprehensible, but (and here it incorporates this world into the larger American society) also a stage of life, with all its pleasures and traumas, that we must all pass through—these teens (and here the teens of modern America) become all our teens. It is this latter that gave *Grease* its commercial appeal to a wider and larger Broadway audience, well beyond the adolescent youth culture it represents—an American audience of another generation that could identify with it and relive (but now knowingly and with laughter) their own past adolescence.

Other commercial rock musicals have gone off in different directions with a youthful (as well as reminiscing) audience as their target. In this, three different musical forms of structuring the rock musical have appeared. One takes the form of original compositions but, as in the long established Broadway tradition of adaptation, often entails an attempt to update existing and hallowed literary sources. These are reset in the contemporary world and presented in a rock format that will ensure their appeal for today's audience. In a sense, they represent a postmodern musical that seeks to break the divide between high and popular culture through hybridity. But this is also a deliberate marketing strategy that demonstrates the existence of an intricate structural relationship between the contemporary capitalist entertainment business and postmodern cultural practices within the musical. Typical examples would be the rock adaptations of Shakespeare's *Two Gentlemen of Verona* (*Two Gentlemen of Verona* [1971]), *The Tempest* (*Return to the Forbidden Planet* [1989]), *Macbeth* (*From a Jack to a King* [1989]), and now a rap version of *The Comedy of Errors* (*The Bomb-ity of Errors* [2001]). In terms of the revival of music theater itself, Gilbert and Sullivan's *The Pirates of Penzance* (1879) and *The Mikado* (1885) have been recreated in rock terms.

The second form is to create biopic and tribute rock musicals that cannibalize rock in terms of its history and the traditions that have formed within it. This is done through a celebration that produces a canon and iconography, using the original rock music itself to dramatize in biographical narrative or revue. *Buddy* (1990), *Elvis: The Legend Lives* (1978), *Good Golly Miss Molly* (1991), *Smokey Joe's Café* (1995), *Boy Band* (1997), *Great Balls of Fire* (1999), *Saturday Night Fever* (1999), *Stop in the Name of Love* (1988), and *125th Street* (2002) represent this trend, and this list is far from exhaustive. Normally these shows, too, have appeared off-Broadway, to be transferred only if they become highly successful.

Finally, a related new form of rock musical has appeared in which the song catalog of a major pop or rock group is used as the musicological basis for the creation of a drama—so the ABBA catalogue is used in this way in *Mama Mia* (2000) and the Queen catalogue in *We Will Rock You* (2002).

A more serious attempt to create a postmodern rock musical, one that resonates with the earlier experimentation of *Hair* and *Godspell*, is Larson's

Rent. Moreover (and again like these two earlier musicals) it seeks to build a radical social critique of America. *Rent*, too, is a conceptual musical but a hybrid that seeks to bridge the gap between high and popular culture through constructing itself as a rock opera in a relation with Puccini's *La Boheme*. Bohemianism makes an art of life and so produces a world that is creatively constructed and inhabited in these terms. It is *la vie boheme* that supplies the metaphor in terms of which *Rent* is dramatically organized. But now the bohemian life represents both individuality *and* community in a social world where difference, the self-creation of identity wrought by the process of aestheticization of daily life, stands at the center. It is the bohemian life that is seen as constituting a truly human existence here. This becomes the foundation of *Rent*'s social and political critique of contemporary America. It is not simply that the artists of America's capitalist and materialist world cannot pay the rent (as in Puccini's *La Boheme*) but that the rent they must pay to inhabit (and be inhabitants) of the American world is constitutive of their souls. The cash-nexus of the capitalist world has turned the soul into the economic medium of exchange through which social relationships are established. Overshadowing this world is the way the American system is produced through the governance of life on its own behalf. This entails embodying the system through the discipline of the body, as opposed to the care of the soul (to put it in Foucault's terms).[4] Here the social problems of youth can be made to surface in the musical in the current manifestations of drugs and AIDS. These displace Puccini's representation of consumption as the new punishment that carries the young off before they can establish a life of creative freedom, carrying the same menace, however, as punitive judgements meted out, as far as conventional society is concerned, for moral wrongdoing.

The bohemian characters of *Rent*, then, represent the positive future made possible by the aestheticization of life despite the fact that they live in a squat in the Lower East Side of Manhattan and they are artists and their outcast attendants—drug dealers, the homeless, and the poor. The central characters are Mark, a filmmaker and the narrator; Roger, an HIV-positive musician who wants to make a social and cultural contribution before he dies; Mimi, a drug-addicted dancer who works in an S-and-M club; Angel, a drag queen; and his lover Tom. However much they may seem to be the social debris of American society, all these figures are concerned with making their "downtown world understandable to the uptown world without selling out. Their love for one another is what makes their life bearable" (Green 1996, 305).

They are, at one level, impossibly romanticized characters in the extremes of their lives, but this romanticization is essential for the social and political critique of America to be driven home. Critics of *Rent* (Steyn, for instance) have rejected it as obsessive in its anti-Americanism and celebration of everything taboo, and they compare it unfavorably as a postmodern hybrid with the classical model to which it seeks to establish intertextuality. It is true, of course, that Puccini had all the resources of nineteenth-century romantic and late-romantic music theater at his disposal to make his opera, whereas *Rent* draws on the more limited resources, perhaps, of the rock musical. But the real center of this critique of *Rent* is not the musical superiority of *La Boheme* but, rather, a claim that the latter is somehow more universal and transcendental in its dramatic portrait of bohemian life. *La Boheme* is certainly not this at all—it is essentially a work situated well within a particular musical and dramatic tradition. Indeed, the romanticism of *La Boheme* is very much located culturally and socially within late-nineteenth-century Europe and the mores and morals of an emergent European capitalism. In *La Boheme,* Mimi's death symbolically marks the social transgression of the bohemians and their lives and is offered as suitably enacted on her, as a woman, for her defiance of the institutional conventions and the patriarchal structures of this world. That *la vie Boheme* is not a genuinely possible life is Puccini's ultimate message in *La Boheme.* In *Rent,* Mimi and Angel, too, die in relation to their social transgression: Mimi of drugs and Angel of AIDS. But the musical does not end on that note of pessimism. Instead, the characters reemerge, in spirit if not in body, to join the rest of the cast in a celebration of living the day in their contemporary lives in the hope that a future can be resurrected from it. The bohemian life is not a phase here but an art of living that is worth fighting for as a better life. Everyday life is claimed for aesthetics and not in opposition to it. The romanticism of *Rent* is a different thing from that of Puccini's *La Boheme.* Even if the former remains idealistic and still largely the prerogative of youth, age is not treated as essentially inimical to it. Moreover, this romanticism restores to the Broadway musical what Steyn complains it has lost, and without which it can never recover—heart. But heart here is not just the heart of Middle America. It involves a sense of an emotional appeal to and direct relation with the audience—what, at a more general level, the musical had always appealed to as popular music theater and genre. It does not revert to the older Americana dream, because it takes on the new American world and gives heart to, perhaps, an originary American Dream that had liberty and equality as its goal and not affluence and consumption. It could be argued that, without rock music as its basis, it would be difficult for *Rent* to find an audience to listen to its message, even if that audience might face problems in entertaining it.

Another serious attempt to create a postmodern musical appeared with the Pet Shop Boys' *Closer to Heaven* (2001). This too sets out to create a sense of contemporary social life in which individuality and community attempt to find expression in a world where difference has moved to the center. This musical, however, speaks for a voice hitherto silenced by the narrative world of heterosexuality and its prescriptive celebration by the musical. *Closer to Heaven* thematizes the gay world, presenting its life and mores particularly in relation to how they have been given self-expression in terms of gay liberation movements of various types, thus becoming institutionalized within the public gay world itself. In this, *Closer to Heaven* responds to the fact that the gay community has become a recognizable social and economic presence in the modern world, and one of manifest significance for the very contemporaneity of plurality in lifestyles and identities. Moreover, in incorporating this world, *Closer to Heaven* deliberately seeks to find a new audience for the musical in terms not only of the gay community but also of youth generally who seek to shape their lives with an emergent postmodern context. In this, it challenges what Marmion has referred to as a musical theater dominated "by the suburban supremacism of Andrew Lloyd Webber and Cameron Mac-Intosh with shows such as *Phantom of the Opera* and *Les Miserables* [and] revivals such as *My Fair Lady* or catalogue musicals such as *Mamma Mia!*" (2001). The Pet Shop Boys, for their part, themselves insist that what they are attempting to create is a musical that is cool. This has much to do with attracting a new audience—for instance, people who go clubbing. "A lot of young people…wouldn't dream of going to a theatre. What we're putting on here is a show we hope they can enjoy and not be put off by the fact that its the theatre or a musical" (quoted in Marmion 2001).

Closer to Heaven creates its postmodern form also in the hybrid relationship that it develops with the traditions of the musical itself. The Pet Shop Boys' understanding of the contemporary musical stage of Broadway and the West End as the now "uncool" that can be made cool implies a regard for the earlier manifestations of musical. Specifically, they claim to have always liked "the high emotional content" of the musical. "That's one of the reasons we've made a lot of dance music. In musicals you can express very strong feelings" (quoted in Marmion 2001). In other words, for them, the musical has heart, and this they seek to develop in a new way for a new audience. It is perhaps not surprising that *Closer to Heaven*, like *Rent*, resonates with heart in this traditional sense. Moreover, the format of *Closer to Heaven* is not that of the blockbuster megamusical but rather of the smaller conceptual musical. The gay world is staged largely in terms of a gay club and the characters who inhabit it: the cabaret and drag show artistes and performers, its owner, his daughter who has returned from the past to rejoin him, and the bar staff, together with others who relate symbiotically to the gay club scene. Their lives and world are treated in terms of a musical comedy that is both sympathetic and ironic by turns and that darkens into tragedy at the end as the negative traits of their gay world are exposed in terms of the consequences they produce. Yet, from this (just as in *Rent*), a new transformation emerges for the hero. From the potential for embitterment that inheres in the gay world, *Closer to Heaven* distills the possibility of a movement into a heaven itself where fun, freedom, individualism, and camaraderie are translated into self-discovery, relationship, and creativity as a responsible social way of being in terms of difference. In this *Closer to Heaven* reasserts the traditional message of the musical that it is love that makes us truly authentic and binds us together in human relationships with one another whether we are, or inhabit a world that is, gay or straight. Without this potential, the musical suggests that the gay community can only be a glittering and ersatz simulacrum of straight community, eaten away at because the seemingly glamorous hedonistic wing merely disguises an ultimately egotistical life on the part of its members, where even pleasures are a source of disconnection, discontent, and destruction. Thus, although the musical is invested with all the fun and exuberance of a riotous campery, it also stages a desperate and manic defense at work, linked to the satisfaction of instinctual desire in the pursuit of selfhood that ultimately fuels exhaustion, atomism, and cynicism. The musical uses the drug-taking of its characters to symbolize this darker projection and to arrive at the climactic and penultimate scene, in which all the characters lie on stage collapsed into drug-induced but completely individualized states of oblivion. They are a collective ensemble, but not a community. The cries for help of the hero's newfound boyfriend and lover go unheard by them, and he dies as a result of his particular and personal drug-trip. This unrelatedness, with its tragic consequence, creates an end to the musical that, nevertheless, offers a "hearted" and utopian message where the characters recognize the need for mutuality and care to prevent their demands for authenticity and self-realization as gays from descending into mere hedonism, egotism, and anomie.

The narrative of *Closer to Heaven*, then, is a tale of love and romance. But it is love and romance in a gay world in which boy meets boy, where the hero and his erstwhile lover find love by awakening to their authentic selves and eventually coming out through a loving relationship with one another. The sexuality of this relationship is not disguised, but recognized to be an essential expression, to the point where the beginning of their romantic union is presented in terms of an explicit sex scene. *Closer to Heaven*, then, opens up the musical to contemporary social reality but remains committed to the traditional concern with love and romance and its expression through music and dance with a high emotional content. In making the "uncool" cool again for a new audience, *Closer to Heaven* utilizes rock music and the creation of dramatic worlds and characters who resonate with the world of plural lifestyles and identities. It also takes characters, and the audience, backstage into the commercial world of rock music. In much of this, it creates a humorous and satirical musical comedy that captures, sympathizes with, and mocks the world it portrays by presenting an ironic but understanding distance. *Closer to Heaven* is above all a musical that is designed to be an entertainment. But, at heart, it is also a musical comedy with a serious intent—it proposes to give a voice to the authenticity of difference, but also chooses to evaluate what would give difference genuine worth. Here the message registers a commitment to the enshrining and establishment of community, albeit in a new form. In short, the utopia *Closer to Heaven* offers is the one that the musical as a popular cultural theater has historically celebrated. In this respect it is, for all its postmodern and deconstructive innovation, consistent with the strongest and most long-lasting traditions of musical theater.

NOTES

1. See also Hastings (1969).
2. See also Zadan (1990).
3. This is, of course, Kurt Weill. See Block (1997, chap. 7) for an account of Weill and the musical.
4. See Foucault (1988).

CHAPTER 6

Modernity, Globalization, and the Megamusical

Steyn (1997) argues that the advent of the conceptual musical and the disappearance of the American Broadway book musical allowed the British musicals of Andrew Lloyd Webber to enter and dominate Broadway from the mid-1980s by taking over the musical's traditional mass middle-class audience. Burston (1998b) agrees about this audience, which he refers to as "lowbrow," but points out that what arrived with the British on Broadway was also an altogether new and different form of the musical—the "megamusical." He sees this as part of a larger transformation in the production of popular music by the electrification or digitalization of recorded music and its creation of virtual environments. This, he argues, is a part of the general global transnationalization of cultural production.

Megamusicals share, according to Burston, a number of essential criteria that set them apart from other music theater productions. These include,

First, markets characterised by rapid global expansion and marked internal growth since 1980...Second, megamusicals are produced and controlled by a select and specific group of highly capitalised globally competent...players. Pioneer British megamusical producers Andrew Lloyd Webber and Cameron MacIntosh, each heading what are now large global companies, have lately been joined by Disney. And the broader field of stage musical production is crowded with new transnational players including Polygram, Viacom and M.C.A. [Finally, the] megamusical's third most distinctive characteristic is its cultivation of specific commercial, technical and aesthetic models of production. This has ensured the replication of any given show with unprecedented meticulousness across a greater number of international venues [to a degree uncommon in] the field of theatrical production even fifteen years ago. (1998b, 205–6)

The result of this has been the globalized transnationalization of music theater along the lines of Fordist methods of mass production, where the essential output is the reproduction of the show on a uniform basis globally. That is to say, the musical has become subject to a

rationalising, industrial logic, including a quality control model implemented and supervised outward from a given metropolitan centre [which is seen by many of those inside music theatre] to replicate technical and artistic production details with such rigour as to delimit the creative agency of performers to a significant degree. Hence the increasing use, by these…insiders, of terms like "cloning," "franchising" and "McTheatre" to describe the megamusical business.

The industrial production of the megamusical to create a show that is essentially standardized, rationalized, and reproducible is achieved primarily through the megamusical's "sonic texts," which reflect an increasing homogenization of both musical sound and acoustics at the level of staging that is in parallel to the highly standardized performance practices and production methods that are employed. This is made necessary by the fact that the megamusical is a global product and subject to the commercial conditions that govern its profitable production within a world market. Central to this standardization is the sound of the megamusical, which is no longer based simply on the radio microphone placed on stage and shared by the performers, but carries through the radio microphone taped to the performers' bodies. This sound and the musical accompaniment is distributed into the theater by loudspeakers around the stage proscenium arch and either side of the audience in the auditorium. The whole show sound is then digitally mixed on a soundboard by the theater technicians. The result is to create a particular sonic text in which the aural realm moves to the forefront and shapes megamusical production and performance practice in two ways: in terms of its volume, which now becomes cinema-sized by comparison with the normal live-theater sound, and of its essential commercial sound, which is that of FM radio, CDs, and TV—a "white" sound scrubbed of all extrinsic noise to give it the homogenized quality that these other media of sound production possess. In this respect, the sound of the megamusical no longer emanates from the performers or is shaped by the acoustics of the theater in which it is performed, but from the sound technology itself. So, as Burston argues, this creates a virtual rather than a live theater, which is further reinforced by the fact that technology now determines the compositional style of the megamusical. The music of the megamusical has to be to brought into line with commercial global songwriting and, particularly, its now typical form, which is that of "soft" rock. In the same way, the performers are disembodied to reduce their interpretative agency. The sound the audience hears from them is not one that is a product of the projection by them of their voices, but of the technology through which their voices (and the orchestra) are projected into the theater. Bodily performance effort is thus considerably diminished. The traditional "belting" singer of Broadway is no longer needed in the megamusical, as the technology produces all the sound and its projection, range, and volume. The result is to produce an audio-visual split. The audience no longer hears what it sees. Instead, the audience is treated to a hyperreal sound and a virtual theatrical production that ensures reproducibility and transferability of the show from one site to another in a completely homogenous fashion. In this way the actors are turned into props, rather than characters embodied by themselves as subjects and agents in which their own identities are central—they become signifiers in the total text of the musical (see Burston 1998a).

There is no doubt that the text thus produced can be spectacular, both aurally and visually. Indeed, according to many critics it is precisely a sense of the spectacular that the audience is expected to take away from a megamusical, as opposed to any specific tunes or performances. Thus the frequently made comments about megamusicals in this respect. It is the spectacle of the crashing chandelier in *The Phantom of the Opera* (1988) and the landing of the helicopter in *Miss Saigon* (1989) that constitute the real show, rather than the lyrics, songs, and performances. The Disney-created shows *Beauty and the Beast* (1994) and *The Lion King* (1997), for instance, are particularly notable for their extravaganza qualities. Even the effort to create a megamusical trading on global multiculture, like the recent *Bombay Dreams* (2002), becomes essentially wedded to spectacle.

The sonic change, then, that characterizes the megamusical corresponds with the ascendancy of a spectacular visual aesthetic in which there occurs a simplification of music, words, and narrative. With it, according to many critics, "live" music theater loses the characteristics that form precisely the value of an "authentic" live theater. Instead these are replaced by the sonic environment of recorded music (and often that experienced in private and domestic listening spaces as well as the cinema) and a drama of spectacle to end the

particular sense of interconnectedness between performer and listener: a sense of union which is understood by many if not most musical performers to diminish the more it is mediated by audio technologies which augment...the audio visual split...from one theatrical "room" to another—a sense of communion between two groups is affected [a dialogical authenticity] which is impossible to create in any other fashion. For many working in the musicals business, the unique, minimally mediated, live or quasi-live quality of this communication continues to constitute the essence of theatrical experience. (Burston 1997, 215)

The hyperreality and virtuality of the megamusical, Burston argues, is a requirement of the industrial and commercial logic of which it is part. The show must be homogenized, standardized, and rationalized to make it transferable from site to site (its producers insist that this is not actually standardization but an attempt to ensure that the show has the same high quality wherever is it produced). This standardization also reflects the nature of the global audience for the megamusical. It is a growing audience (and hugely so) and essentially one that has been brought up on cinema, FM radio, CDs, TV, and pop concerts, and therefore carries with it the sound environments of these other media. It recognizes that pop music is well established as the global music. Digitized sound conformity is expected. In the same way, it is argued, the megamusical is not reflexive and text-driven but rather a theater of spectacle, which equates it, in terms of drama, with these other mainstream and mass media. Moreover, the megamusical makes use of these other media for its construction. It is worth noting here how this kind of show is able to use stars from other media, who are not music theater–trained, as performers, and so tie itself to established audiences. For Burston, following Adorno, the audience for the megamusical, partly because of its experience of other popular cultural media and entertainment, is essentially passive.

Familiar ... with the giant sounds of contemporary cinema or the even acoustics of television, the growth of segments of the stage musical's increasingly global audience share more contemporary sonic tastes: tastes that position the auditor in a more passive role of reception ... Producers, musicians and designers all regularly divide the history of the audience reception of the musical into two eras. In the first and only recently superseded era, pre-dating the widespread usage of radio microphones, audiences "listened." In the second, current era, they merely "hear." (1998a, 214)

Steyn (1997) refers to the "maximalism" of the megamusical to characterize its style of melapoesis and drama. Traditionally, the musical was a popular artistic genre organically connected to popular culture, musically by the vernacular nature of its song and dance and dramatically by narrative, lyric, and dialogue that was contemporaneous with and engaged the society of its time. This gave it its essential vitality and relevance. But, in this, the musical was also essentially American: as Steyn would perhaps put it, the musical oozed America (and, for most of the time, celebrated it). For him, the British megamusical (although this could be extended to megamusicals generally) lacks both vernacular status and contemporaneity, because it is neither related to the tradition of the musical nor to contemporary society. Crucially, it lacks any specific localized cultural character or identity that would provide a source to give it a content through which to form itself as a reflexive musical-theatrical expression. Instead, it is about maximum value, maximum technology, and maximum money. Thus Steyn quotes, with approval, Lionel Bart's comment that very little has changed about the contemporary musical except its commercial drive (in terms of merchandising, for instance) and the new ability for exact reproductions so that many productions of the same show can be staged around the world (see 1997, 173). This echoes, of course, Burston's view that spectacle and sound establish the essential character of the megamusical. With this kind of show it is the treatment rather than the text that is central, a quality that follows from the transnational global nature of the megamusical.

There is an element, musically, of experiment in the megamusical, and that is its typically sung-through composition, which gives it the musical style of an opera. But in this too, as a critic like Steyn would again maintain, it is possible to argue that megamusicals become like something else, in this case like cinema (particularly silent cinema), proceeding dramatically through gestures, images, and music. So once again the megamusical is aligned dramatically with the general industrialized and global transformation of popular culture and its products. Moreover, even in this operatic experiment, it could be suggested that the new musical typically loses it specific character as a musical. For Banfield, opera and the musical are essentially different forms.

In opera, traditionally, the music commands an exclusive viewpoint on the drama...it cannot be resisted or resist itself...In the musical, however, music...[or] song...has traditionally behaved much more self-consciously and *presentationally*, that is, as one mode of representation rather than its governing medium; and indeed we could say the same of dance, comic dialogue and all other stage topoi that make up a show. Correspondingly, music is often the subject of representation on stage: it can often not just move in and out of the drama but in and out of itself. (1993, 6–7)

Steyn would seem to concur when he writes about the tension of a musical residing in the movement from dialogue to underscored speech, then to the verse and chorus of song (see 1997, 278). The effect for him of the operatic sung-through form of the megamusical is to leave one with a swamping score, singing out information since everything is sung, which loosens the relationship between song and lyrics. It is no longer the case, as it is very specifically in the book musical and also in the conceptual musical, that the lyricist has to find a lyric idea that indicates the moves in song that are constitutive of the music theater and drama of the musical. The megamusical, because of its operatic form, finds it extremely difficult to make a musical distinction between trivialities and big character soliloquies, because big and small moments carry the same melodic weight.

Essentially then, the megamusical, for all its overwhelming size, has been understood as a diminution of the real tradition. The centering of the megamusical around the treatment of the text rather than on the text itself, stemming from the industrialization of its production and performance practices, has been thought to empty it of content or deflect content dramatically onto its form, at least for many critics.

It is not difficult to find confirmation of such views, where spectacle, universal sound qualities, and so on become everything. Schönberg and Boublil's *Les Miserables* (1986), for instance, reproduces *The Phantom of the Opera*'s operatic and spectacular form, but with very little engagement. Using Victor Hugo's novel as its basis, it tells the very full narrative of the traditionally valorized hero Jean Valjean over a period from 1815 (after he has been released following 19 years spent on a chain gang, the punishment for stealing a loaf of bread) to the 1832 student uprising in Paris. Throughout the sequence of events that follows his release, Valjean is relentlessly pursued by the fanatical police inspector Javert, who, after chasing his quarry through the sewers of Paris, drowns himself because he has violated his obsessive code of justice by allowing Valjean to escape. The point being that *Les Miserables* is precisely and only a saga, and spectacle constitutes its *raison d'être* rather than content. In this context various critics have pointed to the historical vagueness of the show. It is about some revolution, but who exactly is revolting against whom and what they are revolting about is far from evident. The authors of the show have responded with the suggestion that this vagueness is a strength, arguing that *Les Miserables* carries a generalized sense of revolt against injustice that is applicable to all times. They point out that it has inspired audiences against authoritarian political regimes when performed in Eastern Europe. It is difficult, however, to see the force or accuracy behind such extravagant claims. The fact is that *Les Miserables* is dramatically blank in terms of content—and is filled instead, by spectacle.

Miss Saigon, by contrast, intends a specific critical perspective and involves an anti-American thrust. Set in the Vietnam War, Puccini's *Madame Butterfly* is here updated to create a modern operatic story showing the clash of two cultures. The story begins with the fall of Saigon in 1975 and focuses on Kim, a young rural Vietnamese woman who comes to Saigon looking for work. On her first meeting with Chris, a marine guard at the United States embassy, they fall in love. Without knowing she is pregnant, Chris gets evacuated home and marries. A few years later he and his American wife come back to find Kim, who pleads with Chris to take their son back to the United States. To make sure he does, she kills herself, thus making Chris himself entirely responsible for the child. The drama of *Madame Butterfly*, then, is given contemporary relevance by virtue of its setting and exposure and through the Engineer figure, emblematic of a cruel greed that will survive under any circumstances. But, as Mellers (1996) argues, its model manages to achieve a much more reflexive and critical relationship to the issue of modernity, imperialism, and the clash of cultures. Puccini created a musical and dramatic language, inherited from Verdi, that had become increasingly sentimental and popularist and so readily lent itself to the expression of romance and suffering. In this respect, it shares a degree of parallel ground with the twentieth-century musical. Moreover, *Madame Butterfly* "potentially fused the old type of musical theatre with the new. Its very story is about the clash between the Old World and the New (forward-looking, scientific, materialistic, competitive)" (20–21). In thinking that, for a time, he might buy love until he marries, and so contracting a marriage Japanese-style with Butterfly, Pinkerton trivializes and exploits the relationship with her—while she believes that she has truly married him, which entails sacrificing her Japanese identity for a Western one. The music associated with Pinkerton is

as brashly assertive and as "Western" as the Stars and Stripes anthem that follows him around, and is at the opposite pole to Butterfly's music, which is melodically rooted in non developing "oriental" pentatonicism and is harmonically rootless in augmented fifth chords and whole-tone progressions. The collocation of these antithetical musical techniques, as of the two human beings they render audible, can end only in disaster. (20–21)

So, as Mellers goes on to argue, "Puccini's projection of the social contexts in which his creatures move are as brilliant as his revelation of their identities" (21–22). In this respect, *Madame Butterfly* becomes a contemporary drama and parable about the modem world. *Miss Saigon,* by contrast, is unable to achieve this musical and dramatic realization of culture clash. The music, loud soft rock, is undelineating and, once again, the spectacle takes over the drama—this time, in the form of a helicopter landing on the stage to rescue Chris as Saigon falls to the Vietcong. The lyrics, through which ideas around imperialism, exploitation, and culture clash are presented, though vernacular, are dramatically ineffective and rarely expressively communicative. But it is not just the comparison with *Madame Butterfly* that suggests the musico-dramatic failure of *Miss Saigon* as a musical about modernity. As we have seen, Sondheim's *Pacific Overtures* manages a powerful address on similar themes, and in musico-dramatic terms that preserve the melapoesis of the musical and thus its distinctiveness as a genre.

The poor state of the megamusical may not be universal, but where it fails the problem does seem to stem from its replacement of content by a form in which spectacle and sound are constitutive of its nature. Lloyd Webber's *Cats* (1982) classically illustrates the triumph of staging over content, where the differentiation between the cats, which is the drama, is primarily carried by the staging and not by musical characterization. This problem is borne out not only by the megamusicals that are original compositions but also by the revival of old Broadway hit musicals reshaped in megamusical terms. One example is *Crazy for You* (1992), which combined numbers from the

Gershwins' *Girl Crazy* (1930) with other Gershwin numbers to play up and maximize the potential of an all-singing all-dancing extravaganza. A second is the 1994 production of *Show Boat* (1927), in which the set and production mustered all the technological resources of theater to cross musical with cinematic techniques. Here the point was reached where the *mise-en-scène* overshadowed the narrative and the drama turned into a mere series of tableaux, a cavalcade. Kern's serious address on the course of American life and history through the personal dramas of its characters was seriously undermined, if not entirely obscured. This suggests that, for all the exceptions, partial and otherwise, Burston is generally right to argue that the megamusical is essentially market-driven and a product of a global capitalist cultural industry brought to music theater. The megamusical is a show that largely lacks a specific national content, and utilizes a kind of universal technological sound. In its spectacle, it can be taken away as an experience that often requires relatively little of its audience. Above all it is a show that can be reproduced and merchandised globally.

As Burston suggests, the centralizing of production is closely linked to the ideology of the contemporary world of global capitalism—neoliberalist and celebratory of the market, especially in terms of the seemingly now triumphant victory of capitalism over socialism. He points out that the three major theatrical centers for the musical—Broadway, the West End, and Toronto—are sited in countries in which the government actively promotes a cultural policy that is essentially geared to the market financing and provision of the arts. In America, Reaganism supplemented deregulation inside and outside the cultural sector with a sustained attack on the National Endowment for the Arts as lefty and immoral. This legacy was taken over by President Clinton. Moreover, it is conjoined with the war of attrition faced by the American Corporation for Public Broadcasting, in which telecommunications legislation has turned the *de facto* revitalization of corporate conglomeration in broadcasting into a *de jure* situation. In Britain, from Thatcher on, there has been a constant tilting of cultural provision toward the commercial in which state subsidy for the arts has been systematically reduced. This forces the Arts Council and its clients to operate on market principles, promoting the commodification of popular culture and leaving experimental theater with little source of funding. In Canada, state-subsidized cultural institutions have been starved of funds, and the grant to the Canada Council has steadily fallen. So theater is forced to produce works for a mass market in order to survive, which is partly why the megamusical came to take off in Toronto.

Of course, the tie between the musical and commerce is in no sense new. But in the past the relationship managed to sustain the art as well as the entertainment value of musical theater. The problem of the global megamusical is whether the musical is being reduced to entertainment alone. This seems to be an even more glaring issue when musicals that have genuine artistic provenance have difficulty in finding a popular audience to entertain.

Clearly this formulation of the state of the modern megamusical is more than simply justified. It is in many respects compelling, but it is important to realize that it is not the whole story. In its extreme version, it represents too total a criticism, as even Steyn and Burston recognize. The megamusical is often overpackaged and anodyne, but, equally, it can and has created music drama with some success and within the traditions of music theater. In this sense, even with the megamusical, there are elements of continuity. Pete Townshend's *Tommy* (1993), for instance, is a rock opera in which the rock music is original and far from anodyne in the use it makes of vernacular to construct a drama that takes up the contemporary world thematically. It tells the story of a four-year-old boy who loses all his senses after witnessing his father killing his mother. Unable to communicate, he later becomes a pinball wizard and develops into a messianic superstar. Spectacle (and thus treatment) remains central to *Tommy*'s musico-dramatic construction, with the plot being developed by impressive sets and video projections, but the show is more than just spectacle.

Equally, a sung-through musical can work as a musical theater. Lloyd Webber's *The Phantom of the Opera*, for instance, has a story and characters that are absolutely made for its broad sweeping melodies and operatic form. It is the story of a virginal woman (Christine) who is caught between two different men, the Phantom and Raoul, and the two different kinds of love they offer. In this Christine is presented with the choice of erotic love, through which she can take up a career in the theater as an artistic and self-determining but deviant person, or domestic love, in which she will embrace the traditional role of wife and mother and submit herself to this. Christine and Raoul's duet ("All I Ask of You") presents this second choice, and, aware of the danger of the first choice, Christine asks Raoul to protect her from making it ("Angel of Music"). Musically, as Burston has shown, the score throughout represents the opposition between erotic and marital love in terms of atonality and tonality. The Phantom's music is atonal and dissonant (particularly the opera that he has composed, *Don Juan*), just as his erotic love and tutelage are sinister. Raoul's love is presented in tonal music that celebrates a commitment to bourgeois values and the bourgeois worldview. This conflict is also paralleled theatrically by further sets of binary oppositions—night and day, black cloaks and white dresses, art against life, and sin against virtue. Christine, in the end, chooses a marital destiny, because she cannot accept the love and world proffered by the Phantom. In this way the very music of *The Phantom of the Opera* continuously trades on Western and nineteenth-century tonal normatives to persuade us of the correctness of this choice (which is never questioned) as the proper choice for a woman. Thus Lloyd Webber's own well-known commitment to a conservative and retrospective worldview

is posed through the interplay between tonality and atonality. Not only
would Christine's choice of the Phantom threaten the stability of the social
order and its basis in traditional heterosexual relationships, but atonality
in music is itself presented as a form of chaos in Western culture. *The Phantom of the Opera* thus becomes a megamusical that is formally integrated,
albeit in conservative ways. It carries a very powerful ideological message, which is essentially that of the necessity of maintaining the traditional values of the bourgeois world. Form and content, then, are
consistent in *The Phantom of the Opera;* there is a harmony between the dramatic and ideological terrain it configures and the fact that it is romantic
melodrama that bases itself on a model taken from a nineteenth-century
opera.

The relation between form and content in Lloyd Webber's *Sunset Boulevard* (1994) may be even more integrative. Among other devices, this show
differentiates the characters musically. For Norma Desmond (the central
character), for instance, Lloyd Webber writes music that, according to Steyn,
approximates a silent film score. In song she sounds like an unearthly figure, characterized by ethereal 4/4 ballads, with strange string and wood-
wind arrangements that have a hypnotic-like quality. These orchestrations
are "elusive" and "ambiguous" and help constitute "a surprisingly psychological score" (1997, 282). In an interesting reversal of tradition, the musical
here, instead of being absorbed into the film medium, recovers the cinematic.[1]

However forceful, then, the Burston account of the commodification of
the megamusical may be, there are the exceptions, where spectacle
becomes functional and drama is restored to what is so often "mere" narrative. These are important, not least because they indicate something
about the continued vitality of musical theater.

THE MEGAMUSICAL AS MODERN POLITICAL TEXT,
MYTH, AND FABLE: THE CASE OF *EVITA*

Lloyd Webber's *Evita* (1978) is a further exception. On the cusp of the
megamusical, it is far from empty. It actually offers a powerful myth,
fable, and political text that is rooted in the modern world. Here the spectacle of music theater proves itself an efficient allegory of the politics of the
global world that has itself increasingly become a stage, and it does so in
a critical and realist manner. Yet this show has often stood for the vacuity
of modern musical theater. One characteristic and typically critical dis-
missive view of *Evita* is that of Brustein:

The political implications of *Evita* are the least convincing aspect of the
work…what apparently attracts [the authors] to Eva Peron is her surefire blend of
sex, showbiz and ambition; she is, in short, another superstar who experienced a

similar rise from poor beginnings to great influence. I suspect the real subject of Rice and Webber is success, its rewards and human cost and that has as much political, religious or intellectual significance as one finds in *Aida* or *Madame Butterfly*. (1979, 26)

This is echoed by Swain, who sees *Evita* as

an opera which trivialises all emotion as mere means to an end, there is no possibility of dramatic reflection…Even as a study of power, *Evita* does not work well because Eva is only shown singing about, and never moving among…her people, the source of power…The portrayal, in both the lyric and music, of Eva Peron and Che as political symbols rather than as human characters, eliminates the ambiguous aspects, the hidden dimensions which can make drama out of history. (1990, 307)

Brustein and Swain are mistaken in their criticisms. In both there is a failure to understand the nature of the twentieth-century politics that *Evita* thematizes in its representation of a particular kind of mass expression. Of these politics, *Evita* is a precise, prescient, and articulate theatrical realization. As a musical of politics it has a deep critical intention and thrust. More so than the film version,[2] the stage musical *Evita* is firmly centered on the issue of power and politics and their nature in the twentieth-century world, and sex, showbiz, and ambition play a central part in the story it tells. But Brustein is mistaken to think entertainment is its theme and not politics. Rather, *Evita* shows how these ingredients and their particular forms lie at the heart of modern politics. In a world in which mechanical reproduction, mediatization, globalization, and the aestheticization of the everyday life have become foundational, a correspondingly aestheticized politics of myth, charisma, and spectacle have followed. Swain fails to see that *Evita*'s theatricalization of Eva, Juan Peron, and Che as symbols captures precisely how and in what way this power and politics work. Therein lies its value and importance as a popular work of art. It offers a powerful reading of modern politics, not as a historico-factual record, but as an imaginative and dramatic encounter with its nature. On this basis, it stands as a vital political text about modernity, one that pursues that other traditional function of art in terms of moral purpose and critique. In *Evita* the issues of ambition and power, and their forms of animation, are the central concerns of a moral and critical address, albeit formulated as entertainment.

Evita recounts the tale of Eva Peron and how she achieved the mythical status that she continues to have in Argentina and beyond. It traces her beginnings as an illegitimate child of a landowner born to a poor rural family and follows her rise to the pinnacle of power and position in Argentine politics and society as "Evita"—the very icon and symbol of Argentine nationhood itself. This rise is charted from Eva's first move to Buenos Aires in search of stardom, which she achieves in film and theater, to her meeting with Juan Peron, whose mistress she becomes and whom eventually she will marry. The union between Eva and Juan Peron is struck as a power pact whereby through the Peronist movement the couple will, and do, take political control. As "Evita," Eva comes to be both the nation's figurehead and center of power. This transformation, from Eva Peron to Evita, is the central narrative focus of the musical.

Evita entails a story of glamour and stardom, but, for all its setting in Peronist Argentina, it is not the insidious glamorization of fascism that some have claimed. Rather, it articulates how fascism used spectacle, myth, and glamour as major vehicles for its politics and suggests, by extension, how much this has come to typify the nature of modern mass politics generally, whether right, left, or center, in the mediatized, globalized world. The main political thrust is to show that Eva Peron, transfigured into Evita, is essentially an image constructed in terms of myth and charisma, and how this image is invested with power and a politics of myth thus created and sustained. It engages modern popular culture to highlight its role in the making of modern mass politics. *Evita* is no celebration of this process, but, rather, its theatrical articulation. Moreover, Eva's myth and the world in which she and mass politics flourishes become the subject of a critical address delivered not only through the characterization of Eva and Juan Peron, but also through the figure of Che and what he symbolically represents.

The latter's key critique is achieved partly through the radical commentary that punctuates the show. Thus the musical begins with the scene of mass mourning at Eva's funeral and with Che's first song. This establishes the political theme of the musical and its engagement with Eva and her world. In "Oh What a Circus," Che reflects on how all Argentina has come out in a frenzy of sorrow for an actress who is treated as a goddess and saint—Santa Evita. He interrogates the real significance of her death by pointing out that, once the smoke of the funeral has cleared, people will see the reality of how she, in fact, achieved nothing by doing nothing. The pointedness of this reflection and the accuracy of his analysis of this emotional scene captures modern mass politics precisely[3] and shows the acute sensitivity of *Evita* to it. Throughout the show, a series of songs establishes Che as the vocal vehicle for the exposure of the mythologization of politics that Eva's rise so dramatically represents. In "Revolving Doors" the tawdry route to power is revealed, in "High Flying Adored" the basis for Evita's status is shown as hollow, in "And the Money Kept Rolling In" the corruption behind her rise is exposed, and in "Waltz for Che and Eva" the whole basis of Evitaism/Peronism becomes dependent not only on deadly repression but actual killing.

Evita's interrogation of modern politics, however, is not confined simply to Che's privileged intervention. It is also realized, most immediately, in the periodic critical dialogues between Che and Eva as the former rises to and establishes her power and, indeed, in the wider dramatization of Eva's rise. The story of the latter is clearly not just some tale of stardom and its pitfalls, although stardom is an essential part of its texture. Nor is *Evita* the story of a tragic fall in the conventional sense. In terms of the classical model, Eva is more like the characters who act as the *deus ex machina* through which the hero/heroine is typically tempted, exploited, and brought down than the heroic center itself. She is Lady Macbeth rather than Macbeth, or Iago rather than Othello. Even more, she is the new hero-ine (or hero) created by the modern world of commodification and con-sumption as the charismatic means for the construction of mythical status in terms of popular culture. The people need to adore her, and in moder-nity this means that she must dazzle as an icon of fashionable beauty.

The fated character of Evita, then—and she is truly fated—depends not on a tragic flaw but rather on the operation of a dynamic that binds Eva herself so inexorably to her myth and its popular construction. Her reality becomes the iconic political identity that she comes to possess as part of the structures and strategies that fascist politics deploys. In this way Eva's tragedy is tellingly twentieth-century in nature. She becomes the victim of the mythic status she actively sought to construct and manipulate—the monster that takes over and effaces her human identify. Here the politics of *Evita* moves well beyond issues about personal ambition per se to dramatize style as the engine of a kind of political power.

It is in this respect that *Evita* can be read as a calculating anatomy of political process, rather than an individuated biography. Engagement with character becomes largely secondary to fascination at watching the power process at work, and sentiment is thus situated at one remove. There may be some poignancy in Eva's death at the end of the musical, but even here the pathos belongs largely to the victim herself and her com-plete submission to the Evita myth. The show itself, in the end as in the beginning, makes clear what Eva has done. It fully realizes the monster that has been created.

Evita presents a modern fable textualized in a corrosive aestheticized politics of spectacle. Moreover, the musical accentuates this by graphically drawing on the nature of the specific disease from which Eva Peron died. As she is eaten up by the monster of the myth of her charisma in the pro-cess of its (and her) aggrandizement, so her body is literally eaten up too by the cancer that devours her. The death of identity is replicated by the death of the body in a unity of simile. "Eva" dies away to muteness as *Evita* ends with her silence as its final scene. Only the image that is her myth is left on stage. Her true tragedy—and it is one that belongs to the modern world—is that she can engage in image-construction but not con-trol its effects, and so cannot manage the power this releases.

Evita, then, addresses the aestheticized politics of modernity on all its various levels through a coherent and critical dramatic realization of its nature. Both Eva and "the people" who are her followers take their political existence from their symbolic formation and the symbiotic relation created between them. This is not to deny, however, that *Evita* is also a product of the culture industry and of the technological and media resources within it that commodify its forms. Indeed, things could hardly be otherwise. It started life as a concept of a musical in a recording and developed as a stage musical only after the success of this. Its production was conceived of as a total package, and it was this totality, in the same form, that was reproduced in all of its stagings worldwide. The creation of the film was a continuation of this process. *Evita* was a commercial proposition designed for international consumption. It represents the industrial revolution that has taken place in a live theater that has become transnational in both scope and structure. *Evita* belongs very much, in short, to the theatrical world that Burston describes as big global business entailing larger capital investment, bigger and more numerous venues, and the attainment of a level of standardization in production that had never previously been known in the theater.

Evita is entertainment and so constructed to maximize its entertainment value through spectacle, the provision of meaty roles for star performers, the writing of hit tunes within a popular format and a vernacular libretto, audience-identifiable characters created through the biographicalization of story, and so on. In all these ways and more *Evita* is an obvious product of culture industry. But *Evita* is also something else. It sustains the hope of Walter Benjamin, against Adorno and Marcuse, that even an industrialized popular culture can become capable of mobilizing potentialities in ways that give it both artistic depth and a critical edge. *Evita* does this. In terms of the musical as a popular musico-dramatic cultural form, *Evita* involves a number of innovations: its through-composition instead of dialogue and numbers marries the musical with opera to break the high/low culture divide in an interesting way. The dramaturgical use of Che as a figure who is an internally reflexive voice weaving in and out of the action both narratively and dialogically extends the dramatic scope of the show and increases the possibilities of its sophistication. The integral dramatic use of the *mise-en-scène*, through the exploitation of technological resources, extends and deepens the range of what can be theatrically articulated. The music adopts a variety of popular and operatic forms to create a considerable flexibility of dramatic usage. In all these ways *Evita* stays within its popular form of music theater but extends its boundaries.

But more, *Evita* is an articulate and critical voice stemming from popular culture. It speaks of its own world of commodification, aestheticization, and mass consumption. *Evita* is not a voice that is mere entertainment nor is it just a passively distracting and manipulating voice of a culture industry. It is a critical engagement with its world. In theater, it captures and explores the theatricalization of politics. Imagery is made imaginal to look at it. A popular icon, Che, is used to strike down the iconographies of mass popular culture. Myth is now shown to be the vehicle for agency as well as narration and representation. The suspension of disbelief that theater entails for its entry becomes articulate to voice itself as an increasing condition of modernity where all the world is, in effect, becoming a stage. *Evita* takes up and reuses the critical possibilities (to which Benjamin hopefully pointed) of allegory and makes it a vehicle to see through as well as see with the modern world. In these ways it represents a continuation of musical theater tradition, rather than its inexorable demise.

NOTES

1. See also Perry (1993).

2. To a certain extent the film of *Evita* decenters the political radicalism of the stage musical. By transforming the character of Che into an Everyman figure, the sharp edge of his critique is eroded. This mutation captures, perhaps, what Baudrillard argues is the turn from the modern to the postmodern in the character of mass politics: the refusal of the mass to engage with the hyperreal world of images that constitute the postmodern world and that now becomes the only political strategy available to its members as a response. The film also accentuates the biographical exploration of Eva Peron's personality and life as against the politics and power that form and animate her existence and position. More specifically, it undermines the latter by introducing a new song—"You Must Love Me"—that entirely jars, by creating a sense that her relationship with Juan Peron was a romantic one as opposed to one of power. It is the latter that the stage musical insists on. Finally, the whole film is overshadowed by Madonna's impersonation of Eva Peron to produce a conflation between Madonna and Eva, which suggests that superstardom—and its success, rewards, and perils—is the show's central theme.

3. It is, actually, highly resonant of British responses to the death of Princess Diana.

CHAPTER 7

On and Off Broadway:
A Postscript

The musical historically developed out of and in relation to American popular culture, and in this it always remained commercial theater. Indeed, as has been argued, this was central to how the musical was vitally and reflexively tied to American popular culture as expression, ideology, and myth. Now the world and popular culture that the musical stemmed from has changed, and, with it, its home has changed, including Broadway itself. In America and on Broadway, the economics of theatrical production have created a major shift. The economic costs of producing a live musical have risen astronomically, which means that new musicals will only be commissioned and mounted if it seems that their success can be guaranteed. A very long run is essential to such success. In the 1920s, an economically successful musical might achieve a run of between 450 and 500 performances; by the 1980s, an economically successful run would require more like 1,500 performances, and often much more than this. The last really economically successful American musicals ran for greater and even more enormous lengths on Broadway—*A Chorus Line* (1975) ran for 6,137 performances, *Annie* (1977) for 2,377, *42nd Street* (1980) for 3,486, and *La Cage aux Folles* (1983) for 1,761. The megamusicals have overtaken even these performance figures, but under quite new commercial and technological conditions of production. In this changing context, fewer musicals are produced and many have originated off-Broadway.

So the musical theater business has inevitably become concerned with the search for surefire success, which has meant turning essentially to those composers, performers, and producers who, on the basis of their historical record, can guarantee it. In this way, Broadway no longer nurtures composers and performers as it once did. This nurturing was a crucial and creative part of how the musical developed as an American vernacular genre of music theater and music drama. It is not surprising that the well of musicals, composers, performers, and producers who once constituted Broadway (and to whom its theater business could turn for guaranteed success) has run dry. Broadway has lost the star names it made and is unable to create enough in the way of output to create new ones. Thus Broadway now has to bus in stars from other media areas. Sadly, too, ranks of the personnel of Broadway have been decimated by AIDS. The British and megamusical have largely replaced the American and traditional musical. The glorious seventy-year tradition, proceeding through the birth of the distinctively American musical with the likes of Bolton, Wodehouse, and Kern, to the complex structural ambition of the Rodgers and Hammerstein musical play, to the new levels of integrated choreography of, for instance, Agnes de Mille and Jerome Robins, has been displaced by what many would see, including Steyn, as products outside the key traditions—the lushness of "through-composed operetta," for instance, or "dance-free" chamber opera. Indeed, Steyn is one of those writers who captures the dearth of the once much more thriving and typically American musical stage with considerable passion. He is wrong to assume, however, that the American musical is completely dead: its character has inevitably changed to take it in the directions that make it unable to simply follow and ape its old tradition. The problem is whether commerce will give sustenance to musicals that take this direction.

That, of course, depends to a large extent on whether a market can be found for them or produced by them. In this the musical faces the paradox of a Western culture that is both globalizing and yet subject to ever greater differentiation. On the one hand, the musical tries to reconstitute itself as megamusical; on other hand, it seeks to capitalize on niche markets, appealing to the new diversity that specifically flows from lifestyle identities. The musical has set out to cater to audiences that have different and diverse cultural interests, through rock and "connoisseur" musicals, for instance. But these responses, to a large extent, have taken place off-Broadway and entail a different kind of musical from that of the traditional song-and-dance or book musical. The musical, then, has fragmented into a variety of forms as its audience has become socially differentiated, and these forms enjoy different relationships with the traditions that formed the musical as an American and vernacular genre of music theater and music drama.

Finally, the globalization of the culture industry in terms of the generation of the megamusical has ended the role of Broadway as the central venue of the musical. Now the musical is a genre produced and performed worldwide and in a whole series of venues, even if New York, London, and Toronto are the primary ones and the production of megamusicals originates in these metropolitan centers to be reproduced glob-ally. In one sense, this variety of location is not entirely new in terms of New York and London. There is and always has been a British form of the musical, stemming from the forms of live popular entertainment of nineteenth-century Britain and crossed with European imports, which also had an influence on the American musical. But it tended to remain parochial and arguably lacked the development of a real tradition. When one thinks of the chief composers of British musicals—Coward, Novello, Ellis, Wilson, Bricusse and Newly, Bart, and so on—one is faced with the fact that the British musical is a patchy tradition. These figures composed a whole variety of music theater—in the form of operettas, comedies, romantic musicals, revues, and so on—but they had no real center after the demise of British musical comedy post-1918. Many historians of the musical identify the British contribution in terms of Gilbert and Sullivan, but see little coming after to in any way compete with the mastery of the book musical. Morley, in his study of the British musical, argues that: "the British stage musical has never achieved on its home territory the domi-nance that its American counterpart has had on Broadway . . . [Moreover,] the arrival of the American musical in London [especially post-Second World War] was to make all English musicals seem overnight about thirty years out of date in terms of choreography, orchestrations, lighting, sets, costumes and action. British producers and composers alike went into a prolonged and understandable shock" (1987, 7–10). As Mordden (1984) argues, what British composers fell back upon to compete was period-piece nostalgia (for example, Sandy Wilson's *The Boy Friend* [1954]), Dick-ensian familiarity (Lionel Bart's *Oliver* [1963]), or British salt of the earth (*Me and My Girl* [1937]). No theatrical organization was specifically set up in relation to musicals in Britain at this point to create an organized collec-tivity of producers, directors, and performers as "showbiz." This latter only came as American musicals started to enter the West End after the Second World War to the point where the West End, through London pro-ductions, developed both the companies and the performers to take on Broadway. This development led, in turn, to productions of American musicals and their performers being transferred in either direction.

The advent of the megamusical changed all this, with the British taking the lead in the creation and production of such musicals. But this is, of course, a different story, and one that has nothing to do with the niche that the British musical had established for itself vis-à-vis the American musi-cal. It is the story of the development of a transnational culture industry in which the new musicals have a global identity. Where the musical is going, then, becomes an interesting question. At the same time, the nature of its relationship with its origins becomes a complex issue.

For all the shifts from Broadway, however, the connection between the musical and America is far from dead. At the very least, it will always be possible to maintain the originary theater life of the musical through the revival of the canonical works within its tradition. But what the future musical might entail and how this future can maintain the tie between the musical and popular culture (which has hitherto supplied the musical with its life) in other ways than through the global megamusical is open to speculation. In this, the future of the megamusical may itself not be entirely secure. The commitment to form over content and spectacle over text, to create a global product for a global audience, opens up the field that can be treated in megamusical terms but also closes down any specific localized cultural character or identity to the musical. This undermines both its vernacularity and contemporaneity and thus its ability to engage with an existent social world. The link between the musical and popular culture increasingly reduces itself to the technological rather than the dramatic, which carries the risk of producing an empty show (if not showing off) about nothing achieved at huge economic cost. In this respect, it is interesting to note how, and increasingly, many new megamusicals in recent years have been gigantic turkeys rather than geese laying golden eggs—*Moby Dick* (1992), for instance, and also *Martin Guerre* (1995), *Whistle Down the Wind* (1998), *Toulouse-Lautrec* (1999), *Notre Dame de Paris* (1998), *Napoleon* (2000), and so on. The virtual worlds thematically and theatrically created by megamusicals could become their downfall. Since they are addressed to a global audience of "anybody," there is no "somebody" to relate these worlds to. They can become virtual in the worst sense of being nobody's world. Thus the megamusical is stuck with a dilemma as a popular cultural form, because it has tended to abandon specific people as its cultural referent. In this respect, the contemporary world of commerce and the market begins to threaten the popular vitality of the musical, whereas, with the Broadway musical in its heyday, commerce and the market provided a means to foster it.

Yet here it is interesting to see how two of the major players on the global market, Cameron MacIntosh and Andrew Lloyd Webber, have reconsidered the musical and its successful contribution in this respect. The first has created a hit on the London stage with a musical that recovers its musical comedy tradition (*The Witches of Eastwick* [2000]); the second has composed a new musical that is rooted in a particular society—that of Britain—so a "something" and a "somebody" is at work here (*The Beautiful Game* [2000]). A further opening for the musical might be to celebrate global culture as multiculture and so address the experience of multiculturality that characterizes many modern societies. Rahman's *Bombay Dreams* (2002) attempts this in what is effectively a West End appropriation of a Bollywood musical film. In being set in Bombay, this captures Indo-Asian otherness for Britain while simultaneously constructing Indo-Asian hybridity as a new British identity. It clearly registers the penetration of Indian culture into ordinary British life. The problem is that this musical is not sure whether to celebrate Bollywood or mock it. In practice it does both, but the mockery is far from kind. *Bombay Dreams* emphasizes the sheer escapism of Bollywood, the romantic absurdity of what passes for drama in Bollywood, the apparent laughability of many of Bollywood's standard artistic forms. Paradoxically, the musical only really comes alive when it operates in terms of these forms and traditions. This means that this show, like most megamusicals, falls back on spectacle for its primary effect. Similarly much of the music of this show incorporates the standard soft rock so typical of the megamusical. The danger of *Bombay Dreams* is that it possesses the same kind of multiculturality as chicken tikka masala. It becomes a multiculture reduced to homogeneity. In this respect *Bombay Dreams* is not a triumphant achievement, but rather shows how difficult it is for the musical to achieve a more positive relationship with global culture. Like *La Cava* (2000) and *Napoleon* (2000) before it, *Bombay Dreams* remains stuck in the attempt to fish for a global version of an evening out.

Appendix: Musicals Referred to in the Text with Main Composers, Lyricists, and Book Writers

This appendix excludes the early West End musical comedies listed in chapter 1. For details of these shows, see Gänzl (1986).

Annie (1977)
Music: Charles Strouse
Lyrics: Martin Charnin
Book: Thomas Meehan

Annie Get Your Gun (1946)
Music and lyrics: Irving Berlin
Book: Herbert and Dorothy Fields

Anything Goes (1934)
Music and lyrics: Cole Porter
Book: Guy Bolton, P. G. Wodehouse,
    Howard Lindsay, and Russel
    Crouse

The Arcadians (1909)
Music: Lionel Monckton and Howard
    Talbot
Lyrics: Arthur Wimperis
Book: Mark Ambient and Alexander
    M. Thompson

Are You There (1916)
Music: Ruggiero Leoncavallo

Lyrics: Albert de Courville
Book: Edgar Wallace

Assassins (1990)
Music and lyrics: Stephen Sondheim
Book: John Weidman

Babes in Arms (1937)
Music: Richard Rodgers
Lyrics: Lorenz Hart
Book: Richard Rodgers and Lorenz Hart

The Beautiful Game (2000)
Music: Andrew Lloyd Webber
Lyrics and book: Ben Elton

Beauty and the Beast (1994)
Music: Alan Menken
Lyrics: Howard Ashmen and Tim Rice
Book: Linda Woolverton

Bells Are Ringing (1956)
Music: Jule Styne
Lyrics and book: Betty Comden and
    Adolph Green

The Black Crook (1866)
Music and lyrics: Various
Book: Charles M. Barras

Bombay Dreams (2002)
Music: A. R. Rahman
Lyrics: Don Black
Book: Meera Sya

The Bomb-ity of Errors (2001)
Music: Kevin Shand
Lyrics and book: Andy Goldhey

Boy Band (1997)
Music: P. Quilter
Lyrics and book: C. Miller

The Boy Friend (1954)
Music, lyrics, and book: Sandy
   Wilson

The Boys from Syracuse (1938)
Music: Richard Rodgers
Lyrics: Lorenz Hart
Book: George Abbott

Brigadoon (1947)
Music: Frederick Loewe
Lyrics and book: Alan Jay
   Lerner

Buddy (1990)
Music and lyrics: Buddy Holly
Book: Alan Jones

Cabaret (1966)
Music: John Kander
Lyrics: Fred Ebb
Book: John Masteraff

Call Me Madam (1950)
Music and lyrics: Irving Berlin
Book: Howard Lindsay and Russel
   Crouse

Camelot (1960)
Music: Frederick Loewe
Lyrics and book: Alan Jay Lerner

Can-Can (1953)
Music and lyrics: Cole Porter
Book: Abe Burrows

Candide (1956)
Music: Leonard Bernstein
Lyrics: Richard Will, John Latouche,
   and Dorothy Parker
Book: William Helman

Carousel (1945)
Music: Richard Rodgers
Lyrics and book: Oscar
   Hammerstein II

Cats (1982)
Music: Andrew Lloyd Webber
Lyrics: T. S. Eliot, Trevor Nunn, and
   Richard Stilgoe

Chicago (1975)
Music: John Kander
Lyrics: Fred Ebb
Book: Bob Fosse and Fred Ebb

A Chorus Line (1975)
Music: Marvin Hamlisch
Lyrics: Edward Kleban
Book: James Kirkwood and Nicholas
   Dante

Closer to Heaven (2001)
Music and lyrics: Pet Shop Boys
Book: Jonathan Harvey

Company (1970)
Music and lyrics: Stephen
   Sondheim
Book: George Furth

The Cradle Will Rock (1938)
Music, lyrics, and book: Mark
   Blitzstein

Crazy for You (1992)
Music: George Gershwin
Lyrics: Ira Gershwin
Book: Ken Ludwig

Damned Yankees (1955)
Music and lyrics: Richard Adler
Lyrics: Jerry Ross
Book: George Abbott and Douglass
   Wallop

The Desert Song (1925)
Music: Sigmund Romberg
Lyrics: Otto Harbach and Oscar Ham-
   merstein II
Book: Otto Harbach, Oscar Hammer-
   stein II, and Frank Mandel

Dreamgirls (1981)
Music: Harry Krieger
Lyrics and book: Tome Eyen

Du Barry Was a Lady (1939)
Music and lyrics: Cole Porter
Book: Herbert Fields and B.G.
   DeSylva

Elvis: The Legend Lives (1978)
Music and lyrics: Various
Book: Jack Good and Ray Cooney

Evita (1978)
Music: Andrew Lloyd Webber
Lyrics: Tim Rice

Face the Music (1932)
Music and lyrics: Irving Berlin
Book: Moss Hart

Fiddler on the Roof (1964)
Music: Jerry Bock
Lyrics: Sheldon Harnick
Book: Joseph Stein

Floradora (1899)
Music: Leslie Stuart
Lyrics: Ernest Boyd Jones and Paul
   Rubens
Book: Owen Hall

Follies (1971)
Music and lyrics: Stephen Sondheim
Book: James Goldman

42nd Street (1980)
Music: Harry Warren
Lyrics: Al Dubin
Book: Michael Stewart and Mark
   Bramble

From a Jack to a King (1989)
Music, lyrics, and book: Bob Carlton

Funny Face (1927)
Music: George Gershwin
Lyrics: Ira Gershwin
Book: Fred Thompson and Paul Ger-
   ard Smith

Funny Girl (1964)
Music: Jule Styne
Lyrics: Bob Merrill
Book: Garson Kanin

*A Funny Thing Happened on the Way to
   the Forum* (1962)
Music and lyrics: Stephen Sondheim
Book: Burt Shevelove and Larry Gelbart

A Gaiety Girl (1893)
Music: Sidney Jones
Lyrics: Harry Greenbank
Book: Owen Hall

Gay Divorce (1932)
Music and lyrics: Cole Porter
Book: Samuel Hoffenstein and Ken-
   neth Webb

Girl Crazy (1930)
Music: George Gershwin
Lyrics: Ira Gershwin
Book: Guy Bolton and John McGowan

Godspell (1971)
Music and lyrics: Stephen Schwartz
Book: John Michael Tebelak

Good Golly Miss Molly (1991)
Music: Various
Musical compilation, lyrics, and book:
   Bob Eaton

Good News (1927)
Music and lyrics: Ray Henderson,
    B.G. DeSylva, and Lew Brown
Book: Laurence Schwab and B.G.
    DeSylva

Grease (1972)
Music, lyrics, and book: Jim Jacobs
    and Warren Casey

Great Balls of Fire (1999)
Music and lyrics: Various
Book: Richard Cameron

Guys and Dolls (1950)
Music and lyrics: Frank Loesser
Book: Joe Swerling and Abe
    Burrows

Gypsy (1959)
Music: Jule Styne
Lyrics: Stephen Sondheim
Book: Arthur Laurents

Hair (1968)
Music: Galt MacDermot
Lyrics and book: Gerome Ragni and
    James Lado

Hello Dolly (1964)
Music and lyrics: Michael Stewart
Book: Jerry Herman

HMS Pinafore (1878)
Music and libretto: W.S. Gilbert and
    Arthur Sullivan

I'd Rather Be Right (1937)
Music: Richard Rodgers
Lyrics: Lorenz Hart
Book: George S. Kaufman and Moss
    Hart

I Married an Angel (1938)
Music: Richard Rodgers
Lyrics: Lorenz Hart
Book: Richard Rodgers and Lorenz
    Hart

Into the Woods (1987)
Music and lyrics: Stephen
    Sondheim
Book: James Lapine

In Town (1892)
Music: F. Osmond Carr
Lyrics and book: Adrian Ross and
    James Leader

Irene (1919)
Music: Hal Tierney
Lyrics: Joseph McCarthy
Book: James Montgomery

Jubilee (1935)
Music and lyrics: Cole Porter
Book: Moss Hart

Jumbo (1935)
Music: Richard Rodgers
Lyrics: Lorenz Hart
Book: Ben Hecht and Charles
    McArthur

The King and I (1951)
Music: Richard Rodgers
Lyrics and book: Oscar Hammerstein II

Kismet (1953)
Music adaptation and lyrics: Richard
    Wright and George Forrest
Book: Charles Lederer and Luther
    Davis

Kissing Time (1919)
Music: Ivan Caryll
Lyrics and book: Guy Bolton and P.G.
    Wodehouse

Kiss Me Kate (1948)
Music and lyrics: Cole Porter
Book: Sam Spewack and Bella
    Spewack

La Cage aux Folles (1983)
Music and lyrics: Jerry Herman
Book: Harvey Fierstein

La Cava (2000)
Music: Laurence O'Keefe and Stephen
    Keeling
Lyrics: Laurence O'Keefe and John
    Chaplin
Book: Dana Broccoli

Lady Be Good (1924)
Music: George Gershwin
Lyrics: Ira Gershwin
Book: Guy Bolton and Fred Thompson

Lady in the Dark (1941)
Music: Kurt Weill
Lyrics: Ira Gershwin
Book: Moss Hart

Leave It to Me (1938)
Music and lyrics: Cole Porter
Book: Bella Spewack and Sam
    Spewack

Les Miserables (1986)
Music: Claude-Michel Schönberg
Lyrics: Herbert Kretzmer
Original book: Alain Boublil and Jean
    Marc Natel

Let Them Eat Cake (1933)
Music: George Gershwin
Lyrics: Ira Gershwin
Book: George S. Kaufman

The Light Blues (1916)
Music: Howard Talbot and Herman
    Finck
Lyrics: Adrian Ross
Book: Mark Ambient and Jack Hulbert

The Lion King (1997)
Music and lyrics: Elton John and Tim
    Rice
Book: Roger Allers and Irene Mecchi

A Little Night Music (1973)
Music and lyrics: Stephen
    Sondheim
Book: Hugh Wheeler

Mlle Modiste (1905)
Music: Victor Herbert
Lyrics and book: Henry
    Blossom

Mama Mia (2000)
Music and lyrics: ABBA
Book: Catherine Johnson

Mame (1966)
Music and lyrics: Jerry Harman
Book: Jerome Lawrence and Robert E.
    Lee

Man of La Mancha (1965)
Music: Mitch Leigh
Lyrics: Joe Darion
Book: Dale Wasserman

Martin Guerre (1995)
Music: Claude-Michel Schönberg
Lyrics: Herbert Kretzmer and Alain
    Boublil
Book: Alain Boublil and Claude-
    Michel Schönberg

Me and My Girl (1937)
Music: Noel Gay
Lyrics and book: L. Arthur Rose and
    Douglas Furber

Merrily We Roll Along (1981)
Music and lyrics: Stephen
    Sondheim
Book: George Furth

The Merry Widow (1907)
Music: Franz Lehár
Lyrics and book: Victor Leon and Leo
    Stein

The Mikado (1885)
Music: Arthur Sullivan
Libretto: W. S. Gilbert

Miss Dolly Dollars (1905)
Music: Victor Herbert
Lyrics and book: Glen McDonagh

Miss Saigon (1989)
Music: Claude-Michel Schönberg
Lyrics: Richard Malby Jr. and Alain
    Boublil
Book: Alain Boublil

Moby Dick (1992)
Music: Hereward Kaye and Robert
    Longden
Lyrics and book: Robert Longden

The Most Happy Fella (1956)
Music, lyrics, and book: Frank Loesser

My Fair Lady (1956)
Music: Frederick Loewe
Lyrics and book: Alan Jay Lerner

Napoleon (2000)
Music: Timothy Williams
Lyrics: Andrew Sabiston
Book: Andrew Sabiston and Timothy
    Williams

Naughty Marietta (1910)
Music: Victor Herbert
Lyrics and book: Rida Johnson
    Young

No, No Nanette (1925)
Music: Vincent Youmans
Lyrics: Irving Caesar and Otto Har-
    bach
Book: Frank Mandel and Otto Har-
    bach

Notre Dame de Paris (1998)
Music: Richard Cocciante
Lyrics and book: Luc Plamondo

Of Thee I Sing (1931)
Music: George Gershwin
Lyrics: Ira Gershwin
Book: George S. Kaufman

Oh Kay (1926)
Music: George Gershwin
Lyrics: Ira Gershwin

Book: Guy Bolton and P.G. Wode-
    house

Oklahoma (1943)
Music: Richard Rodgers
Lyrics and book: Oscar Hammerstein
    II

Oliver (1963)
Music, lyrics, and book: Lionel Bart

125th Street (2002)
Music and lyrics: Various
Book: Alan Jones

On Your Toes (1936)
Music: Richard Rodgers
Lyrics: Lorenz Hart
Book: Richard Rodgers, Lorenz Hart,
    and George Abbott

Pacific Overtures (1976)
Music and lyrics: Stephen Sondheim
Book: John Weidman

Pal Joey (1940)
Music: Richard Rodgers
Lyrics: Lorenz Hart
Book: John O'Hara

Panama Hattie (1940)
Music and lyrics: Cole Porter
Book: Herbert Fields and B.G.
    DeSylva

Passion (1994)
Music and lyrics: Stephen
    Sondheim
Book: James Lapine

Peggy Ann (1926)
Music: Richard Rodgers
Lyrics: Lorenz Hart
Book: Herbert Fields

The Phantom of the Opera (1988)
Music: Andrew Lloyd Webber
Lyrics: Charles Hart

Book: Richard Stilgoe

Pins and Needles (1937)
Music and lyrics: Harold Rome

The Pirates of Penzance (1879)
Music: Arthur Sullivan
Lyrics and book: W. S. Gilbert

Porgy and Bess (1935)
Music: George Gershwin
Lyrics and book: DuBose Heyward
    and Ira Gershwin

Red, Hot, and Blue (1936)
Music and lyrics: Cole Porter
Book: Howard Lindsay and Russel
    Crouse

Rent (1996)
Music, lyrics, and book: Jonathan
    Larson

Return to the Forbidden Planet (1999)
Music and lyrics: Various
Book: Bob Carlton

Rose Marie (1924)
Music: Rudolph Friml
Lyrics and book: Otto Harbach and
    Oscar Hammerstein II

Rosy Rapture (1915)
Music: Herman Darewski
Lyrics and book: J. M. Barrie

Sally (1920)
Music: Jerome Kern
Lyrics: Clifford Grey et al.
Book: Guy Bolton

Saturday Night Fever (1999)
Music and lyrics: The Bee Gees
Stage adaptation by Nan Knighton et al.

The Shop Girl (1894)
Music: Ivan Caryll
Lyrics and book: H.J.W. Dan

Show Boat (1927)
Music: Jerome Kern
Lyrics and book: Oscar Hammerstein II

Shuffle Along (1921)
Music: Eubrè Blake
Lyrics: Noble Sissy
Book: Flournoy Miller and Aubrey Lyles

Silk Stockings (1955)
Music and lyrics: Cole Porter
Book: George S. Kaufman, L.
    McGrath, and Abe Burrows

Singin' in the Rain (1952)
Music and lyrics: N. H. Brown and
    Arthur Freed
Book: Betty Comden and Adolph Green

Smokey Joe's Café (1995)
Music and lyrics: Jerry Lieber and
    Mike Stoller
Book: Stephen Helper and Jack
    Viertel

The Sound of Music (1959)
Music: Richard Rodgers
Lyrics: Oscar Hammerstein II
Book: Howard Lindsay and Russel
    Crouse

South Pacific (1949)
Music: Richard Rodgers
Lyrics: Oscar Hammerstein II
Book: Oscar Hammerstein II and
    Joshua Logan

Stop in the Name of Love (1988)
Music: Various, arranged by Jon
    Miller and Wayne Findley
Lyrics: Various
Book: Bill Kenwright

Strike Up the Band (1930)
Music: George Gershwin
Lyrics: Ira Gershwin
Book: George S. Kaufman (1930 ver-
    sion by Morria Rykind)

The Student Prince (1924)
Music: Sigmund Romberg
Book and lyrics: Dorothy Donelly

The Sultan of Sulu (1904)
Music: George Ade

Sunny (1925)
Music: Jerome Kern
Lyrics and Book: Otto Harbach and
    Oscar Hammerstein II

Sunset Boulevard (1994)
Music: Andrew Lloyd Webber
Lyrics and Book: Christopher Hamp-
    ton and Don Black

Sweeney Todd (1979)
Music and lyrics: Stephen Sondheim
Book: Hugh Wheeler

Sweethearts (1913)
Music: Victor Herbert
Lyrics: Robert B. Smith
Book: Harry B. Smith and Fred De
    Gresac

Tip-Toes (1925)
Music: George Gershwin
Lyrics: Ira Gershwin
Book: Guy Bolton and Fred Thompson

Tommy (1993)
Music and lyrics: Pete Townshend
Book: Pete Townshend and Des
    MacAnuff

Too Many Girls (1939)
Music: Lorenz Hart
Lyrics: Richard Rodgers
Book: George Marion Jr.

Toulouse-Lautrec (1999)
Music: Charles Aznavour
Lyrics: Dee Shipman
Book: Shaun McKenna

Two Gentlemen of Verona (1971)
Music: Galt MacDermot
Lyrics: John Guare and Mel Shapiro
Book: John Guare

West Side Story (1957)
Music: Leonard Bernstein
Lyrics: Stephen Sondheim
Book: Arthur Laurents

We Will Rock You (2002)
Music: Queen
Lyrics and book: Ben Elton

Whistle Down the Wind (1998)
Music and lyrics: Andrew Lloyd
    Webber
Lyrics: Jim Steinman

Whoopee (1928)
Music: Walter Donaldson
Lyrics: Gus Kahn
Book: William Anthony McGuire

The Witches of Eastwick (2000)
Music: Dana P. Rowe
Lyrics and book: John Dempsey

The Wizard of Oz (1902)
Music: Paul Tietjens and A. Baldwin
    Sloane
Lyrics and book: L. Frank Baum

References

Adorno, T. 1967. "Perennial Fashion: Jazz." In *Prisms*. London: Spearman.

Adorno, T., and M. Horkheimer. 1993. "The Culture Industry: Enlightenment as Mass Deception." In *The Cultural Studies Reader*, ed. S. During. London: Routledge.

Altman, R. 1987. *The American Film Musical*. Bloomington: Indiana University Press.

Babington, B., and F. Evans. 1985. *Blue Skies, Silver Linings: Aspects of the Hollywood Musical*. Manchester: Manchester University Press.

Banfield, S. 1993. *Sondheim's Broadway Musicals*. Ann Arbor: University of Michigan Press.

Barrios, R. 1995. *A Song in the Dark*. Oxford: Oxford University Press.

Bell, D. 1960. *The End of Ideology*. Glencoe: Free Press.

Benjamin, W. 1973. *Illuminations*. London: Fontana.

Bettelheim, B. 1978. *The Uses of Tales. Enchantment and the Meaning and Importance of Fairy Tales*. Harmondsworth: Penguin.

Block, G. 1997. *Enchanted Evenings: The Broadway Musical from "Show Boat" to Sondheim*. New York: Oxford University Press.

Bordman, G. 1980. *Jerome Kern: His Life of Music*. New York: Oxford University Press.

———. 1981. *American Operetta*. New York: Oxford University Press.

———. 1982. *American Musical Comedy: From "Adonis" to "Dreamgirls."* New York: Oxford University Press.

———. 1985. *American Musical Revue*. New York: Oxford University Press.

———. 1986. *American Musical Theatre: A Chronicle*. New York: Oxford University Press.

Bradbury, M., and J. McFarlane. 1976. *Modernism: A Guide to European Literature 1890–1930*. Harmondsworth: Penguin.

Bratton, J.S., R. Cave, H. Holder, B. Gregory, and M. Pickering. 1991. *The British Empire and The Stage 1790–1930.* Manchester: Manchester University Press.

Brogan, H. 1990. *The Penguin History of the United States of America.* Harmondsworth: Penguin.

Brustein, R. 1979. "Sex and Power in New York Theatre." *New Republic.* 10 November, 181–183.

Burston, J. 1997. "Enter Stage Right: Neo-Conservatism, English Canada and the Megamusical." *Soundings* 5: 19–31.

———. 1998a. "Theatre Space as Virtual Place: Audio Technology, the Reconfigured Singing Body and the Megamusical." *Popular Music* 17, no. 2: 45–61.

———. 1998b. "The Megamusical: New Forms and Relations in Global Production." Ph.D diss., University of London.

Burton, H. 1994. *Leonard Bernstein.* London: Faber & Faber.

Cox, H. 1969. *The Feast of Fools.* Cambridge: Harvard University Press.

Crook, S., J. Pakulski, and M. Waters. 1992. *Postmodernisation: Change in Advanced Society.* London: Sage.

Cruse, H. 1997. *The Crisis of the Negro Intellectual.* New York: Morrow.

Dennison, T. 1963. *The American Negro and His Amazing Music.* New York: Vantage Press.

Elias, N. 1994. *The Civilising Process: The History of Manners and State Formation and Civilisation.* Oxford: Blackwell.

Engel, L. 1972. *Words without Music.* New York: Macmillan.

Erenberg, L. 1984. *Stepping Out: New York Nightlife and the Transformation of American Culture 1890–1930.* Chicago: University of Chicago Press.

Ewen, D. 1959. *Complete Book of the American Musical Theatre.* New York: Holt.

Feuer, J. 1993. *The Hollywood Musical.* Basingstoke: Macmillan.

Filmer, P., V. Rimmer, and D. Walsh. 1999. "*Oklahoma:* Ideology and Politics in the Vernacular Tradition of the American Musical." *Popular Music* 18, no. 3: 381–395.

Foucault, M. 1988. *The History of Sexuality Volume 3: The Care of the Self.* London: Pelican Press.

Freedly, G. 1978. "The Black Crook and the White Fawn." In *Chronicles of the American Dance from the Shakers to Martha Graham,* ed. P. Magriel. New York: Da Capo.

Gänzl, K. 1986. *British Musical Theatre.* Vol. 1. Basingstoke: Macmillan.

———. 1995. *Gänzl's Book of the Broadway Musical: 75 Favourite Shows, from "HMS Pinafore" to "Sunset Boulevard."* New York: Schirmer.

Gänzl, K., and A. Lamb. 1989. *Musicals: Gänzl's Book of the Music Theatre.* New York: Schirmer.

Garrison, W.L. 1835. "Declaration of the Sentiments of the Anti-Slavery Convention." *The Liberator.* November, i–xii.

Geertz, C. 1975. *Interpreting Cultures.* London: Hutchinson.

Gilbert, D. 1940. *American Vaudeville, Its Life and Times.* New York: Dover.

Gilroy, P. 1993. *The Black Atlantic: Modernity and Double Consciousness.* London: Verso.

Goldberg, I. 1958. *George Gershwin: A Study in American Music.* New York: Frederick Ungar.

———. 1961. *Tin Pan Alley: A Chronicle of American Popular Music.* New York: Frederick Ungar.

Gordon, J. 1992. *Art Isn't Easy: The Theatre of Stephen Sondheim.* New York: Da Capo.

Gottfried, M. 1979. *Broadway Musicals.* New York: Abradale Press.

Green, S. 1971. *Broadway Musicals of the 1930s.* New York: Da Capo.

———. 1986. *The World of Musical Comedy.* New York: Da Capo.

———. 1996. *Broadway Musicals: Show by Show.* Milwaukee: Hall Leonard.

Habermas, J. 1974. "The Public Sphere: An Encyclopedia Article." *New German Critique* 3, 37–87.

Hamm, C. 1979. *Yesterdays: Popular Song in America.* New York: W. W. Norton.

———. 1983. *Music in the New World.* New York: W. W. Norton.

Hamon Jr., W. 2000. *Raising Cain: Blackface Performance from Jim Crow to Hip Hop.* Cambridge: Harvard University Press.

Hanes Harvey, C. 1996. "Holy Yumpin Yimminy: Scandinavian Immigrant Stereotypes in the Early Twentieth Century Musical." In *Approaches to the American Musical,* ed. R. Lawson-Peebles. Exeter: University of Exeter Press.

Harvey, D. 1990. *The Condition of Postmodernity.* Oxford: Blackwell.

Hastings, M. 1969. *America 1968: The Fire This Time.* London: Victor Gollancz.

Hirsch, F. 1989. *Harold Prince and the American Musical Theatre.* Cambridge: Cambridge University Press.

Horn, D. 1996. "Who Loves You Porgy? The Debates Surrounding Gershwin's Musical." In *Approaches to the American Musical,* ed. R. Lawson-Peebles. Exeter: University of Exeter Press.

Hyman, A. 1975. *The Gaiety Years.* London: Cassell & Collier Macmillan.

Idelsohn, A. Z. 1932. *A Thesaurus of Hebrew Oriental Melodies.* Berlin: Breitkopf.

Ilson, C. 1989. *Harold Prince: From "Pyjama Game" to "Phantom of the Opera."* Ann Arbor: University of Michigan Press.

Jacobson, D. 1997. *The Immigration Reader: America in a Multidisciplinary Perspective.* Oxford: Blackwell.

Kerman, J. 1998. *Opera as Drama.* Berkeley: University of California Press.

Kislan, R. 1980. *The Musical: A Look at the American Music Theatre.* Englewood Cliffs, N.J: Prentice-Hall.

Kivy, P. 1988. *Osmin's Rage: Philosophical Reflection on Opera, Drama, and Text.* New Jersey: Princeton University Press.

Lamb, L. 2000. *150 Years of Popular Music Theatre.* New Haven: Yale University Press.

Lawson-Peebles, R., ed. 1996. *Approaches to the American Musical.* Exeter: University of Exeter Press.

Lederman, M. 1983. "The Life and Death of a Small Magazine." In *Modern Music 1924–46.* Monograph 18. New York: Institute for Studies in American Music.

Lerner, A. J. 1986. *The Musical Theatre: A Celebration.* New York: McGraw-Hill.

Lipset, M. 1960. *Political Man.* New York: Doubleday.

Lott, E. 1993. *Love and Theft: Blackface Minstrels of the American Working Class.* New York: Oxford University Press.

Lubel, L. 1956. *The Future of American Politics.* New York: Doubleday Anchor.

Major, J. 1963. *Roosevelt of the New Deal: 1932–1940.* New York: Harper & Row.

Marcuse, H. 1964. *One Dimensional Man.* Boston: Beacon Press.

Marmion, P. 2001. "The Revived Musical." *Evening Standard Hot Tickets Supplement*, 10 May.

Mates, J. 1987. *America's Musical Stage: Two Hundred Years of Musical Theatre.* New York: Praeger.

McQueen-Pope, W. 1949. *Gaiety: Theatre of Enchantment.* London: W. H. Allen.

McShane, M. 1994. *Down the Asphalt Path: The Automobile and the American City.* New York: Columbia University Press.

Mellers, W. 1964. *Music in a Newfound Land: Themes and Developments in the History of American Music.* London: Barrie & Rockcliff.

———. 1996. "From Butterfly to Saigon: Europe, American and 'Success'" In *Approaches to the American Musical,* ed. R. Lawson-Peebles. Exeter: University of Exeter Press.

Mitchell, B. 1955. *Depression Decade: From New Era to New Deal.* New York: Rineheart.

Mordden, E. 1983. *Broadway Babies: The People Who Made the American Musical.* New York: Oxford University Press.

———. 1984. *Better Foot Forward: The History of the American Musical Theatre.* New York: Grossman.

Morley, S. 1987. *Spread a Little Happiness: The First Hundred Years of the British Musical.* London: Thames & Hudson.

Nathan, H. 1946. "Charles Matthews, Comedian and American Negro." *Southern Folklore Quarterly,* no. 10: 28–39.

Perry, G. 1993. *"Sunset Boulevard": From Movie to Musical.* London: Pavilion Books.

Pickering, M. 1997. *History, Experience, and Cultural Studies.* Basingstoke: Macmillan.

Postlethwaite, T., and B. McCouchie. 1989. *Interpeting the Theatrical Past.* Iowa: University of Iowa Press.

Price, C. 1989. "England IV and England X." In *The New Grove Handbooks in Music: A History of Opera,* ed. S. Sadie. Basingstoke: Macmillan.

Ramshaw, M. 1989. "Jump Jim Crow! A Biographical Sketch of Thomas D. Rice." *Theatre Annual* 17: 31–42.

Richmond, K. 1995. *The Musicals of Andrew Lloyd Webber.* London: Virgin Publishing.

Riesman, D. 1950. *The Lonely Crowd.* New Haven: Yale University Press.

Rodgers, R. 1975. *Musical Stages.* New York: Random House.

Rogin, M. 1998. *Blackface, White Noise: Jewish Immigrants in the Hollywood Melting Pot.* Berkeley: University of California Press.

Shaw, A. 1985. "Popular Music from Minstrel Song to Rock 'n' Roll." In *One Hundred Years of Music in America,* ed. P. H. Lang. New York: Da Capo.

Shils, E. 1955. "The End of Ideology?" In *Encounter.* Vol 8, No 3: 20–35.

Slobin, M. 1982. *Tenement Songs: The Popular Music of the Jewish Immigrants.* Urbana: University of Illinois Press.

Smith, C., and G. Litton. 1981. *Musical Comedy in America.* New York: Theatre Arts Books.

Southern, E. 1997. *The Music of Black Americans: A History.* Rev. ed. New York: W. W. Norton.

Starr, L. 1984. "Towards A Revaluation of Gershwin's *Porgy and Bess.*" *American Music* 2, no. 2: 17–28.

Steyn, M. 1997. *Broadway Babies Say Goodnight: Musicals Then and Now.* London: Faber & Faber.

Swain, J.P. 1990. *The Broadway Musical: A Critical and Musical Survey.* New York: Oxford University Press.

Thomas, H. 1995. *Dance, Modernity, and Culture: Explorations in the Sociology of Dance.* London: Routledge.

Toll, R. 1974. *Blacking Up: The Minstrel Show in Nineteenth Century America.* New York: Oxford University Press.

Traubner, R. 1983. *Operetta: A Theatrical History.* New York: Doubleday.

Twain, M. 1924. *The Autobiography of Mark Twain.* New York: Harper & Row.

Walsh, D. 1996. *American Popular Music and the Genesis of the Musical.* Goldsmiths Sociology Papers, no. 1. London: Goldsmith's College.

Waxman, C. L., ed. 1969. *The End of Ideology Debate.* New York: Simon & Schuster.

Well, A. 1989. *Black Musical Theatre: From Coontown to Dreamgirls.* Baton Rouge: Louisiana University Press.

Whitcomb, I. 1988. *Irving Berlin and Ragtime America.* New York: Limelight Editions.

Wilder, A. 1972. *American Popular Song: The Great Innovators 1900–1950.* New York: University of Oxford Press.

Williams, R. 1966. *Modern Tragedy.* London: Chatto & Windus.

Wolfe, T. 1971. *Radical Chic and Mav-Maving the Flak-Catchers.* New York: Bantam Books.

Zadan, C. 1990. *Sondheim and Co.* New York: Harper & Row.

INDEX

(Songs and show titles are indexed by title.)

About the Authors

DAVID WALSH is Senior Lecturer in the Sociology Department of Goldsmiths College at the University of London. He publishes and teaches in the area of sociological theory and the sociology of culture with particular emphasis, in recent years, on the sociology of music and music theater.

LEN PLATT is Senior Lecturer at the University of London, where he runs a part-time undergraduate program in cultural and social studies. He has published widely on literary cultures of the early 20th century, and is currently advisory editor of *The James Joyce Quarterly*. He is the author of *Joyce and the Anglo-Irish: A Study of Joyce and the Literary Revival* and *Aristocracies of Fiction: The Idea of Aristocracy in Late-Nineteenth and Early-Twentieth Century Literatures*.